Living Theravada

Living Theravada

Demystifying the People, Places, and Practices of a Buddhist Tradition

BROOKE SCHEDNECK

SHAMBHALA

Shambhala Publications, Inc.
2129 13th Street
Boulder, Colorado 80302
www.shambhala.com

Excerpt from the Metta Sutta on p. 183 used with permission by Amaravati Publications.

Cover art: Laos, Luang Prabang, Wat Sen, with morning
    procession of monks. © John Seaton Callahan / Getty
Cover design: Sarah Schulte

9 8 7 6 5 4 3 2 1

First Edition
Printed in the United States of America

Shambhala Publications makes every effort to print on acid-free, recycled paper.

Shambhala Publications is distributed worldwide by Penguin Random House, Inc., and its subsidiaries.

LIBRARY OF CONGRESS CATALOGING-IN-PUBLICATION DATA
Names: Schedneck, Brooke, author.
Title: Living Theravada: demystifying the people, places, and
    practices of a Buddhist tradition / Brooke Schedneck.
Description: Boulder: Shambhala, 2023. | Includes bibliographical
    references and index.
Identifiers: LCCN 2022021979 | ISBN 9781611809718 (trade paperback)
Subjects: LCSH: Theravāda Buddhism.
Classification: LCC BQ7185 .S34 2023 | DDC 294.3/91—dc23/eng/20220609
LC record available at https://lccn.loc.gov/2022021979

Contents

Introduction

Lived Theravada Buddhism

Imagine walking onto the grounds of a temple in Bangkok, Thailand. You notice the grand, brightly colored structures all around you. After your eyes have adjusted to the glimmering gold, the layout of the space comes into focus and you begin to take in the extremely detailed artistry making up these buildings. Your attention turns to a group of lay Buddhists wearing white, chatting and adjusting the offerings they are making to look aesthetically pleasing. Next you hear chanting drifting out from a hall where monks have gathered. Many of the monks are seated in a line, chanting together, while others are still arriving or carrying out monastic duties. You walk into this hall and take a seat on the floor in the back. Some of the laypeople are holding chanting books and reading from them, but it strikes you how many, who are not even monks, know the chants by heart. You notice immediately the elegance with which these men and women move, paying respect to monks and bowing to the golden Buddha statue. Your attention turns from people to the iconography as you take in the large array of statues behind the monks. As you continue to look around, you spot a large case beside you. It holds amulets, or small clay figures, with prices affixed. As the chanting quiets, you see all the monks close their eyes and sit still in meditation for about ten minutes until a bell rings, marking the end of the session. Everyone leaves.

As you can see, a visit to a Buddhist temple is a full sensory experience. This experience is an example of *lived religion*—that is, observing and participating in what is happening around you in a religious environment. Lived religion considers the practices and beliefs of individuals, which may be contradictory and inconsistent, and how they are incorporated into daily life. Instead of focusing on the abstract ideals of a religion as expressed in authoritative texts or leaders, lived religion reveals how people apply these various expressions to their everyday lives.

This book will help you understand the experience of lived Buddhism in four Theravada Buddhist countries of mainland Southeast Asia: Cambodia, Laos, Myanmar, and Thailand. Theravada Buddhism is also present within parts of Vietnam, Malaysia, Indonesia, Sri Lanka, Bangladesh, and Nepal—and of course there are diasporic communities of Theravada Buddhists throughout the world. However, limiting the scope of this book to four countries allows for a more focused understanding of lived Theravada Buddhism.

Theravada Buddhists consider themselves to be holders of the Buddha's words as recorded in the Pali Canon—a collection of scriptures recorded from oral tradition—and they can be conservative in their protection of the Buddha's teachings. Although this conservative orthodoxy is present in the tradition, a parallel stream of flexibility and openness also exists. This flexibility can be easily seen in diverse manifestations of Theravada Buddhism throughout history. Devotional statues and images that seem to be outside of Buddhism, including the Hindu god Ganesha and the former king of Thailand, Rama V, are part of the Theravada Buddhist complex.

This book will guide you through both aspects of lived Buddhism: the conservative and the popular. We will look closely at various formal monastic traditions alongside seemingly opposing features such as protective tattoos. Meditation practice, aimed toward the final Buddhist goal of enlightenment, or *nibbana*, seems incompatible with the practice of making a wish in front of a Buddha statue for the more tangible goal of something like a new car. The latter is often labeled or even dismissed as "popular Buddhism," belittling people for trying to achieve health, wealth, and success in education or their careers rather than focusing on deep understanding of Buddhist truths. However, popular Buddhism is popular for a reason—it provides the practical reassurances needed in times of uncertainty. And there is nothing wrong with that. You will not find the word *superstition* used in this book to describe any popular practice. This is intentional. Superstition is most often used derogatorily to put down others' practices as silly and unnecessary. Popular practices are meaningful and important while adding the crucial element of fun. However, to maintain itself as a world religion, Buddhism also needs an otherworldly aim, nibbana, and the path out of suffering as the ultimate aspiration. I aim to strike a balance here, as the tradition does, between elite and popular, high aspirations and temporary relief.

While much of this book attempts to reconcile tensions and provide an overview of lived contemporary Theravada Buddhism, it does not provide a comprehensive summary of Buddhist teachings. There are many good academic textbooks on the Buddha's teachings, which look deeply into the texts of Buddhism. Instead, we will explore these teachings and their contradictions and connections, and how they affect decisions and daily lives of regular Buddhists in Southeast Asia. Buddhism is more than texts and monastic ideals, which we will understand through specific topics and examples that provide a deep understanding of lived Theravada Buddhism today. This book won't discuss a detailed background on the history of Southeast Asian kingdoms and nation-states. I have largely left out conversations of Buddhism and the state, which would stray from this book's focus on modern-day lived Buddhism. However, woven throughout is the context you will need to understand differences of practice within each country. I have tried to maintain a balance of information about all four countries as much as possible. This is challenging, however, because there is much more academic research undertaken in Myanmar and Thailand than Cambodia and Laos.

After living in Thailand and teaching courses on Buddhism for over a decade, I have found that students and travelers often conclude that lived Buddhism is largely inaccessible—it appears too foreign because of the unfamiliar languages, aesthetics, and behaviors. Of course, this foreignness is part of the excitement and fun! But, at the same time, the difference of the temple environment, awkward interactions with monks, difficult meditation practices aimed at taming an unruly mind, and unexpected sacred objects can be overwhelming. Through teaching on Buddhism in Southeast Asia in American classrooms and in study-abroad courses in Thailand, I have created a curriculum investigating lived, contemporary Theravada Buddhism. This book aims to be a guide to understanding Buddhism as a lived tradition within mainland Southeast Asian societies, giving a complex picture of Theravada Buddhism today.

Why Theravada Buddhism?

Theravada translates as "the way of the elders," indicating that the tradition considers itself to be the most authoritative and pure, going back to the time of the Buddha. Theravada Buddhism is distinguished by canonical literature preserved in the Pali language, beliefs and practices that derive from these texts as interpreted by a monastic lineage, along with rituals sponsored and attended by laypeople in temples. Key characteristics include the monastic alms round, temporary ordinations, and the practice of generosity through offering food, money, and service to the temple.

A combination of factors helped Theravada Buddhism take root in mainland Southeast Asia: (1) the spread of powerful ideas and objects through missionaries and trade, (2) moral legitimation of kings through the monastic sangha, (3) possibilities for varying levels of commitment for ordinary people, and (4) the incorporation of previous religious systems.

Buddhism, as a world religion with universal values, arrived in mainland Southeast Asia beginning between the seventh and eighth centuries C.E. through the teachings of pilgrims, traveling monks, and scholars who signified the cosmopolitan nature of Buddhist culture. Kings and kingdoms became deeply engaged with these ideas in mainland Southeast Asia in the eleventh and thirteenth centuries. The king's role as *dhammaraja* (upholder of the Buddhist law) and *cakkavatti* (universal monarch) allowed this figure to be powerful but also accountable. The archetypal Buddhist monarch is the Indian king Asoka (270–230 B.C.E.), who supported Buddhist institutions and missionaries, allowing Buddhism to spread throughout Asia.

Buddhism gave rulers a cosmic framework in which they had a central place. Monks acted as advisors and supporters to monarchs because the monastic institution depended on the success of the royalty. But the political and religious relationship was not always symbiotic. When kings tried to reserve the place of highest merit for themselves, their subjects might turn to local monks with abilities in healing and magic. Political leaders of kingdoms and nation-states of mainland Southeast Asia have consistently tried to control the power of popular Buddhism. However, so far, no ruler has been completely successful. Within Theravada Buddhism, power and merit can reside with the rich and powerful but can also be powerfully demonstrated in the ascetic, forest-dwelling, reclusive monks.

Buddhism's dispersion throughout Southeast Asia was not just a top-down affair led by monks and kings. Instead, the Buddhist moral vision was one that could be shared by regular villagers, merchants, and upper-class people alike. As Theravada became the dominant religious system of the region, it encompassed older traditions rather than degrading or purging them. This complementarity rather than competition allowed for Theravada Buddhism to become a civilizational force in this region.

Historical Context of Theravada Buddhism in Southeast Asia

Lived Buddhism is observable today because of a centuries-long history of acculturation, incorporation, and assimilation into the region. Mainland Southeast Asia is divided between hills (the uplands) and valleys (the lowlands). The lowland people are mainly the Buddhist majority groups of the Tai, Burman, Khmer, and

Lao people. The hills predominately comprise indigenous ethnic minority groups, which were formerly called hill tribe groups. The indigenous minority groups have historically followed spirit religions, however in the modern period, some have converted to the world religions of Buddhism or Christianity due to these religions' missionary efforts.

Before Buddhism and Indian culture arrived in Southeast Asia, locals in both the hills and the plains conceived of their world as inhabited by spirits, which mirrored nature's kindness and beauty along with its destructive powers. Seeking assistance from these spirits and ancestors became a way to control one's life and guard against misfortunes such as ill-health, untimely death, and natural disasters. Keeping the spirits happy through offerings remains an important part of the spiritual landscape, which now is closely connected to the broader framework of Theravada Buddhism. Legends and epic tales of gods and mythical creatures from India found their way onto the lowlands of Southeast Asia through itinerant merchants, travelers, and holy men known as brahmins. These elements of Indian civilization laid a new foundation on top of the indigenous spirits and folklore already present there.

The early period of Indianization used ideas of mandala kingdoms, where the structure of the capital and geography of the landscape were meant to mirror the cosmos itself. Mount Meru, a cosmic mountain, is the center of the universe and the mythical home of the gods in Indian cosmology. Capital cities of ancient Southeast Asian kingdoms contained structures likened to Mount Meru, most famously represented by the stupas of the ninth-to-fifteenth-century Angkor kingdom of present-day Cambodia. By the end of the thirteenth century, Theravada Buddhism began to dominate as Pali scriptures replaced the predominance of Sanskrit inscriptions and monks with begging bowls outnumbered the brahmin priests, while elements of Hinduism remained alongside. The ruins of these ancient kingdoms can be visited today, including Ayutthaya and Sukhothai in Thailand and Bagan in Myanmar.

After the kingdoms period, by the eighteenth century, much of mainland Southeast Asia became colonies of France and Britain. Britain colonized present-day Myanmar, while the French held control of Cambodia and Laos. Colonialism was an affront to Theravada Buddhism, with colonial leaders and officials actively belittling Buddhist traditions. Thailand was able to avoid direct and formal colonization but was certainly influenced by Western powers during this time. Colonization and migration opened the country to residents from India and China. Today, Indian communities remain in Myanmar with Chinese communities having established themselves throughout Southeast Asia.

After colonization, new and independent governments used the language of Buddhism and Buddhist socialism to create independent nations. The nation-states' borders mirrored the maps created by the colonial powers. All four governments used Theravada Buddhism in various ways to bind their new nation together. Prioritizing Buddhism led to feelings of alienation among groups that were not part of the Buddhist lowland majority. In 1948, when U Nu became the first prime minister of the independent Burma, his attempt to establish Buddhism as the state religion was met with resistance from non-Buddhist minorities. The successors to this failed attempt at modern Buddhist kingship were a series of military governments, which shifted from a secular orientation in the 1960s to control over Buddhism starting in the 1980s. This long history of colonization, armed rebellion, and military rule has contributed to Myanmar being one of the poorest countries in Southeast Asia.

In Thailand, as the modern nation-state was forming, Buddhist kings attempted to harness the power of Buddhist nationalism by controlling the monastic institutions through standardized monastic education and missionary programs that sought to convert non-Buddhist highlanders as a means of creating loyalty toward the national government. Partly due to its avoidance of colonialism, Thailand has become more developed and prosperous than its neighboring countries. At the same time, this prosperity is fragile due to fluctuating democratic and military governments.

In Laos and Cambodia, once the French colonial period ended,

Theravada Buddhists experienced repression through communist governments. In both countries Buddhism was used as a common bond to rally against the French, which was subsequently displaced by communist ideals. Cambodia's Khmer Rouge, in power between 1970 and 1975, persecuted much of Buddhism in the country, destroying monasteries and forcibly disrobing monks. Similarly, the communist government in Laos, the Pathet Lao, began by using the unity and power of Buddhism, but by 1975 it had created a secular communist regime, where monks were encouraged to disrobe and earn their own livelihoods. Cambodian Buddhism gradually returned as the Khmer Rouge lost power. In Laos, the communist government decreased its secular, socialist position, taking a pragmatic stance toward the rootedness of Buddhist culture and traditions in the population, and Buddhism regained some of its significance in public life. Both countries continue to experience poverty and underdevelopment but are working to resuscitate Buddhism's place in their national heritage.

Today mainland Southeast Asian countries are nation-states, with communist, democratic, and military governments. There are megacities, such as Bangkok, with high population density as well as rural villages in the mountains without paved roads or electricity. People with enormous wealth live alongside a stable middle class and those barely surviving on the little money they make each day. The highlanders traditionally lived very different lives from lowlanders with distinct and various languages, clothing, and religious practices. Today, the lives of lowlanders and highlanders converge more closely as highlanders move into provincial cities, with improved transportation, economies, and infrastructure.

Foundational Teachings

To understand lived Buddhism, some background knowledge of the scriptural canon and teachings, known as the *dhamma*, is necessary. More of these basic Buddhist teachings and their origins will be sprinkled throughout the book, related to each chapter's topic.

	Population	Percent identifying as Buddhist	Monastics	Official religion
Thailand	70 million	93%	300,000 male monks; 41,000 active temples.	No official religion. Buddhism is the privileged religion, and kings of Thailand are the main patrons and upholders of Buddhism.
Myanmar	55 million	81%	500,000 male monks, male novices, and female precept nuns; 15,000 pagodas. Highest percentage of monks in relation to population in mainland Southeast Asia.	No official state religion. Government shows preference for the majority religion, Theravada Buddhism.
Cambodia	16 million	98%	4,000 temples; monastic population still recovering from decimation of Theravada Buddhist traditions during the Khmer Rouge (1975–79).	Buddhism (officially recognized since 1989).
Laos	7 million	67%	22,000 monks; 5,000 temples.	Communist country with no state religion.

(figures are approximations)[1]

Statistics and Facts

Buddhist Scriptures Overview

Although this book focuses on lived Buddhism, much of the practices Theravada Buddhists enact are based on Buddhist teachings.
Today, these teachings are accessed through texts, the most authoritative of which are combined into the Pali Canon, which record
what are believed to be the Buddha's words and provide information on the early Buddhist communities. The Pali Canon is divided
into three parts, called the *Tipitaka*, or Three Baskets: (1) the *Sutta
Pitaka*, collections of stories and poetry expressing the Buddha's
teachings; (2) the *Vinaya Pitaka*, stories and discussions regarding
the rules of monks; and (3) the *Abhidhamma Pitaka*, the philo-
sophical and metaphysical explanation of Buddhist teachings and
concepts. These texts passed through oral recitation and memory
from shortly after the Buddha's death, around the fifth century
B.C.E., until the texts were written in Sri Lanka to ensure the teachings' preservation. It is difficult to know exactly when it was written
down, but by the fifth century C.E., the Pali Canon existed as a fixed
written collection of texts. According to Theravada tradition, the
oral canon was established at the First Buddhist Council, a gathering of five hundred enlightened monks, shortly after the Buddha's
death. Periodically in Buddhist history, five other councils have
been called to preserve the purity of the texts and resolve conflicts
regarding them.

Pali is considered to be a pure, sacred language that is important
because of the meaning it conveys and the power it communicates
through the words themselves. Monks who have been ordained
even for a few years can memorize large portions of the daily chanting book, of which much comes from the Pali Canon. Other monks
will take to memorizing large portions of the Pali Canon as part
of their education in the monastic institution. However, understanding and analysis of these texts takes considerable study, which
only some monks have as their focus. Knowledge of and interest in
Pali literature varies depending on locality, institution, and even
individual monk, but it is widely seen as impressive and valuable.

In mainland Southeast Asia, Myanmar is known for its scholarship on the Abhidhamma, export of insight meditation, and prides itself as a stronghold of pure Theravada Buddhism. Thai Buddhists are considered to be holders of the orthodox tradition through their preservation of the Vinaya. Both statements of conservatism belie a rich diversity of traditions underneath the surface. For instance, Cambodia has a reputation for magical and supernatural expertise, while Lao Buddhism is closely connected to spirits.

Buddhist texts provide many of the important ideas incorporated into the lived religion today. One aspect of Theravada Buddhism is essential to know before studying contemporary expressions: cosmology.

Buddhist Cosmology

Religious cosmology is meant to be explanatory: Where were we before we were born? What will happen when we die? Theravada Buddhists, to varying degrees, see the world colored by ideas of *kamma*, samsara, rebirth, and nibbana. Since Theravada Buddhists use Pali instead of Sanskrit, the terms in this book will be in Pali, unless otherwise specified. I will refer to *kamma* and *nibbana* instead of the more familiar Sanskrit terms *karma* and *nirvana*. These four concepts are the core of Buddhist cosmos.

> *Kamma* includes all intentional acts, which mold one's consciousness in such a way that it eventually affects one's rebirth. Good kamma results in rebirth in fortunate realms and bad kamma, in the unfortunate ones.
> *Samsara* is the phenomenal world in which one is born, dies, and is reborn. It is suffering to experience this over and over again.
> *Rebirth* occurs because of one's kamma. One continues to be reborn in samsara as their kamma keeps them connected to the cycle of rebirth.
> *Nibbana* is the experience of full realization and end of

suffering. When one attains this state, one no longer creates new kamma, but one has to experience the results of past kamma created before the attainment of nibbana.

Instead of one world, Buddhist cosmology is broken into three: (1) the world of the five senses, which include humans and animals, as well as other realms with lower gods, demigods, demons, and hell beings; (2) a world of pure form containing gods with only two senses (sight and hearing), along with consciousness; and (3) a world of no form, the highest heavens of pure consciousness only. Within these three worlds exist six types of beings:

1. Gods   4. Animals
2. Demigods   5. Demons or ghosts
3. Humans   6. Hell beings

Generally, gods in the formless sphere, with some exceptions, live for millions of years in blissful meditative states but eventually exhaust all positive kamma that brought them there and fall to one of the lower realms. Demigods are powerful beings but are jealous of the higher gods, always feeling and acting upon their anger and aggression, resulting in injuries and death to themselves. Humans can experience the range of emotions, unlike most of the other types of beings. We have enough happiness and joy to feel satisfied but also enough pain and suffering to be motivated toward practice. Because of these experiences, we create good and bad kamma as humans, and we can pursue Buddhist study and practice. Human form is the ideal place to seek nibbana.

In contrast to humans, animals do not have the capacity to pursue the religious path as their lives are filled with suffering and focus on survival. Demons, also known as hungry ghosts, traditionally are depicted as afflicted with greed but are never able to satisfy their desires. Hell beings are tortured in response to their bad kamma. These beings must exhaust the bad kamma that caused rebirth there and then they can be reborn in any of the realms, depending on which kammic seeds come to fruition next.

There is a hierarchy to the three worlds, but there is no ladder to ascend. One's kamma sends a being up or down the hierarchy. Even if you are a human in this life, you could be a god in the next life or settle for a long period of torment in one of the hell realms. If anything in Theravada Buddhism is like a theistic God, it's not the Buddha or any of the gods in the upper worlds; it is kamma. Kamma is made up of our own actions—what we choose to do based on our mental intentions. Depending on these actions, we can stay in samsara or we can take steps toward understanding reality and achieve liberation from this cycle.

Kamma is often depicted in English-language popular culture as an instant kind of revenge. However, kamma in Theravada Buddhism is a long game. Most frequently, a Theravada Buddhist will attribute positive or negative circumstances in their current life to their immediate past life and will endeavor to create good kamma in this life to be reborn in one of the fortunate realms. However, our actions from any past life could affect us at any time in this life, and any action we do now could come back to us at any future lifetime.

The Four Noble Truths

In addition to Buddhist cosmology, there are other basic teachings that are necessary to understand lived Theravada Buddhism more fully. The Buddha's first teaching after his nibbana experience was his central message about the nature of suffering and the way out of suffering. This is expressed as four statements called the Four Noble Truths:

1. There is suffering.
2. There is an origin to suffering.
3. There is cessation to suffering.
4. There is a path to the cessation of suffering.

These four simple sentences declare that the main problem of existence is suffering. The cause of this suffering is our greed and attachment. Because there is an origin, then there logically will follow a way to cease the problem. This cessation is nibbana. The fourth truth, the path leading to nibbana, is expressed in another list. This path has eight components shown in the Eightfold Path.

The Eightfold Path

The practices of the Eightfold Path are as follows:

1. Right View
2. Right Intention
3. Right Speech
4. Right Action

5. Right Livelihood
6. Right Effort
7. Right Mindfulness
8. Right Concentration

Because eight steps are a lot to remember, the path is broken down further into three main parts: (1) morality (Right Speech, Right Action, Right Livelihood), (2) meditation (Right Effort, Right Mindfulness, Right Concentration), and (3) wisdom (Right View, Right Intention). In following this path, morality provides a foundation for one's mental stability in concentration, which can then contribute to insight. Although the path is tiered, it is not as if one masters morality and then moves on to concentration, and then wisdom. All three can continually be practiced as they reinforce one another. Theravada Buddhist laity primarily concentrates on the foundation of morality, and people participating in meditation retreats or practicing in monastic settings are able to explore the meditation and insight parts of the path more easily.

The Eightfold Path urges us to penetrate our ordinary way of seeing the world and understand the universal truth of reality. This reality is described by the Three Marks of Existence: (1) impermanence (*anicca*), (2) suffering (*dukkha*), and (3) non-self (*anatta*). Once we can accept and recognize these fundamental aspects of our existence, we will reduce and eventually eliminate our suffering because we will stop expecting that we should not suffer, things should not change, and we have control. Our attachment to ourselves is a cause of dis-ease. The Buddha, in his nibbana experience, discovered that we do not have a permanent inner substance or soul we can call our own. We tend to believe that relationships, homes, money, and enough objects will bring us permanent happiness. Buddhist teachings state that they will not because of impermanence: these things are all inconstant, unreliable, and beyond our control.

Structure of This Book

This book is divided into three parts, centered around basic categories of lived Buddhism: sacred places and objects, people, and practices. I begin with place in chapter 1. The most important space for Buddhists to practice lived religion is the temple. The temple serves as a place to live the monastic life and make offerings as a layperson but also to showcase Buddhist values through art and imagery. Chapter 2 focuses on Buddhist objects, including Buddha statues, relics, and protective devices such as amulets or tattoos.

Monks and laypeople feature in every chapter; however, part 2 focuses particularly on their roles within Buddhist practices and spaces. Male monks take a variety of forms, from forest to city, from beloved to controversial, and chapter 3 gives an overview of this diversity in contemporary mainland Southeast Asia. Roles for women in Theravada Buddhism are less obvious. Chapter 4 features examples of laywomen, precept nuns, and female monks. All these categories bring different opportunities and challenges to women, which are not part of the male Buddhist experience. In chapter 5, I illuminate the ways Theravada Buddhists have related to religious minority groups. Instead of feeling secure in their majority status, many Theravada Buddhists have felt the need to protect and defend their dominance.

Part 3 centers on Buddhist practices. Popular lay Buddhist practices, such as making wishes and vows to various statues and deities, are illustrated in their staggering variety in chapter 6. Chapter 7 looks at the practice of meditation and the meditation retreat phenomenon in Thailand and Myanmar. If you are traveling to mainland Southeast Asia, two appendices offer information on where to attend meditation retreats and proper etiquette inside a temple. Refer to the bibliography, which is organized according to chapter subjects, for further exploration of any of the topics covered here.

The tone of this book is neither disparaging nor praising of the tradition. I take a critical look at contemporary Buddhism through these chapters, discussing monks considered both praiseworthy and corrupt, popular lay practices some would label as being against the Buddhist teachings, and orthodoxy that presents a hindrance to gender equality. I attempt to describe these phenomena through the perspectives of Buddhists, but of course the choice of content and tone is my own. Nevertheless, my aim is that through this presentation of topics and case study examples, readers will get a picture of the comprehensive and complex system of lived Buddhism in Theravada Buddhist countries today.

PART ONE

Sacred Places and Objects

CHAPTER 1

The Temple

Entering the gates of Wat Srisuphan in Chiang Mai in northern Thailand provides a great view of the main physical features of the temple before you. Straight in front is the main worship hall; to the right is the ordination hall, where Buddhist men are ordained in a formal ceremony. In between these two buildings is a statue of Ganesha, the Hindu elephant-headed god, along with devotional materials people can donate to the temple or use at home. Although Wat Srisuphan has typical characteristics, Buddhist temples do not follow a single template. The word *temple* is used to describe not just one building but a complex filled with gathering places, living spaces, and public spaces. Because all temples cannot meet the demands of all people, there is a wide variety of purposes for individual temples.

This diversity is seen not just nationwide but also within regions of each country, depending on the history and communities of worship surrounding the space. City temples most often have finely crafted buildings and more accommodation for monks, while village temples are often simpler in construction and only have space for the few monks who live there. A famous temple that holds a sacred relic or Buddha temple has many buildings and spaces for worship, while a secluded forest temple might have only one common space for gathering once per day. These Buddhist sacred sites serve many functions, but in aggregate the Theravada Buddhist temple contains a balance of beauty, solemnity, devotion, togetherness, leisure, and fun.

The Buddhist temple or monastery—*wat* or *vat* in Thailand, Cambodia, and Laos; *phongyi khaung* in Myanmar—encompasses many aspects of the Buddhist tradition. Although this is not the only space where one can practice Buddhism, it is the main space to encounter Buddhist aesthetics, lay Buddhist practice, and monastic living. Through the intricate artwork and practitioners' use of the space, temples visually display the Buddhist cosmos, along with its teachings and values. These doctrines and beliefs are communicated through murals, which depict the Buddha's life story; huge pagodas, which contain tiny relics of the Buddha's body; and the atmosphere of the environment itself, which Theravada Buddhists say makes one feel calm and at ease.

Temples are often very old, historic structures, but they continually serve a variety of needs and modern demands. Ancient Buddhist kingdoms in South and Southeast Asia developed the concept of a *dhammaraja*, a Buddhist king who rules in accordance with the teachings of the Buddha while supporting and sustaining the dhamma through sponsorship of temples. In Theravada Buddhism today, along with royal temples, many temples are maintained through the support of the lay Buddhist communities. In addition to being sacred sites, monasteries are part of local communities, often providing parking lots, animal shelters, picnic spots, childcare centers, and village meeting locations. Partly because of this entanglement between those living nearby and those living inside the temple, community supporters offer food, clothing, and monetary support to maintain the monastic way of life and the temple's structures.

Temple Layout

The temple is most simply a private residence for monastics. Monks need a space apart from the domestic life to mark the distinction between ordained and laypeople. In the traditional village, a single temple is the center of both religious and social life. In contemporary Southeast Asian cities, there are many temples close together, enmeshed within diverse urban communities.

Spiritual Symbolism

Temples have one main entrance, marking the arrival into a sacred space. Buddhist symbols, such as a wheel representing the Buddha turning the wheel of dhamma upon his first teaching, decorate this entrance. This boundary between inside and outside the temple can also be signaled with a guardian figure keeping away evil people and spirits. These guardians, including dragon serpents called *naga*, are mythical creatures from within the Indian and Buddhist cosmology. In Thailand, mythical lions (*singh*), demons (*yak*), and half-animal and half-human figures (*kinnari*) are prominently featured. These figures are similarly depicted on temple building doors and walls.

Temples are also protected and supported by the presence of divinities (*deva*). Devas come from the lower realms of Buddhist heavens and are depicted with crowns and royal costumes. *Apsara*, seen in Cambodia, are celestial dancers whose movements delight the gods. Gods from Hinduism, such as Brahma and Vishnu, function as supporters of Buddhism. Brahma, recognized by his four heads, often has his own shrine area of a temple, while Vishnu on his eagle mount (*garuda*) can be seen on temple building doors, protecting the entrance. Shrines to local spirits can be found on the edges of temples. In Cambodia, the northeast corner generally contains a shrine called *anak ta vat*, referring to the indigenous spirit of the temple.

The layout of the temple is designed to represent the Buddhist cosmos, with the mythical cosmic mountain and home to the gods, Mount Meru, symbolized by a stupa. Stupas, also known in English as pagodas, are dome or bell-shaped structures. Their design is derived from ancient burial mounds of India. They have become a symbol of Buddhism and have been important in the dissemination of the religion in Southeast Asia. The stupa, with three tiers of pedestals, symbolizes the three worlds of desire, form, and absence of form, which make up samsara. The tip of the stupa, consisting of concentric rings, portrays the many levels of heavens, with the peak representing nibbana. Stupas can come to a point, or they can have a cone shape called *krang* in Cambodian architecture.

Not all temples contain stupas, but if they do, this structure will usually be the first one from which the temple expands. Buried within or underneath stupas are relics believed to originate from the Buddha's own body, such as one of his hairs or a tiny piece of bone, or from the cremation of a famous king or monk in the area. Buddhists pay respect to the relics by circumambulating (walking around) the stupa three times, usually chanting praise to the Triple Gem (Buddha, Dhamma, Sangha) and carrying candles, flowers, and incense. After completing the three rounds, each practitioner lights their candle and incense, and places their flower nearby, while making a wish for their future health and happiness.

Communal Spaces

The simplest temple would consist of one main gathering place with sparse accommodations. But there are many possibilities for temple structures beyond this, including features such as a stupa, funerary monuments, ordination hall, library, classrooms, crematoria for funerals, meditation center, and multipurpose pavilions, as well as stores selling devotional offerings, amulets, souvenirs, coffee, and convenience items. Often temples provide benches or picnic tables in outdoor seating areas for rest or meal breaks. One can also find fortune tellers, lottery-sellers, food stalls, or outdoor massage stations at the edges of some temples.

One of the most important communal structures in a temple is the *vihara*, a roofed hall where followers worship and gather. This hall is rectangular in shape, with thick pillars to support the tiered roof. The vihara is used as a place for monastic ceremonies, communal gatherings on holidays and holy days, and dhamma talks, as well as to make offerings. For most of the year, the vihara is a quiet place to reflect on the detailed artwork and Buddha statues displayed all around, but during Buddhist holidays and holy days, the vihara can be packed with people.

Lay Buddhists often visit the vihara to pay respect to the Buddha statue there, prostrating three times to acknowledge the Triple

Gem. The altar at the vihara is an abundant place to experience Buddhism, as it is filled with a large central Buddha image, which in Myanmar is often encircled by a light board emanating outward like an expansive halo. This main image is surrounded by many smaller images—disciples of the Buddha in respectful poses turned toward him, wax figures of revered monks in the nation or region, and photographs of royalty—along with offerings like large candles and gold and silver trees.

Other Typical Temple Features

If a temple has an ordination hall, it is often the most ornate building. In some temples, one building might function as both the vihara and ordination hall. The ordination hall, the only space where men can become monks, is indicated by eight boundary markers called *sema* stones. Buried underneath these stones are large, heavy iron balls marking the eight cardinal and subcardinal points of the building, with a ninth buried in the center of the building. In Cambodia, sema stones are placed around the vihara. During the multiday sema consecration ceremony in Cambodia, laypeople place offerings in the holes, such as money and other items symbolizing the security of a good life.

Other optional areas of the temple include a manuscript library for safeguarding sacred texts; a bell tower or drum hall to signal the routines of monastic and village life; and a bodhi tree, often girded with sticks and decorated with sashes for ornamentation and good luck. Some temples have monastic schools on the premises. Temples with meditation centers have large cafeterias, meditation halls, and accommodation for lay meditators. Other temples have halls dedicated to important sacred artifacts. These fully enclosed or open-air halls can include a collection of relics, a large footprint of the Buddha, or the remains of an important monk who lived at the temple.

Living Quarters

Many temple buildings are off-limits for casual visitors, as they are living spaces for monastics and other residents. Monks study, sleep, and keep their personal possessions in these simple accommodations, which can be a single hut (*kuti*) in the forest or a thin mattress on the floor of a big room shared with many other monks. Some city temples contain a building with small, dormitory-style rooms for resident monks. The abbot and senior monks might have larger accommodations, also serving as receiving areas and an office.

Laypeople may stay at a temple if they have fallen on hard times, are students needing free rent, or have relations in the temple. These accommodations often have shared bathroom facilities. There are also rows of latrines in public temple spaces marked for use by laypeople and monks.

Large kitchens, found in temples with many residents, are used with special care when a meal is sponsored by donors during an auspicious occasion, such as a senior monk's birthday. A sponsored meal can also mark a new business venture or commemorate a relative's death. Some temples possess cars, which laypeople donate for monks' traveling duties, while others that need transportation might arrange for a paid driver on a regular basis, or a lay driver could offer their services as merit.

This diversity of temple layouts is part of the adaptive quality in Buddhism in Southeast Asia. The variation is a result of layers of rich history and culture.

Temple Murals

Temple murals—located in the vihara, ordination hall, or other halls—are an important medium for expressing Buddhist narratives. In the early twentieth century, murals were less common in non-elite temples. In temples with limited resources, Buddhist stories and narratives were depicted on cloth and then hung on special occasions. Today, especially in Thailand and Cambodia, visitors can appreciate detailed mural paintings in many temples.

In a few temples, murals depict Buddhist teachings not through narrative but through artistic imagination and symbols. Murals can also incorporate local folk stories, regional legends, scenes of sacred places in India, and epic tales from Hinduism. The Ramayana is often featured in Theravada temples, with illustrations of the hero Lord Rama and his loyal assistant, the monkey-god Hanuman. The Ramayana, called *Phra Lak Phra Lam* in Laos, is often featured in images of Rama that are often carved on doors of Lao temple buildings. Murals act as educational devices to concretize Buddhist ideas, promote understanding, and familiarize youth with their religion.

Careful observers will get a sense of the Buddhist cosmos through mural scenes. The world of the gods is high up near the ceiling of the temple hall to mark their status, sometimes filled in with stupas and palaces befitting a heavenly realm. Theravada Buddhists speak of making merit for the purpose of going to heaven or for helping deceased family members to reach there. Reaching the heavenly realms seems an attainable and imaginable goal for Buddhists, partly because it is depicted in temples, whereas reaching nibbana seems extremely remote and abstract. Tavatimsa, known as Indra's heaven, is popular in murals with imagery of royal and divine symbolism. This heaven is portrayed as a paradise, with beauty and pleasures abundant. Indra, king of the gods and supporter of Buddhism, is typically identified by his green skin and crown, either seated or flying. His heaven is considered an ideal reward for merit-making Buddhists.

Scenes of our world, the world of five senses, depict humans' daily life, hell realms, or narratives of the Buddha. Different countries have various stories and texts, which become popular ways of disseminating morality. In Thailand, for example, the story of *Phra Malai* recounts a monk's cosmological travels, instilling a sense of fear for committing actions that would result in being born in hell realms and an aspiration toward merit-making to achieve the reward of a more fortunate rebirth. Temple murals are not always thought of as original art; instead, painting and copying Buddhist scenes can be an act of Buddhist devotion. However, original art-work and architecture is possible—for example, Wat Rong Khun, or the White Temple in Chiang Rai, Thailand, depicts characters from the movie trilogy *The Matrix* and Japanese cartoons as part of Buddhist cosmology.

The most frequent depictions on the walls of temples, however, are the life story of the Buddha and the last ten lives of the Buddha (*jatakas*).

The Buddha's Life in Murals

Scenes from the Buddha's life will be instantly recognizable to lay Buddhists and monastics alike entering a temple building. Depend-ing on how big the hall is, you might only see the basic highlights of the story. If there is not much space available, the most important moments portrayed would typically be: the Buddha's birth, the four encounters, renunciation of palace life, calling the earth to witness, nibbana, first teaching, and death, all of which I'll highlight below.

BIRTH. The Buddha, or Prince Siddhartha Gotama, is born unusu-ally, out of the side of his mother, Queen Maya, under a sala tree in Lumbini, present-day Nepal. The mural depicts the baby upon his birth, with gods and devas appearing in the sky to celebrate this wonderful moment along with Queen Maya and her attendants. The newly born baby walks on seven lotus flowers and declares that this is his final birth. After this, the baby forgets his intention to become a Buddha in this life, and his future is left open to some dramatic tension.

THE FOUR ENCOUNTERS. The father of the Buddha, King Suddho-dana, upon hearing the prediction that his son could be a great mon-arch or a great religious leader with either many royal subjects or spiritual disciples, decides to tip the odds in his favor by essentially trapping his son in the palace and giving him all the comforts one could ever want, reasoning that this would cut any spiritual longing. However, this plan backfires when the gods help to orchestrate a consequential moment.

When Prince Gotama is finally able to sneak out of the palace, he is immediately faced with four encounters. Murals illustrate the prince observing a sick person, an old person, a dead person, and a renouncer—that is, a person who has left the householder life. After these four encounters, Gotama cannot take his trivial life in the palace anymore and he flees, against the wishes of his family, to join the renunciant life.

RENUNCIATION OF PALACE LIFE. By this time, Prince Gotama has a wife and son. Many temples will mark his parting by depicting the prince gazing upon his family as they are sleeping, right before he escapes in the night. The *bodhisatta*—Pali for the Sanskrit term *bodhisattva*—flees with an attendant on horseback, the hoofs of the horses held up by a deva so that their departure remains silent. At the same time, Mara blocks the way of the Buddha's departure, trying to convince him of the pleasures of the world and that he does not need to renounce his householder life. Because Mara is one of the high-ranking gods within the realm of desire, he is opposed to anyone trying to escape his domain of power. After reaching far enough away from the palace, the future Buddha is depicted cutting off his hair as a symbol of his renunciation.

CALLING THE EARTH TO WITNESS. Next, the future Buddha encounters Mara again. Mara has been watching the bodhisatta since his departure and attempts to prevent his enlightenment through (1) an armed attack, which is often depicted in murals with lots of armor and armies filled with demon creatures; (2) assertion of superior merit; and (3) an attempt at seduction carried out by Mara's daughters. This seduction scene can sometimes occur after the enlightenment. Mara's assertion of his own superior merit is followed by the bodhisatta proving him wrong through calling the earth to witness his lifetimes of meritorious activities. Gotama is depicted with his left hand, palm up, on his lap and his right hand facing down, with fingertips touching the earth. This gesture signals the Earth Goddess Thorani to bear witness to Gotama's good deeds through a flood of water, which is the manifestation of all the bodhisatta's accumulated merit.

ENLIGHTENMENT UNDER THE BODHI TREE. After defending himself against Mara, Gotama is ready to reach his goal of nibbana, the end of suffering. This is represented by the Buddha sitting alone and cross-legged with hands in a meditation posture underneath a bodhi tree in Bodh Gaya, present-day India.

THE FIRST TEACHING IN DEER PARK. Prince Gotama does not actually become a Buddha when he reaches nibbana but when he shows others the way. In the scene of his first teaching, Gotama Buddha is sitting with hands raised and connected in the teaching gesture of setting the wheel of dhamma in motion. This hand position represents this important moment of his teaching career, his first preaching in Deer Park, in present-day Sarnath, India.

MAHAPARINIBBANA. As the Buddha ages, he builds the *sasana*, or the Buddhist institution, by collecting disciples and expanding the monastic and lay communities until his death, in his eighties, from food poisoning. Most murals depict the Buddha laying on his side upon his death, with his disciples nearby crying as he enters his final state of nibbana known as *mahaparinibbana*. The Buddha's relics, which appeared after his cremation, live on in pagodas across the world. Before his death, the Buddha developed the Triple Gem, or the Three Refuges. These include the Buddha himself, the Dhamma, and the Sangha, the community he established. Buddhists can take refuge in these three precious things as they follow the path to nibbana.

Jataka Tales in Murals

Second in visibility at Theravada temples after the Buddha's life story is his previous life stories, especially the last ten before he became the Buddha. These jataka tales reveal the importance of kamma and how it is carried across lifetimes. They are the narratives of Buddhism, which reveal the Ten Perfections one needs to become a fully realized Buddha:

Giving
Morality
Renunciation
Wisdom
Effort
Patience
Truth-telling
Resoluteness
Loving-kindness
Equanimity

The most popular and well known of these stories is the Buddha's most recent life before his Buddhahood, the Vessantara Jataka. In this story, the future Gotama Buddha, named Prince Vessantara, realizes the perfection of generosity and is born with the urge to be extremely giving, which produces the narrative tension of the story. Upon giving away his kingdom's precious white elephant to a neighboring kingdom, his subjects are displeased, and they force Prince Vessantara and his family into exile in the forest. On their journey away from the kingdom, Prince Vessantara gives away his chariot and all his possessions. The only things he has left are his wife and two children. They make do in the forest, procuring food and wearing animal skins, until Vessantara must also give away his family members. Fortunately, his children are taken care of by the gods and no harm comes to them. The Buddha gives his wife, Maddi, to a god in disguise who immediately returns her, allowing

Vessantara to complete this perfection of generosity. This is a compelling and frustratingly patriarchal narrative, which reveals the commitment to generosity for someone aiming to become a Buddha. All ends happily, however, with the family back together and Prince Vessantara coronated as king after his kingdom forgives him.

Jataka stories are extraordinary and compelling examples of Buddhist values. Buddhists, whether ordained or lay, are not expected to live up to these ideals all the time. These narratives are meant to inspire motivation to keep training one's mind and serving others, so it makes sense that they are often prominently depicted in temples.

Buddhist Teachings on Murals

One unusual but revealing theme in mural painting is the depiction of Buddhist teachings in abstract form. At Wat Suan Mokkh in Surat Thani, Thailand, murals depict teachings for all to understand Buddhist dhamma. This temple contains a Spiritual Theater, dedicated to murals that evoke Buddhist teaching, through the efforts and vision of Buddhadasa Bhikkhu (1906-93). This well-known monk reinterpreted Buddhist teachings through his writing, which remains extremely influential in Thailand to this day. In fact, his writing in Thai represents the largest corpus of thought published by a single Theravada thinker. But his murals showed another side of his concern, not for the scholarly but for the regular people.

Buddhadasa Bhikkhu wanted Buddhism and nibbana to be as accessible and relevant to laypeople as it was to monastic renunciants. Through murals he sought to increase lay access to nibbana and set in motion seeds of liberation. Though one might not understand deeply all the dhamma and be liberated from suffering by looking at a mural, one could have a flash of understanding that could begin a transformation. And this transformation is not only meant for Thai Buddhists, as the murals have an international quality to underscore that the dhamma is beyond cultures and nations. There are quotes from the Bible for Christians and images of the

Ten Bulls or Ten Ox Herding Pictures used in the Zen tradition of Mahayana Buddhism.

Local Temple Stories

Some murals in rural temples depict their own local customs and cultures. For example, in the village of Li in northern Thailand, the murals at Wat Pra Bhat Huai Tom depict daily life at the temple, with monks preaching to and interacting with the villagers, who are part of an ethnic group known as Karen. The Karen villagers depict themselves in their distinctive cultural outfits worshipping the main teacher, Luang Pu Kruba Chaiyawongsa, who guided them to a Buddhist way of life. In city temples, the story of the founding of a Buddha relic or statue the temple contains might be part of the mural landscape. Wat Suan Dok of Chiang Mai, Thailand, has a mural in the ordination hall that depicts Phra Sumanthera, the monk who discovered a Buddha relic and offered it to the king of the Lanna kingdom. In Cambodia, some of their recent, tragic history can be seen on some murals. At Wat Pol Chen, one mural depicts heaven as an ideal society where one is free to farm, go to school, and worship the Buddha. These everyday occurrences are in stark contrast to the Khmer Rouge, the communist regime responsible for the genocide of about two million Cambodians during 1975-79. Another mural in the same temple depicts a hell realm of Khmer Rouge soldiers forcing a monk to murder other monks.

Temple Festivities and Holidays

The temple can often be a quiet place. In the midday heat of a weekday during the hot season, for instance, there might not even be a monk in sight. However, there will be at least one monk available on premises to receive offerings from laypeople who drop by to donate. When the weather gets cooler in the evening and laypeople have finished work, some may stop by to participate in the evening chanting. This relaxed atmosphere is transformed during

Buddhist holidays with music, dancing, food stalls, and tons of people having fun.

Buddhist holidays are all celebrated based on the lunar calendar. The Buddhist new year, taking place in mid-April, is known as Bi Mai in Laos, Songkran in Thailand, Thingyan in Myanmar, and Chaul Chnam Thmey in Cambodia. It's a time of celebration with families; it's also when many urbanites return to their villages and village temples. Other Buddhist holidays throughout the year also serve as occasions to gather at the temple. The most important days and periods in the Buddhist calendar are:

- Visakha Bucha, full-moon date of the sixth lunar month;
- Asalha Bucha, the day before the rains retreat on the first full moon of the eighth month;
- Magha Bucha, full-moon date of the third lunar month;
- Vassa, three-month rains-retreat period from the eighth lunar month to the eleventh; and
- Kathina, any date following the rains retreat.

Visakha Bucha

Visakha Bucha—recognized as an important international day by the United Nations in 1999, a fact many Buddhists are proud of—is the celebration of three important life events for the Buddha: his birth, enlightenment, and death. This Buddhist holiday focuses on the person of the Buddha, the first of the Triple Gems.

Asalha Bucha

Asalha Bucha marks the turning of the wheel of dhamma in the Deer Park of Sarnath. The Buddha taught the Four Noble Truths and the Eightfold Path to his first five disciples on this day. This day is a remembrance of Dhamma, the second of the Triple Gems.

Magha Bucha

Magha Bucha venerates the Buddha's three important teachings called the *Ovada Patimokkha*: do not commit evil, do what is wholesome, and purify the mind. This date also marks the full coming together of the sangha, ten months after the Buddha's enlightenment. The gathering of 1,250 monks on this occasion represented the flourishing of the teaching because all these monks were enlightened, having been ordained by the Buddha himself. This day highlights the Sangha, the last of the Triple Gems.

Vassa, Rains Retreat Season

During the Buddhist rains retreat season, an annual three-month monastic retreat practiced July through October, temples are busier with monks and laypeople studying and practicing Buddhism. This is especially true for temples with a meditation center, which can swell with participants during this time. Temples may also see an increase in men ordaining temporarily, to try out the discipline of the monastic life. The rains retreat's intensified period in the temple is based on Buddhism's origination in premodern India. During the rainy season, when monks walk on muddy paths, they can potentially harm plants and creatures that are growing and living there. When farmers and laypeople criticized Buddhist monks for their travel during this time, the Buddha made a rule for monks to stay in a fixed location.

At the end of vassa, monks partake in a ritual called the *pavarana*. During this ritual, monks are invited to identify transgressions against their rules committed by fellow monks. In this way, the rains retreat is spent becoming pure fields of merit, observing their own and others' behaviors so that at the conclusion of the intensive period, they can assert to the laity their purity and spiritual potency.

Kathina

The kathina ceremony is the most important, popular, and auspicious occasion for merit-making. This is the date, organized separately by each temple's committee, when laity present monastic robes after vassa has ended, thus facilitating the monastic life for men who just spent three months studying and practicing Buddhism intensely. In November and December, there is usually a kathina happening at some temple every weekend. Because of this timing, the monks are considered highly worthy recipients of this gift.

During these holidays one can expect to see a procession around the temple's sacred landmark, such as the pagoda, sometimes carrying a Buddha statue on parade, followed by a gathering in the main assembly hall, where gifts and donations are displayed. When the monastic portion of the ceremony begins, laypeople get an opportunity to take the Three Refuges, another title for the Triple Gem (Buddha, Dhamma, Sangha), and renew their commitment to the Five Precepts (refraining from harming living beings, taking what is not given, sexual misconduct, lying, and drinking alcohol or taking drugs). This is followed by a dhamma talk or preaching by the abbot or senior monk of the temple, and blessings bestowed upon the laity by the monks. Monks are seated higher than laypeople during formal ceremonies, either behind the monk speaking or on raised platforms lining the sides of the vihara. Evening ceremonies are also popular on Buddhist holy days. People hold lit candles to circumambulate three times around the pagoda or sacred part of the temple, with a chanting session and preaching in the gathering hall that may last through the entire evening.

During weekly holy days (*uposatha*), and based on the phases of the moon, lay Buddhists go to the temple in the morning to make food offerings so that monks do not have to walk on their alms round. The evening chanting might be better attended than usual on a weekly holy day. Some lay Buddhists may not go to the temple, but they will mark the holy day by not eating meat, going to a vegetarian restaurant instead, or donating to a charity. It is considered a meritorious activity if one refrains from eating meat, but this is not required by Theravada Buddhism. It is the act of killing animals that is problematic, less so than eating animals.

Temple fairs are also important events. These occasions occur outside of the Buddhist calendar and are usually in conjunction with a fundraising effort. A temple might recognize the anniversary of the death of an important monk at the temple, the abbot's birthday, or the temple's production of a new batch of amulets they want to make available. These types of events may raise money for a renovation project or to build new accommodations for monks or lay guests and meditators. Maybe they are building a new ordination hall or installing a grand new Buddha statue on the premises. Temple fairs, with laypeople usually providing food for free and having lots of merit-making opportunities, will attract many people to have a fun afternoon while feeling good about giving.

Chanting

At any type of temple celebration, participants will hear wholesome praises of the Buddha, Dhamma, and Sangha and values of Buddhism communicated via chanting sessions. Formal chanting also occurs every day in the morning and evening for the monks and lay guests staying at the temple. Chanting is an important way to let the Buddhist teachings seep in over time and a powerful concentration exercise to be able to keep up with the fast-paced and occasionally melodic rhythms.

The evening chant begins with a bell rung to let all the monks and community members know the ceremony is beginning. In his book *The Traffic in Hierarchy*, the anthropologist Ward Keeler reports from his stay in a temple in Mandalay, Myanmar, that young novice monks and fully ordained monks make two lines and enter the hall to begin the daily ceremony. They face the image of the Buddha, place a cloth on the floor and sit on it, with the youngest monks at the back and the most senior in the front rows. The novices in the back rows probably only know some of the more basic chants but memorize more of the texts as they continue to participate each day. Laypeople, if there are any joining from outside the temple or are living at the temple, sit behind all the monks.

The most common chanting heard during Buddhist holidays is the Passages on Going for Refuge and the recitation of the Five Precepts, with varying versions in different regions. These affirmations occur as a call-and-response with the monk leader.

Saranagamanapatha (Passages on Going for Refuge)

Buddham saranam gacchami
Dhammam saranam gacchami
Sangham saranam gacchami
To the Buddha I go for refuge.
To the Dhamma I go for refuge.
To the Sangha I go for refuge.
Dutiyampi Buddham saranam gacchami
Dutiyampi Dhammam saranam gacchami
Dutiyampi Sangham saranam gacchami
For the second time, to the Buddha I go for refuge.
For the second time, to the Dhamma I go for refuge.
For the second time, to the Sangha I go for refuge.
Tatiyampi Buddham saranam gacchami
Tatiyampi Dhammam saranam gacchami
Tatiyampi Sangham saranam gacchami
For the third time, to the Buddha I go for refuge.
For the third time, to the Dhamma I go for refuge.
For the third time, to the Sangha I go for refuge.

The Five Precepts are first stated by a monk and then the laypeople will repeat the words as a reminder of their basic commitments to a Buddhist lifestyle:

Pancasila (The Five Precepts)

Panatipata veramani sikkhapadam samadiyami
I undertake the rule of training to refrain from killing living creatures.
Adinnadana veramani sikkhapadam samadiyami
I undertake the rule of training to refrain from taking what is not given.
Kamesu micchacara veramani sikkhapadam samadiyami
I undertake the rule of training to refrain from sexual misconduct.
Musavada veramani sikkhapadam samadiyami
I undertake the rule of training to refrain from false speech.
Suramerayamajjapamadatthana veramani sikkhapadam samadiyami
I undertake the rule of training to refrain from consuming intoxicating drinks (and drugs) that lead to carelessness.

Another frequent refrain is to pay homage to the Triple Gem. This praise of the Buddha, Dhamma, and Sangha reminds Buddhists to be humble in their journey toward nibbana and to be grateful that they have these three precious things to help guide the path. The prostration after each exaltation serves as a bodily reminder of this humility and gratitude.

Araham samma-sambuddho bhagava[2]

Buddham bhagavantam abhivademi.
(The Exalted One, rid of defilements,
Perfectly Enlightened by Himself,
I bow low before the Buddha, the Exalted One.) (Prostrate)
Svakkhato bhagavata dhammo,
Dhammam namassami.
(The Teaching, well-expounded by the Exalted One;
I bow low before the Dhamma.) (Prostrate)
Supatipanno bhagavata savaka-sangho,

Sangham namami.
(The Sangha of disciples, who have practiced well,
I bow low before the Sangha.) (Prostrate)

Senior monk leaders follow the basic morning chanting or evening chanting in their chanting book and afterward can pick an
optional chant. If laypeople are present, the monk will call out the
page number of the next chant, and laity usually help one another
to find the right one so they can continue to follow along. Chanting
usually lasts about a half hour to an hour, followed by a short meditation practice to continue calming the mind that began with the
devotion and focus of this daily ritual. This is the main communal
time for the temple. Attendance is not mandatory but is certainly
expected for a monk unless other duties prevent him.

Tourism and the Temple

Temples with standout features—for example, a silver ordination
hall, a big reclining Buddha statue, or a mountaintop glittering
pagoda—are attractive to tourists. In major cities in Theravada
Buddhist countries, many of the top-ten tourist sites are Buddhist
temples. Yangon and Mandalay in Myanmar, Bangkok and Chiang
Mai in Thailand, Vientiane and Luang Prabang in Laos, and Phnom
Penh and Siem Reap in Cambodia—all include temples in recommended itineraries for tourists, both Buddhist and non-Buddhist,
international and domestic.

To capitalize on this popularity, some temples host other cultural
activities, such as traditional dances, music troupes on weekend
nights, or programs where tourists can ask questions about Buddhism or learn the local arts and handicrafts. At other sites, including many of the pagodas in the Sagaing Hills in Myanmar, there are
no formal cultural or religious engagement opportunities, but there
is commerce. Tourists can buy Buddhist art or little trinkets such
as bracelets or bookmarks. Anyone who has been to Siem Reap in
Cambodia will remember the children constantly attempting to sell

books about Angkor civilization and Cambodian history to travelers. For these sellers, international tourists are a way to make daily wages. Some temples popular with tourists host souvenir and coffee shops just outside the main area of the temple. Monks in Thailand I have spoken to about this mixing of religion and commerce reason that ultimately these types of shops allow for more time spent in the temple itself, possibly creating more opportunities to learn about Buddhism.

Since domestic tourists typically have a better understanding of Buddhism, special programs and commerce are not usually directly targeting them. However, there might be unfamiliar local rituals they would like to try out or offerings they would like to make to temples with new and interesting features. For a domestic tourist from a rural part of Myanmar able to make the trip to Yangon, a visit to the famous Shwedagon Pagoda would be a sacred and fun experience. For international tourists from the Theravada region, such as a Thai tourist to Mandalay, part of the trip might be to access a new sacred site or divine figure, to pay respects to revered monks, or to make merit by visiting new temples. In Thailand, day trips to different regions of the country, which incorporate visiting nine temples in one day, have become trendy.

However, there can be conflicts with tourism, as was seen in Wat Suan Dok when a couple displayed their yoga routine in tight and revealing clothing, inappropriate for a temple. In fact, tourists may not be sure how to act in a sacred area. Some international tourists have been disruptive to Theravada temples, taking wedding photos at scenic temple surroundings when this is not a place of romance. Tourists might be loud and affectionate with one another as well. For this reason, Buddhist temples popular with tourists hire security guards and ticket-takers to manage the space. These temples might also charge fees for international tourists, assuming they are not Buddhist and therefore would not donate on their own. For more information on temple etiquette, see appendix 2 on page 207.

Famous Temple Profiles

The general features and practices above are part of many city and village temples. However, there are some temples that have particularly well-known histories, distinct aesthetics, and controversial practices.

Shwedagon Pagoda, Myanmar

The Shwedagon Pagoda is the most sacred site of Myanmar, located in the city of Yangon, atop the Singutarra Hill. Standing over 370 feet high and covered in thin sheets of gold plates, Shwedagon Pagoda is a thriving center of Buddhism in Myanmar today. On the way to the pagoda, there is much commerce of Buddhist books and talismans available. Inside the temple itself, after removing shoes and ascending the stairs, the vast platform and immensity of the pagoda become clear. Monks and precept nuns are usually available to talk with there, many of whom want to show foreigners around and practice English. The space is filled with people, lay devotees, and monks making offerings, reciting prayers, counting beads, reading prayer books, and meditating inside the four image halls that abut the pagoda. The space is also used for nonreligious activities, such as enjoying a picnic or doing schoolwork.

The pagoda is said to date back to the time of the Buddha when eight of his sacred hairs were enshrined in this location. Legend has it that the Buddha himself gave these hairs to two merchant brothers, Tapussa and Bhallika, who offered him rice cakes and honey. These two merchants asked the Buddha for an object to worship, and he pulled out his hairs. The brothers enshrined some of these hairs in what was to become the Shwedagon Pagoda. In his book *Sacred Sites of Burma*, the art historian Donald Stadtner asserts that because these relics almost certainly do not exist at Shwedagon, since its establishment dates from centuries after the Buddha's time, the real contents of the inner core of the pagoda remain a mystery.

Because of its history and powerful myth, the Shwedagon Pagoda also has a history of conflict and struggle. The anthropologists

Janette Philp and David Mercer argue that the pagoda has been a key element in national political struggles, used by protestors against the state during both British colonial regime and military rule. Because kings traditionally patronized Shwedagon Pagoda, receiving great merit, political leaders have tried to tap into this power.

Wat Phra Dhammakaya, Thailand

The Dhammakaya temple noticeably stands out from other Theravada temples. The largest temple in Thailand, it is not a motley collection of offerings of Buddha statues and buildings in different styles. Instead, everything is intentional and uniform. Even the Buddha statue is different here with its sleek, smooth look.

Founded in 1978 on eighty acres of land outside of Bangkok, Wat Phra Dhammakaya is a relatively new temple, and its architecture and features mark it as such. The stupa, completed in 1999, instead of being bell or pyramid shaped, is circular. With its broad base and ball on top, some say the pagoda looks like a flying saucer. You can see this pagoda when descending into Bangkok's Don Mueang Airport. The upper portions contain three hundred thousand golden Buddha images, and inside the stupa are seven hundred thousand of these statues carved with the name of every donor. All of these statues are exactly alike, and all are situated in an extremely orderly and equidistant manner, mirroring the monks who sit on the outer rim of the stupa and the laypeople who are placed in perfect rows below. During Buddhist holiday rituals, the main events take place at the Dhammakaya stupa with several hundred thousand people often in attendance. This happens during mass temporary ordinations or Buddhist holidays such as Magha Bucha Day, when at night each person's candle glows for perfect photographic moments.

Pha That Luang, Laos

Pha That Luang is Laos's most important national heritage symbol and Buddhist icon, located in the country's capital, Vientiane. Built

by King Setthathirat between 1566 and 1567, this stupa historically served as the center of the Lan Xang kingdom in Vientiane. In
1918, during the French colonial period in Laos, the French began a
rebuilding program of important Buddhist monuments. That Luang
needed rebuilding after being destroyed by the Siamese in the early
nineteenth century. The French embarked on this effort to produce a sense of Lao Buddhist national identity distinct from Siam,
attempting to counteract external influence. The Pathet Lao communist government of Laos next used That Luang as the national
symbol and created an annual state-sponsored ritual in November
commemorating the monument. This festival lasts for over a week,
venerating the Buddha's relic in the pagoda. That Luang is part of
the attempt to reinvigorate and embody Laos culture and traditional
values. Today it is the central symbol of the nation, featured on
tourist brochures and banknotes.

Wat Pah Nanachat, Thailand

Wat Pah Nanachat, the international forest temple, is a unique space
in Theravada Buddhism. English is the spoken language at this temple in northeastern Thailand, where foreign monks come to train in
the Thai forest tradition. The vihara of Wat Pah Nanachat contains
a small Buddha statue and altar; it has a marble floor, giving the
space a fresh, clean look. The few other communal buildings have
this same understated but neat aesthetic. Most of the space is taken
by accommodation and meditation areas. Each hut or small room
for lay female guests has a walking path, and plenty of walking in
nature is possible in and around the grounds of the temple. Instead
of monuments as the focal points of devotion, outdoor spaces are
most important, with trees affixed with sayings to contemplate the
nature of the mind.

Wat Mae Kaet Noi's Hell Garden, Thailand

A "hell garden" is not strictly a Buddhist temple on its own, but it is a unique space of Theravada Buddhism in Southeast Asia. Hell gardens are idiosyncratic projects of monks or laity who have a vision of Buddhist cosmology that they want to share with others. The abbot of Wat Mae Kaet Noi in Chiang Mai Province saw visions of hell that he commissioned artists to render into three-dimensional statues.[3] These statues depict torture in the hell realms of Buddhist cosmology. Some of the statues have a mechanical component so that for a small fee one can hear the screams of the person in hell. The victims of their own immoral actions are also portrayed in disgusting shapes, often with long tongues, sinuous legs and arms, and elongated genitals. Signs posted throughout the garden let those who can read Thai know what each person did wrong to receive this punishment. Some of these bad karmic actions include harming one's mother and father or not paying attention to their teacher, as well as taking drugs, cheating on one's spouse, and lying because of greed.

Tiger Temple, Thailand

The Tiger Temple, or Wat Pa Luangta Maha Bua Yannasampanno, located in western Thailand and founded in 1994, demonstrates the degree of latitude some temples are given within Theravada Buddhism. The first abbot of this temple was Ajahn Maha Bua, widely respected as an *arahant* (enlightened person) by Thai Buddhist society and an influential figure within the Thai forest tradition. The temple was, until recently, a popular tourist attraction featuring interactions with tamed tigers, which demonstrates how far it veered from the austere, solitary practices forest monks are known for.

Though Tiger Temple marketed itself as a tiger sanctuary based on a narrative of Buddhist compassion toward tigers and was recognized as a zoo by the Thai Ministry of Natural Resources and

Environment, it received international criticism as well as accusations of drugging, illegal breeding, and physical abuse of the tigers. After an undercover investigation by CEE4Life garnered media attention, the Department of National Parks of Thailand raided the grounds in 2016. They discovered around sixteen hundred illegal tiger parts, including forty dead cubs kept in a freezer. The temple was closed shortly after, and every single tiger was confiscated and moved to a government wildlife breeding station. Since this scandal, the Tiger Temple no longer holds any tigers and the senior monks from the temple maintain that they did not do anything wrong.

Community Temple Profiles

Famous temples often have interesting stories and exciting locations, but they are in the minority. Most temples serve their surrounding community, with no special features or tourist visits. These temples give a sense of the diversity possible within this general framework of Theravada temple structures. I have asked four monks to describe for me the main structures and activities of their temples.

Wat Daowadung, Thailand, with Phra Somsri

At Wat Daowadung, located off a side road in the old city of Chiang Mai, Thailand, the most important activities for monks are chanting, collecting alms, cleaning, performing rituals, and studying. Normally monks only chant in the evening in the vihara, though during the rains retreat, they conduct morning and evening chanting every day with thirty minutes minimum of meditation afterward.

In Wat Daowadung, there are five main areas: vihara, ordination hall, funeral hall, stupa, and the monks' accommodations. The vihara is used in all group gatherings such as kathina, weekly Buddhist holy days, and Buddhist rituals requested by community members. The ordination hall hosts ordination ceremonies and related monastic rituals, and women are not allowed to enter. When a person in the community passes away, their family brings their body to the temple for the monks to chant and dedicate merit to the deceased. The most sacred space, the stupa, is not used much at this temple except for important occasions such as Visakha Bucha, when all monks and laypeople gather to circumambulate three times with candles, incense, and flowers. Monks clean the stupa every three months and ask forgiveness twice a year there (before and after the rains retreat). Monks spend the most time in their private living spaces, where they can sleep, play on the phone, watch TV, talk, practice chanting, and study.

Wat Thmey, Cambodia, with Bhante Bon Sroeun

Located in Kampong Cham Province, Wat Thmey is a rural, country-side temple about ten kilometers from the center of town. Bhante Bon Sroeun has been the abbot of this temple since he was thirty-three years old, after growing up in the village and graduating from a monastic university in Thailand. The focus of this temple is primary education for monks and English education for all villagers. In this small and remote part of a developing nation, education is valued as an opportunity that should be available to all.

The school building features fifteen classrooms with plans to build two more floors in the future. A multipurpose building contains Buddha images for worship, a meditation hall with guest rooms for practitioners, the abbot's office, and a radio station to broadcast Buddhist teachings. The temple's stupa contains the relic of the former abbot. In front of this stupa are the monastic accommodations, which include a library with over twenty thousand books, mostly in Khmer with some in English. In front of this building is a big Buddha statue standing three meters high. In the future, Bhante hopes to build another big building for accommodating more than eighty novice monks. Lastly, there is a small mart, which Bhante rents to a layperson, that sells snacks and drinks to the novice monks and other children who study at the school.

From this example, we can see that a temple is often a work in progress. Bhante's strategy is to begin building and then expand as the donations come. There is no big donor for this temple, so all the supporters work together to pay construction workers for materials and labor. Bhante has his own aspirations for the space but also feels pressure to build as the abbot, to spread education, meditation practice, and teachings of the Buddha to the community.

Naung Ywe Pongyi Khaung, Myanmar, with Venerable Agga Dhamma

Naung Ywe Pongyi Khaung is a village temple of the Pa O ethnic tribe, located in the Shan State of Myanmar. Venerable Agga Dhamma spends most of his time in the Nyong Ywe Education Center, located in the monastery, where he teaches English.

In this monastery, there are two buildings to accommodate monks and novices. One older building houses twenty novices, and a new building houses ten monks. There is also a simple ordination hall, dining hall, and vihara. These spaces are transitioned into classrooms during schooltime. The vihara, at different times during the day, serves as a chanting hall, meeting space, and classroom. Venerable Agga Dhamma, after having benefited from education in Thailand, finds meaning in promoting education. Because opportunities to study are rare in rural, small villages, he is proud to be a part of the Nyong Ywe Education Center. The abbot does not live in this temple, so Venerable Agga Dhamma runs much of the day-to-day operations, especially in the school, as the vice-abbot.

Wat Khounta, Laos, with Phra Sone

Wat Khounta is one of the city temples of Vientiane, Laos, that sends novice monks to monastic high school. It is conveniently located in the city and very close to a main road with restaurants and even a bar on the way to the international airport. This creates a less than peaceful environment for the monks in residence.

In Laos, the main place monks chant is in the ordination hall. This building is in the middle of the temple and is surrounded by an open hall and the monks' accommodations. The community gathers in the hall for merit-making, and monks take their meals there. There is one building for monastic residents, a two-story dormitory for five to six monks and eighteen to nineteen novices. Phra Sone spent much of his time in front of this building where there are big trees and tables. These tables, with much shade, benefit from a nice breeze, and many monastics chat and relax there doing schoolwork.

In Laos, every temple has a bell and drum tower, which is rung in the morning and evening every Buddhist weekly holy day, which takes place on the full and new moons. This practice is part of traditional Lao Buddhist culture. The tower is about twenty to thirty yards high. When he was a novice monk there, Phra Sone loved to ring the bell and beat the drum.

Diverse Purposes of Buddhist Temples

The temple is the quintessential space of Buddhism. It signifies Buddhist values and teachings, reminding visitors and residents of the beauty, sacredness, and compassion of Buddhism. Many Buddhists say they come to the temple to de-stress and feel peaceful. Gazing upon the many Buddha statues with serene faces in temple halls is meant to generate wholesome thoughts. If someone is feeling anxious or unlucky, a trip to the temple might lift their spirits.

Temples tell the story of Buddhism. Through artwork depicting heaven realms and enlightenment, they communicate Buddhist values of openness, friendliness, and calmness. Morality is also taught in temples, which often have artwork portraying hell realms and beings who did not follow the Five Precepts. Temple spaces are set up to produce tranquility through norms and rules so that visitors and residents do not yell, express anger, or provoke violence.

CHAPTER 2

Sacred Buddhist Objects

Buddhism is not just about meditation. It's safe to say that many practicing Buddhists in Southeast Asia are more interested in collecting amulets and lucky Buddhist statues than closing their eyes and being still—and there is nothing wrong with that! Sacred Buddhist objects are not simply decorative or superficial connections to Buddhist values and narratives. Buddhist materials are so significant because they give regular people access to the power of renunciation, the monastic lifestyle, and the study of Buddhist teachings. The Buddha himself has power, as someone who defeated the temptations of Mara and the worldly life. The Buddha's presence and authority, although technically gone after his enlightenment and death, is still apparent through sacred Buddhist objects. These objects can transfer some of that power to others, providing protection from life's uncertainties. Popular protective objects, which will be discussed in this chapter, include statues, images, and relics of the Buddha, along with protective devices in the forms of amulets and tattoos.

Some Buddha statues can be centuries old and are believed to contain immense possibilities for wish-granting. Relics of the Buddha and other important figures such as temple abbots, meditation masters, and kings can be found buried within stupas at temples. Occasionally such relics are on view through glass cases in temple halls designed to showcase a relic collection. Protective devices, made from a variety of materials, can be small or large. Cloths inscribed with diagrams (*yantra*) represent the power of the Buddhist teachings. These diagrams are often found in cars, as places in need of protection from accidents, and on the body as part of sacred tattoo art. Amulets are worn around the neck or can be stored in a special place in one's home, office, or car. These objects are believed to bring protection and merit if the practitioner maintains Buddhist morality.

Objects such as yantra, Buddha statues, and amulets are not sacred in themselves but need to be made powerful through consecration ceremonies using Pali language. As monks recite verses from Buddhist texts, and hold a sacred string, they meditate and send the power of the Buddha into the objects. Relics, however, are inherently sacred as objects that have been a part of the achievement of nibbana. Nothing more is needed to create a relic's power.

These sacred objects are prevalent throughout mainland Southeast Asia, located in markets, temples, cars, and homes and on bodies. The more access one has to sacred power, the more protected one can feel in a world of uncertainty. Uncertainty is a problem for all of humanity; accessing a sense of control over such uncertainty is especially necessary in the developing countries of Myanmar, Laos, Cambodia, and Thailand. From informal wage workers to the wealthy, everyone is looking for some extra assurance in a world full of chaos and possibilities.

In the 1970s, the anthropologist Melford Spiro introduced a three-part system to understand the different goals of lived Buddhism. Although these divisions are in many cases overlapping, they can be a useful orientation to the purposes of sacred Buddhist objects.

Nibbanic Buddhism: The way of practice for Buddhists who aspire to reach nibbana, an extraordinary goal.

Kammatic Buddhism: The way of practice for Buddhists who aspire to a good rebirth in their next life, a more proximate goal for ordinary people. To reach this goal, Buddhists need to create good kamma for themselves.

Apotropaic Buddhism: The way of practice for Buddhists concerned with everyday problems of this world:

protection from bad spirits, curing illness, drought prevention, reversing bad business deals, getting into one's dream college, winning a sports competition, and so on.

This chapter is mainly concerned with this apotropaic dimension, which attempts to harness the power of Buddhism for protection against dangers and add an extra boost of luck to help attain one's dreams for family, relationships, education, and career in this life. The apotropaic orientation does not contradict or dilute the goal of nibbana. The appeal to powerful beings and objects for aid is not in conflict with the values of Buddhism, which in the end is to reduce suffering.

Images of the Buddha

Within Buddhist history, the Buddha image was initially evoked using symbols like a wheel, bodhi tree leaf, lotus, or stupa. But over time, a rich array of possibilities for depicting the Buddha's physical form emerged. Before there were statues made of the Buddha, his presence was depicted by a footprint. The footprint represents a mark left by the Buddha when he walked on the earth and so acts as an extension of his presence and his physical self. Footprints also symbolize the dominance of Buddhism in a region, which has been purified and transformed by the Buddha walking on the land.

If the footprint is big enough, it can portray the 108 symbols of the Buddha's attributes, illustrated in a grid pattern. The Buddha's footprint might also depict a wheel, symbolizing the Buddha's turning the wheel of dhamma. Some footprints are created by artists, but others are purported to be found. After their discovery, a temple may form around them. Buddha footprints are available for viewing in open-air halls in temples such as Wat Fai Hin in Chiang Mai or in the vihara of a temple, such as Wat Phumin in Nan Province of northern Thailand. In many cases the footprint is extremely large, the size of which would be expected of a giant. Whenever I have asked monks and laypeople if they *believe* the Buddha made the giant footprint, I have quickly realized this is the wrong question and assumption. Paying respect and making offerings to a Buddha footprint does not concern belief. Instead, the footprint is connected to the presence of the Buddha and his nibbana, and that is most significant for a sacred object.

Buddha Statues

Today the Buddha statue is the main and most accessible symbol of the Buddha as a religious leader and teacher. These statues can be reminders of what the Buddha accomplished, but they also possess the potency of the Buddha's achievements. Although the depicted form of the Buddha must contain certain features, such as long earlobes and a bump or flame on the top of his head—features that mark him as a member of royalty and a Great Man in the Indian tradition—artists' representations vary. Various ancient kingdoms, time periods, and regions identified by art historians highlight unique stylistic characteristics and innovations.

Along with his signifying distinctions, the Buddha should look beautiful, attracting others through his features. The markers of beauty for the Buddha are similar to those found in premodern India: an oval head, arched eyebrows, a nose like a parrot's beak, broad shoulders, sinuous arms, and hands like lotus flowers. The Buddha is depicted without bones, muscles, or veins. The Buddha can be wearing either diaphanous monastic robes, so you can see his shape, or royal attire, hearkening back to his life before he was a monk. His monastic robes most often leave the right shoulder bare, as monks today wear their robes. To modern eyes, the Buddha statue can appear androgynous or even feminine, with a smooth body and curved hips. In statues, the Buddha is depicted in one of four positions: sitting, standing, lying down, or walking. When seated, the Buddha can (1) have his legs folded one on top of the other in half-lotus, (2) have both feet on top of his thighs in the full-lotus position, or (3) be seated in a chair. In one former kingdom and now the city of Sukhothai in Thailand, the Buddha was depicted as walking. One foot is ahead of the other with his back foot's heel raised. This is known as the Sukhothai Walking Buddha.

Portrayals of the Buddha derive from his life story. Some of the most popular moments to depict are: (1) seated Buddha with right hand touching the earth, calling the Earth Goddess to witness his merit; (2) seated Buddha's enlightenment or meditation pose with right hand on top of the left; (3) standing Buddha indicating fearlessness or protection with one or both hands raised, palms faced outward; and (4) the seated Buddha giving his first teaching with thumbs and index fingers of both hands joined. Calling the earth to witness is a demonstration of the Buddha's power over merit, kamma, and morality. The Buddha's meditative pose evokes his moment of realization. Following this moment, the Buddha stood with his right hand raised in a gesture of fearlessness, conveying a sense of security and serenity that arises from his attainment. One of the most important moments in the Buddha's life was his first teaching, which set the wheel of dhamma in motion. In Thailand there are Eight Buddhas of the Week, with Wednesdays split into two. Thai Buddhists will know the day of their birth and make special offerings to that Buddha statue.

The Buddha statue acts as a reminder of the possibility of nibbana and as a way for devotees to gain merit. The Buddha's field of merit still exists through his presence in relics and images. Sponsorship of a Buddha image is believed to spread and maintain Buddhism, so it is considered a highly meritorious activity. Artists of Buddha statues historically have not been highlighted in Theravada Buddhist chronicles and manuscripts, as their skill lies not in original artistry but in replicating iconographic details. The agency of the artist is, in the end, outweighed by the agency of the Buddha, whose representation must be regulated by the monks and the donor.

Consecration

When an artist creates a Buddha statue, it's just a statue. To become sacred, the image needs to be consecrated through the power of the

Buddha's words spoken in Pali by monks. During consecration, the image is raised on a platform and surrounded by monks. Monks tie white string from themselves to the statue and chant the life story of the Buddha. This message is conveyed to the image through the conduit of the white string. The content of the chanting describes the physical attributes of the Buddha and elements of Buddhist doctrine. The consecration ritual brings the Buddha's power into the statue—but not the Buddha himself.

In northern Thailand, the most frequent time to see Buddha image consecration is at the conclusion of the rains retreat in October, but this ritual can happen at any time. The date is set by the lay sponsor in consultation with the temple abbot. These consecrations may occur simultaneously with the opening of a new vihara or ordination hall. The ritual of a large Buddha statue emplaced as the main image in a hall usually takes place between sunset and sunrise. The recitation of texts and duration may vary depending on the number of monks, the temple, and the number and status of lay sponsors, but all these rituals relate the story of the Buddha's nibbana, instructing both the image and the followers present in the life of the Buddha.

Types of Buddha Statues

There are a few extremely powerful and sacred types of Buddha statues from the period of Theravada Buddhist kingdoms that still are on display today. A king's possession of such a powerful object signals their worthiness of their title and their significant merit status. Other Buddha statues, which don't have a role in deciding the power of kingdoms, are famous for their wish-granting powers or the spectacle of their size.

PHRAJAO TANJAI (*Thai*). To construct a large statue from start to finish can take several months. Usually, an artist will work at the place of manufacture, and the statue will be delivered to a store or directly to a temple. Unique statues, however, can be created at the temple where they will be consecrated, such as the case of the

Phrajao Tanjai. There are about a dozen Phrajao Tanjai in northern Thailand, where this type of statue is the most famous. These statues are not significant for any distinctive artistic style—a casual observer would never know the difference between a Phrajao Tanjai statue and a regular one. The uniqueness lies in the timing of the statue's creation. *Phrajao Tanjai* can be translated as "instant god" or "the revered one that is just in time." The immediacy refers to both the completion of a Buddha statue in just one day and the statue's ability to bring fortune and realize wishes instantly. When a temple seeks to create a Phrajao Tanjai, the ceremony will begin in the evening. A sculptor will attempt to build a small-sized statue before the sun sets on the next day, usually before 6 p.m. If it is not successful, then the image will just be a regular Buddha statue. But if the statue can be completed before the next night, it is seen to be like a miracle, indicating that some god or spirit has helped the ceremony to be completed. If the sculptor finishes their work in twenty-four hours, the consecration ceremony will happen on another evening. Even more amazing is when the sculptor finishes with some time left over for the consecration ceremony to also be completed within the twenty-four-hour period.

One of the most famous statues for its wish-granting powers is the Luangpor Tanjai statue located at Wat Doi Kham, a temple that sits atop Kham Mountain in Chiang Mai. This statue, which is over five hundred years old, is known to grant wishes in exchange for garlands of jasmine flowers. In 2014, a Thai Buddhist named Khankaew Intamul offered 99,999 garlands to this statue after winning four million baht (about 120,000 USD) in the lottery. She attributed her win to Luangpor Tanjai, whom she had asked to aid in her winning first prize in the upcoming lottery. Whenever a winner attributes their luck to this statue, visitors can expect long traffic delays anywhere near this temple. Thai tourists from provinces near and far visit this Buddha statue to make wishes for winning numbers to be called in their favor. While lottery salespeople find a good atmosphere for their product here, the economy for jasmine garland sellers is also boosted by the popularity of this statue.

If you would like to get your dream job, win the lottery, or any other positive outcome, then you can visit Phrajao Tanjai. Once seated in front of the statue: (1) tell it your name and address, (2) your wish, and (3) how many garlands you will offer if you receive the outcome of your request. The information at Wat Doi Kham says that the Phrajao Tanjai will only consider a request for fifty garlands and above. When you visit Wat Doi Kham, you will see a raised platform with hundreds of garlands on it and a small statue behind this. Despite its size, this statue has much power for those who believe it has helped to tip their business deals, exam outcomes, and health in fortunate directions.

PHRA PHUTTHA SIHING (*Thai*). Phra Phuttha Sihing statues are known for their "lion" style. This style contains some plumpness in the form of the body and a lotus bud-shaped flame at the top of the head. The name also refers to one of the Buddha's thirty-two characteristics of a Great Man from the Indian tradition, that of a lion chest. The Buddha is seated either in a meditation or touching-the-earth hand position, with legs in the lotus position. The first Phra Phuttha Sihing image was brought to Thailand from Sri Lanka and was relocated to the early Thai kingdoms before its current location in Bangkok.

Today there are three well-known Phra Phuttha Sihing images: (1) Chiang Mai's Wat Phra Singh, (2) the National Museum of Bangkok, and (3) Nakhon Sri Thammarat's Phra Nakorn Museum. In Chiang Mai, the image is located not in the main vihara but in its own moderately sized hall, elaborately decorated with mural paintings in the northern and central Thai styles. Local belief asserts that the image in Wat Phra Singh has helped to protect Chiang Mai since the sixteenth century. In the two museums, the statues have their own shrine rooms to pay respect.

PHRA KRING (*Thai*). Phra Kring is a bronze Buddha statue that has a small piece of metal placed in a hollow space so that it rings when shaken. The name "kring" evokes the sound of the bell. Phra Kring statues are associated with the Mahayana Buddhist sect and were introduced into Thailand in the mid-nineteenth century for success and protection. This kind of statue is believed to protect against illness and dangers, especially those associated with travel. One monk in Thailand started the phenomenon of Phra Kring during the reign of Rama V (1868–1910). Phra Kring is portrayed with his left hand in meditation pose and his right hand holding a water vase, ready to spray holy water.

MEGA BUDDHA STATUES. Small, medium, and large Buddha statues are often displayed inside temple halls. Mega Buddha statues are a category of their own. These extra-large statues are popular attractions that can be part of a temple complex or exist independently as a site of worship. If a donor commissions a Buddha statue on a mountain, then pilgrims could come to pay respect to it, making extra merit through the effort involved in their journey up the mountain. Others could just see the Buddha on the mountain as they drive by and have the wholesomeness of this image enter their mind. This is the effect and importance of mega Buddha statues— they draw in pilgrims and help to spread Buddhism and curiosity about the teachings. Wat Phra Chetuphon in Bangkok is famous for its beautiful reclining Buddha, which is 50 feet high and 150 feet long. The longest reclining Buddha in the Theravada world is the Winsein Tawya Buddha in Mawlamyine, Myanmar, at 98 feet high and 590 feet long. Thailand has one of the largest seated Buddha statues in Ang Thong Province, known as the Big Buddha of Thailand, or Phra Phuttha Maha Nawamin, at 301 feet high and 206 feet wide. This statue in Wat Muang took almost twenty years to complete. Maha Bodhi Ta Htaung in Monywa, Myanmar, is famous for its Giant Standing Buddha, the third tallest in the world at 380 feet.

Building these statues—often involving thousands of donations large and small, collected over the span of years—conveys individual and communal devotion. Big statues and the ability to build them confirms the store of merit of the abbot or leader in charge as well as the village, kingdom, or nation-state that helped build it. The immensity of the height and length of these statues is awe-inspiring for visitors, who are attracted to such spectacles. The proliferation of large monuments has dotted Buddhist history but has expanded recently in Southeast Asia, increasing possibilities for tourism and pilgrimage. The more monumental sites to visit, the longer tourists will stay in the area, bringing economic gain to the surrounding area.

Singular Buddha Statues

In Theravada Buddhist temples, there are many other types of statues to encounter, including depictions of disciples of the Buddha, legendary monks associated with myths, modern monks from recent history, and various deities. There are a few particularly extraordinary statues that are of great significance in Theravada Buddhism worth pointing to here.

MAHAMUNI BUDDHA. The Mahamuni Buddha statue is the third most sacred site in all of Myanmar, after the Shwedagon Pagoda in Yangon and the Kyaiktiyo Pagoda, also known as the Golden Rock in Mon State, making it the most famous Buddha image in Myanmar. It is now displayed in Mandalay in the Mahamuni Pagoda (also known as the Rakhine Pagoda). This huge statue measures about 12.5 feet high and 6 feet across. The legendary origin story begins when the Buddha and five hundred enlightened disciples flew with their own bodies from India to the Arakan kingdom in modern-day Rakhine State, Myanmar. The Buddha visited because he became aware that the ruler of Arakan at the time, King Candrasuriya, greatly wanted to pay respect to him. When the Buddha was departing, the king requested an image of him to venerate. The gods assembled the statue as a double of the Buddha in every way through materials the king provided. The Buddha himself breathed his own life into it, addressing the image as his double and younger brother.

Because the statue is known for this myth, other kingdoms have tried to take it throughout the centuries. No one succeeded until King Bodawpaya of Burma conquered the Arakan kingdom in 1784.

His army moved the statue to where it now sits in Mandalay. The Burmese were happy to have the sacred object, celebrating their kingdom's power, but this was a devastating loss for the Arakanese, which still resonates today. While chronicles from Rakhine state that the statue had to be tied down so that it would stay away from Rakhine and that it wanted to return, texts from the Burman kingdom explain that the statue wanted to go with King Bodawpaya.

Today in Mandalay, the Mahamuni statue still attracts crowds of visitors daily. Locals and tourists can visit the smaller temples and shops along the road to the Mahamuni Temple selling items to give to monks and devotional offerings. The main way to pay respect to this statue is to press thin sheets of gold leaf paper on its surface. However, only men are allowed to touch the statue, as women are prohibited from entering the platform the statue occupies. Art historian Donald Stadtner estimates that over the last century the Buddha has grown by about twelve tons of gold leaf. The thick layer of gold is placed everywhere except its face. The chief monk, assisted by laymen dressed in white, wash the Buddha's face every morning around 4:30 a.m.

PHRA BANG STATUE OF LUANG PRABANG, LAOS. The Phra Bang statue, from the ancient Lao kingdom of Lan Xang, is still important within contemporary Laos, from which the city of Luang Prabang derives its name. In 1359, the Phra Bang statue was given to King Fa Ngum, the first monarch of the Lang Xang kingdom of present-day Laos, by his father-in-law from the Angkor kingdom to provide legitimacy for his rule. The Siamese, now Thai, have captured the statue twice—in 1782 and 1828—giving it back both times because they attributed periods of chaos to the figure. This Buddha statue is the most revered in all of Laos, protecting the area and its people. The statue itself—in the standing Buddha position with hands raised in the hand gesture of fearlessness—is solid gold and about thirty-two inches tall.

In 1995 Luang Prabang joined the prestigious list of UNESCO's world heritage sites. Part of preserving the city's material culture was enshrining the Phra Bang statue on the site of the old royal palace, which is now the Luang Prabang National Museum. An image hall was completed near the entrance in 2013. This statue still serves as the symbol of Luang Prabang's heritage and is at the center of the Lao New Year celebration in the city. On the fourth and final day of this celebration, the Phra Bang statue is ritually cleansed. The figure is brought out from its image hall and after chanting Pali suttas, the people, ranging from monks to government officials to laypeople, pour water through the throat of a naga, which then washes the Phra Bang statue, purifying the power of the Buddha for another year.

EMERALD BUDDHA. The *Chronicle of the Emerald Buddha*, a text tracking the travels of the Emerald Buddha, states that the statue was discovered by accident in the northern Thai city of Chiang Rai in the fifteenth century. When a layperson was washing a Buddha statue, the stucco chipped off, and when it all was removed, the Emerald Buddha was uncovered underneath. The legendary history of this statue is that a famous ancient Indian Buddhist monk, Nagasena, expressed a wish to create a Buddhist statue for the world. The gods heard the monk's wish, obtained a gem, and sculpted it into the beautiful statue. After its discovery in the Lanna kingdom of present-day northern Thailand, the statue was moved to the Luang Prabang and Vientiane kingdoms of Laos before being captured by the Siamese and was finally installed in Bangkok in 1784 as the central statue signifying Buddhist protection and power during the current lineage of the Thai monarchy, the Chakri Dynasty.

The figure, at just nineteen inches wide and twenty-six inches high, depicts the Buddha meditating in seated lotus position. It is made of jasper—a green stone; not real emerald—and clothed in golden costumes. Green adds to the appeal and power of this statue, as this color would be correlated with the god Indra, fertility, and wealth. During the beginning of each of the three seasons, the king of Thailand changes the outfit of the Emerald Buddha so that its costume matches the weather. For example, during the cool season, a gold-mesh shawl is draped over the statue. Many souvenirs from Bangkok depict replicas of the Emerald Buddha in its three costumes. Once inside the hall housing the Emerald Buddha in the famous Wat Phra Kaew, officials enforce the rule of no photography.

These Buddha statues, despite their diverse materials, all derive from miraculous origins. Once Buddhist actors place meaning and sacredness onto the image, a Buddha statue can become part of national history, a political tool, a confirmation of morality, and a powerful symbol, as well as a reminder of the Buddha. Statues are interactive, inviting others to project onto them and engage with them. They can grant wishes and have protective powers, especially when proper veneration is displayed, which expresses the apotropaic orientation toward Buddhist objects. At the same time, a kammatic and nibbanic framework can be applied to Buddha statues. The sight of the Buddha is thought to bring peacefulness and wholesome thoughts, providing inspiration, motivation, and reassurance. This inspiration can be directed toward good karma and rebirth or the pursuit of nibbana.

Buddha Statues Outside the Temple

Buddha statues do not just exist in temples but can also be found throughout the public sphere in mainland Southeast Asia. Taxi cabs are one common place to encounter Buddha statues in Bangkok, especially on the dashboard. The Emerald Buddha, with its three costumes, is a favorite protector, as is the Chinnarat Buddha, considered the most beautiful, with its frame of mythical animals. Buddha statues can be many different colors and shine with resin or glass, or they can be made from metal, ceramic, or wood. As well, Buddha statues can be kept on a home altar or in one's restaurant or place of business. Not all images of the Buddha are treated so respectfully, though, nor are they all situated in appropriate places.

The Knowing Buddha Organization (KBO) is an organization created by Acharawadee Wongsakon, a Thai laywoman, successful entrepreneur, and meditation teacher. Michael Jerryson, a scholar of Buddhist studies, records the origin of Acharawadee's determination to found the KBO. She was traveling in France when she happened upon The Buddha Bar. Once inside she was distraught to find a Buddha statue in the middle of the bar. The incongruity of the bar atmosphere, including drinking and dancing, with the sacredness she associates with the Buddha led her to establish KBO. Since 2011, the organization has tracked over one hundred cases of disrespect and files lawsuits against companies and restaurants that use the Buddha image inappropriately. The Buddha's head on a toilet seat cover or a door mat, or decorating a garden, for instance, are all inappropriate places. The organization has fought against models posing in front of Buddha images for *Maxim* magazine, and Buddha images on skateboards, beer cans, headphones, and many more. Since a Buddha statue is a sacred object, it should be on altars, proper places of worship, as Christians would want for representations of Jesus on the cross. This Buddhist organization wants Buddhism to be treated with equal respect. This misuse of the image of the Buddha can be considered a form of cultural appropriation. Instead of treating the Buddha figure as a sacred object, as it would be in its own cultural context, non-Buddhists are appropriating the image in inappropriate ways into nonsacred spaces.

In Myanmar, there is no such organization leading the charge against blasphemy of the Buddha image, but the government has brought charges against foreigners damaging religion. When a bar in Myanmar used an image of the Buddha wearing headphones in their promotional materials, the bar manager, a foreign national from New Zealand, was arrested for insulting religion. Under Myanmar law, insulting or damaging any religion has a maximum sentence of two years in jail. The bar owners and management team have apologized for their ignorance. However, their court appearance led to the maximum sentence.

Travelers and foreign residents should be careful to treat the Buddha image with respect. If you buy a Buddha statue in mainland Southeast Asia, make sure it is not an antique. At some locations where statues are sold, you will be given or may have to ask for a certificate confirming that the statue is under one hundred years old. When you carry the Buddha statue home, the customs officers may ask to see the certificate verifying that you are not taking an antique out of the country. You can also have your Buddha statue consecrated. It will not be as long a process as a statue being consecrated in a temple, just a simple blessing. Then your Buddha statue becomes a holy object. Make sure to respect that by placing the statue somewhere high in your house, and not in dirty places such as your front lawn or in the bathroom!

Relics

While images are made and manufactured, relics are created or discovered. Relics, as tiny fragments of the remains of the Buddha and other enlightened figures, are portable and thus can easily propagate and create new centers of Buddhism, contributing to the success of Buddhism as a missionary religion. Where enshrined, relics create sites of pilgrimage and opportunities for merit-making in specific locations.

After the Buddha's death, as described in the *Mahaparinibbana Sutta*, when his remains were cremated, only bones remained; there were no ashes or particles of skin, flesh, or tissue left behind. The text details how upon the Buddha's death in the fifth century B.C.E., representatives from eight different kingdoms divided these relics and enshrined them in eight stupas. Beginning in the third century B.C.E., King Asoka, in his legendary act, gathered the relics from these eight stupas and redistributed them into eighty-four thousand stupas throughout his kingdom. These relics eventually spread further throughout Asia. According to early Buddhist commentaries by the authoritative fifth-century C.E. monastic commentator Buddhaghosa, five thousand years after the Buddha's parinibbana, all the Buddha's relics will assemble at the place of the Buddha's enlightenment, Bodh Gaya. Then the relics will re-form into the shape of the Buddha's body, and after performing some supernatural feats, this relic body will disappear, signaling the end of the Buddhist era until a new Buddha arrives and starts the process over again.

Relics give a sense of the physical presence of the Buddha and evidence of the possibility of enlightenment for followers, instilling faith and motivation. They are believed to contain the agency to move and multiply on their own, demonstrating the Buddha's continued presence in the world. The relic is thought to emit power and energy, protecting the area where it is located. There is no way to definitively prove these small particles have their origin in the body of Gotama Buddha. However, belief and proof are not necessary, nor is faith. Simply being in the presence of a relic and having respect for the sacred object is the point.

Although relics are tiny, often looking like a bean or small piece of crystal, they are immensely sacred because they are pieces of holy people—most importantly, the Buddha himself. Because these objects are so sacred yet so small, they require a big marker of their status. Therefore, relics are enshrined in the huge and symbolic stupa structure. Some relics, buried far within stupas, can never be seen, while others are more accessible. Relics of recently deceased monks or even disciples of the Buddha can be on display in relic chambers of temples. Other relics are taken out for display at special times. To celebrate the international meditation center's anniversary where I was practicing and conducting research, in Wat Chom Tong in Chiang Mai, their relic—a part of the Buddha's skull— was brought out for all participants. The ritual involved us paying respect by pouring water over the glass case that enshrines the relic.

Besides the most common form of body relics, there are also relics of use or contact and objects of commemoration. Relics of use are objects that the Buddha owned such as alms bowls and robes. Objects of commemoration represent the Buddha, such as a sculptural image. Like Buddha statues, relics ground Buddhist institutions and inspire travel and exchange. This power has been harnessed by Buddhist kings and nation-states and can become a symbol of national renewal.

Relic Tales

Relics have their own biographies. Their tales reveal how they came to be interred in various stupas, adding to the power and legend of the Buddha's enlightenment. Relics of the Buddha also connect Buddhism to royalty through their intimate link with kings. The king is necessary in ancient and modern relic tales to activate the relic and create the circumstances, patronage, and monuments necessary for the populace to express their devotion and respect.

In the *Chronicle of Flower Garden Monastery*, Phra Sumanthera, acting on a vision he received from a god, discovered a relic, which he presented to King Kuena of the Lanna kingdom. King Kuena invited the relic into a golden vessel, which was installed in a stupa at the monastery of the same name as the chronicle, Wat Suan Dok, which literally translates as "flower garden temple." The relic performed miracles such as floating and shining luminously and multiplying itself into two. The second one was eventually enshrined in the stupa of Wat Phrathat Doi Suthep.

Some stupas enshrine multiple relics, especially in Myanmar. Inscriptions and epigraphs reveal what is enshrined in a stupa, which can also include paintings and images of the arrival of the relic from its original location. For example, the Kaunghmudaw Pagoda in Sagaing, central Myanmar, enshrines both a tooth relic and an alms bowl from Sri Lanka, but the pagoda also contains unspecified relics, hair relics, stupas studded with jewels, and jeweled images from many countries. In Burmese chronicles, these relics tell the story of a sixteenth-century Sri Lankan king named Dhammapala who sent relics in exchange for military assistance. Exchange of relics creates alliances and competition between kings, particularly between Sri Lanka and mainland Southeast Asia and among closer, smaller kingdoms.

In northern Laos, one relic tale reveals the theme of the Buddha foretelling the future of his relics while he was still alive. At the future site of the pagoda named Chiangteum in the district of Muang Sing, the Buddha told of the enshrinement of his neckbone, whetstone, and razor. The anthropologist Paul Cohen translates this mythical history, which begins with the Buddha journeying to the top of the mountain Chiangteum. After spending some time there eating and drinking, the Buddha declared that three relics should be buried at the top of this mountain as a place of worship. After the Buddha's death, one of his disciples buried the relics as instructed. Today the stupa is protected by four guardian spirits and is celebrated each year by a festival consisting of cleaning and decorating the reliquary and climbing the mountain to make offerings.

Relic stories even extend to modern history. Juliane Schober, a scholar of Burmese Buddhism, writes of the ways relics are used to strengthen political ties, as occurred when China presented a tooth relic in 1994 to Myanmar as part of a forty-five-day tour of the country. The tooth was taken throughout central Myanmar along with two replicas. These replicas were left behind and established in north Yangon and south of Mandalay. This Buddha relic served as a legitimation for the military government at the time, since they were able to bring such a sacred object to the people of Myanmar. Although the Burmese people remained suspicious of the government after the violent quashing of their popular resistance in 1988, worshipping a tooth relic was still an important merit-making opportunity. The Chinese tooth relic was intended by the state to promote a vision of a unified Burmese Buddhist nation, but the resistance of the people was still apparent.

In Cambodia, the anthropologist John Marston describes how almost a million people joined a procession of relics in 2002. These relics, originating from Sri Lanka, had initially been installed in a stupa in front of Phnom Penh railway station in 1957 and were being relocated to a stupa on the hill in Oudong, signaling legitimization of the government because they could orchestrate such sacred movements. The fact that this new emplacement of the relic generated such enthusiasm can be interpreted as a step toward increasing the unity of the country under Buddhism after the devastating genocide under the communist regime of the Khmer Rouge in the latter part of the 1970s.

Besides relics of the Buddha, "mummified" monks also receive some notoriety in Southeast Asia. Instead of cremation, some important monks' bodies are preserved and on display because of wealthy patrons' wishes or plans to cremate the body, which never takes place. Villagers in one rural Cambodian temple preserved their former abbot's body for one year, intending to cremate it. The disciples found that the body had not deteriorated in that time and so it now sits in a glass case in the monks' eating hall, dressed in robes and covered with a white cloth. Although the body does not look like a living person, it still has skin covering the body.

In Thailand, a "mummy monk" is on display in Wat Khunaram on the island of Koh Samui. Luangpor Daeng died in seated meditation in 1973, and his body has been kept in that position inside a glass case ever since. For tourists, this is an unusual divergence from their beach vacation, but for Thai Buddhists, the site of a monk's body in only slight decay offers a visual reminder of the power of the Buddha's teachings. Luangpor Daeng's long meditation sessions and simple life are believed to be the reasons for his body's amazing preservation. Attractions such as these mummy monks can bring income and donations to temples, especially during special occasions when visitors can watch the ceremonial changing of the deceased monks' robes.

Protective Devices

Protective devices, or objects that offer protection, are ubiquitous in Buddhist mainland Southeast Asia. Photographs of famous monks and images of Buddha can be thought of as protective devices, even though they are not formally blessed. Instead, they contain a link to the power and possibility of nibbana through the Buddha's disciples. Although the Buddha is of course extremely important, he is also in some sense a distant and unknowable figure. Monks who are from one's region or whom one's parents worshipped may be easier to feel close to, and these monks are believed to offer protection through the power of their realization. In Thailand, one of the most widely depicted monks is the legendary figure Luang Por Tuat, who is believed to protect against car accidents. Somdet To (Somdet Phra Puttajan To) is also popular because he is believed to be able to endow his image with magical powers. Luangpor Sot Candasaro's picture is ubiquitous because of his skill in meditation and widely held belief that he is an arahant.

Photographs are common items obtained at temples or even at market stalls. However, tattoos, amulets, and yantra are more complex objects of protection. On their own, these items are just ink, cloth, clay, and other natural materials. However, with the power of Buddhist blessings (*paritta*) and verses of teachings (*gatha*), these regular objects are made sacred. Meditation masters' power can be transferred to amulets, which others can tap into when worn. Protective devices have a long history in Cambodia, where they are produced by chanting gatha by a *gru*, a male practitioner and usually former monk who has learned techniques of protection and healing. The accessibility of such power can only be attained by the few who can dedicate much of their time to the mental and moral discipline of the monastic life and meditation. Protective devices are a way to share in this power for those without the time or ability needed to create this sacredness.

Paritta and Gatha

Throughout Theravada Buddhism, traditional paritta are found in the collection of twenty-four discourses selected from the Sutta section of the Pali Canon. These oral recitations and representations of the words infuse power into sacred objects described below: yantra, tattoos, and amulets. Paritta recital is effective because it is believed to be an assertion of truth. If one is established in truth, then the power of that truth can be used to gain protection. Paritta also recall wholesomeness, which can in turn bring material wealth through concentration and confidence. The most well known are taken from the *Mangala Sutta*, *Ratana Sutta*, and *Karaniya-metta Sutta*. Here's an excerpt from a common example:

Mangala Sutta (Discourse on Blessings)[4]

Many deities and men have pondered on blessings longing for
safety, Tell, then, the highest blessing.

Not to consort with fools, with the wise to consort and to
honour the honourable: this is the highest blessing.

Living in befitting places, in the past to have made merit, and
with oneself rightly guided: this is the highest blessing.

Much knowledge (of the Truths) and skills, well-trained in
discipline and speech which is well spoken: this is the
highest blessing.

Support of mother and father, cherishing of wife and children,
ways of work without conflict: this is the highest blessing.

Giving and conduct according to Dhamma, helping relatives,
unobstructive kamma: this is the highest blessing.

Restraint, abstinence from evil, refraining from intoxicants,
heedfulness in Dhamma: this is the highest blessing.

Respectfulness and humility, contentment and gratitude, the
timely hearing of the Dhamma: this is the highest blessing.

Patience and meekness when corrected, and sight of samanas,
timely discussion of Dhamma: this is the highest blessing.

Ardent effort in the holy life, insight into the Noble Truths,
and the realization of Nibbana: this is the highest blessing.

Though in contact with worldly dhammas yet his mind is
not moved, griefless, dustless, secure: this is the highest
blessing.

By doing such things as these (men) are everywhere
victorious, and go everywhere in safety: this is the highest
blessings.

Monks can chant paritta directly to an individual layperson, such
as after having received food on their alms round; to a whole group
through sprinkling water (which feels very refreshing on a humid
day in Southeast Asia); or to someone receiving a sacred string tied
around their wrist. The water or string, in addition to the words,

transfers the protective power of the paritta. These paritta recitals can be part of a simple request for blessing or as part of a multiday ceremony. In March 2020, monks gathered at Bodh Gaya to chant these types of blessings aimed toward the end of the COVID-19 pandemic. Although the paritta are in Pali, these chants are not exclusively foreign and without meaning for laypeople. Instead, paritta, which contain Buddhist doctrines, can educate about the dhamma. In addition to aiding this-worldly needs, paritta can create mindfulness and concentration. In this way, paritta can be seen partially as a compromise between laypeople concerned with their success and merit and monks who are providing a Buddhist educational experience.

While a paritta can be a longer discourse, a gatha (verse) is a shorter blessing of a few lines. Here is an example of a short blessing:

Sumangala Gatha (Verses of Excellent Blessing)[5]

May there be for you all blessings, may all the Devas guard
    you well,
By the power of all the Buddhas, ever in safety may you be.
May there be for you all blessings, may all the Devas guard
    you well,
By the power of all the Dhamma, ever in safety may you be.
May there be for you all blessings, may all the Devas guard
    you well,
By the power of all the Sangha, ever in safety may you be.

The Sumangala blessing uses the power of the Buddha and the Triple Gem to bestow safety and protection. Another example, which the Thai Buddhism scholar Justin McDaniel has called the most powerful text in Thailand, is the *Jinapanjara Gatha (Verses on the Victor's Armor)*. This gatha is known and chanted throughout Thailand every day by monks but also many laypeople. Here is McDaniel's translation of the first three of fifteen verses:

The Buddhas, those bulls of men, having defeated Mara
    and his elephant, [each] having established [his own]

victory seat, they drank the ambrosia of the Four Noble
Truths.
The Buddhas, the sonorous teachers, the twenty-eight guides
beginning with Tanhankara, they are all fixed on my head.
The Buddha is fixed on my head. The dhamma is in my eyes.
The sangha, the holder of every virtue, is fixed on my
chest.[6]

This chant emphasizes not the doctrines or teachings of Buddhism
but the power of the Buddha, Dhamma, and Sangha. Another
famous gatha is the *Itipiso*, which contains verses in praise of the
Triple Gem in 108 syllables, a sign of completeness and perfection.
The first part, in fifty-six syllables, is a recollection of the Buddha.
This part of the gatha enumerates the qualities of the Buddha:

Thus indeed is he, the Blessed One: the Holy One, fully enlightened, endowed with clear vision and virtuous conduct, sublime,
knower of worlds, incomparable leader of men to be tamed, the
teacher of gods and men, enlightened and blessed.[7]

Paritta and gatha are the foundation for protective devices such as
yantra, amulets, and tattoos.

Yantra

Yantra are physical representations of these protective words,
believed to be able to have a real effect on the world. The geomet-
ric design of the yantra acts as a kind of support for the sacred
sequences of the gatha. These designs are not made to be read but
to evoke the power of the gatha. Yantra are drawn onto the body
as tattoos, on pieces of cloth, or directly on the objects in need of
protection. The cloths can be varying sizes and are usually red or
yellow in color and made from cotton in a rectangular shape. These
cloth diagrams are hung in one's vehicle or home to prevent poverty,
ill-health, or accidents. The design can also be inscribed on small
sheets of metal and then rolled into a casing and worn on one's body.

When a new house is consecrated, monks might be called to chant protective paritta and gatha and to draw a yantra in a prominent place, such as the front door.

Some yantra consist of grids with square shapes containing syllables of a gatha written in each of the squares. Yantra diagrams can also be formed into shapes such as a candle, the top of the Buddha's head, or a stupa. Others are shaped into Hindu deities, mythical creatures, or powerful animals such as lions and tigers. Inside the shape, characters are written in Pali in a script considered ancient and sacred. Producing yantra requires much training and is only done by those adept in the arts of asceticism with knowledge of Buddhism.

Sacred Tattoos

Sacred tattoos are a more permanent form of protective devices. These magical tattoos are believed to be incredibly powerful in Theravada Buddhism, protecting against danger and evil spirits and attracting positive things such as luck, wealth, and health. Tattoos can influence the wearer, making them more confident or articulate, or they can inspire others whom the wearer meets to be friendly or nonaggressive toward them. Some tattoos can motivate respect and submission, while others inspire romantic attraction or love. Others still are meant to create invulnerability against animal bites or accidents. Tattoos only become sacred tattoos after a tattoo master consecrates them with the appropriate gatha. Tattoo masters can be monks or laypersons who have studied the art of tattooing and the Buddhist languages and texts necessary and are able to concentrate the mind. After the tattoo is applied, the consecration ceremony consists of the master reciting the syllables within the yantra, animating its power. As a last step, the master blows on the tattoo. Modern-day tattoos protect people working in hazardous jobs, such as construction or roadwork, or protestors against the government. In Myanmar, the Shan people practice the art of sacred tattooing. Sacred tattoos are most popular in Thailand today overall.

Cambodia and Laos, with their histories of war and communism, have lost some of the knowledge associated with sacred tattooing.

There are many examples of magical tattoos from Thailand, where sacred tattoo artistry has become world-famous. The *Yant Amnaj* depicts twin tigers walking toward a central yantra diagram and is often displayed on soldiers and police interested in increasing their status and influence. A tattoo depicting four Buddhas helps protect its wearer from bullets. The Hindu god Hanuman featured in a battle scene from the Thai version of the Hindu epic the Ramayana, confers the power and agility of a monkey. Tattoos of the Hindu god Ganesha offer success and removal of obstacles. Angelina Jolie helped to make famous the *Ha Taew Yant* and her tattoo artist Ajahn Noo Kanpai. This tattoo, which consists of a row of five lines, (1) prevents unjust punishment, (2) reverses bad fortune, (3) protects against black magic, (4) creates good luck and success, and (5) attracts the opposite sex.

The sacred tattoo is believed to work in conjunction with Buddhist morality. The basic Five Precepts must be followed for the tattoo to be effective. There might be other rules to follow as well, such as avoiding eating certain foods at particular times, not emotionally or physically hurting your parents, or not slandering anyone's mother. Some foreigners might get a tattoo without believing in their power or not understanding the actions they need to take to make the tattoo effective. In this case, the person has a beautiful tattoo but not a sacred one. In 2011, Thailand's Ministry of Culture considered banning tattoo parlors from giving tourists tattoos of the Buddha, believing that when foreigners see these tattoos as fashion, they disrespect the religion and cause offense.

Amulets

Amulets are abundant in mainland Southeast Asia. They likely began as small votive tablets to help remind one of the Buddha. Today amulets can also portray images of famous kings, monks, or Hindu gods. They are considered effective as protective devices, especially if made by a monk famous for their power connected to Buddhist training, especially meditation and morality. Amulets are made from clay mixed with natural ingredients such as dried flowers, herbs, seeds, and pollen. They can also be made from wood, stone, ivory, resin, or metal. Many are made using a mold containing the pressed image of a monk on one side and a yantra on the other side. When encased in metal and attached to cords, they can be worn around the neck. A person might wear an amulet discretely under a shirt, while others might make their amulets very public by placing the cord containing multiple large amulets outside of their shirt. The most valuable amulets are made by famous magic monks and would be of the first generations of these amulets. Rumors about particular amulets helping people avoid disastrous situations increase demand. Amulets are marketed in magazines, newspaper articles, and books, which describe their powers and popularity.

You can often find amulets inside or outside of temple grounds. Amulets sold at temples are usually newer ones produced at that monastery or are commercially made and not high value. The sales from amulets are used by many temples to fund building projects. There are also amulet markets. Bangkok's most famous location to buy amulets is the Tha Phrachan Amulet Market, near The Grand Palace. Collectors often spend their time at market stalls here with magnifying glasses, judging the value and authenticity of the amulets on offer. Experts evaluate amulets by their age, the monk who sacralized it, and proof of efficacy through stories. Valuable amulets are sacralized in batches by senior monks enjoying national praise and respect. Each of these batches should have a special authenticating mark, which helps identify fakes. The most famous creator of amulets in recent history was Luang Phor Khun, whose amulets had high price tags because of beliefs in their power to multiply one's fortunes.

Another example of a popular amulet is the Chatukham-Rammathep. The amulet began production in 1987 when the first batch was made to fund the city pillar of Nakhon Si Thammarat in southern Thailand. The two founders of this city, legendary deities known as Chatukham and Rammathep, are believed to be able to help fulfill wishes and provide protection, and they are depicted on the amulet. The amulet's success grew as advertisements and marketing published stories of its power, reaching peak popularity around 2006. Phra Phayom Kalyano, the abbot of Wat Suan Kaew, a temple outside of Bangkok, is known for his outspokenness concerning materialism and Buddhism. Phra Phayom was heavily critical of the craze over these amulets, stating that it did not display the essence of Buddhism. His intention was to direct Thai people away from attachment to material wealth and draw attention back to the "core" of Buddhism.

In Thailand, the commercialization of Buddhism has been labeled *puttha panit*. Selling religious products, some say, reveals the greed of monks. The widespread sale and expansion of the amulet trade is one source contributing to the idea that Buddhism has become too commercial. The materialism and consumerism associated with religious objects, in particular protective devices such as amulets, are thought by some critical monks and laity in Thailand to be destroying Buddhism, weakening the tradition and culture in Theravada societies because it can lead to greed, one of the root defilements. Because these religious commodities are tied to achievement of wealth, they appear to be only for this purpose. However, magical Buddhism itself is not a problem. There is nothing controversial about protecting one's body from harm or one's car from an accident, asking a wish-fulfilling statue for financial ease, or hoping amulets bring luck. It is when these magical pursuits are abused that critical Buddhists charge foul play on the monastic institution or individual monks.

Powerful Buddhist Objects

Buddhist sacred objects are an important part of the lived experience of Theravada Buddhism, especially pertaining to the apotropaic orientation toward practice. These items and practices bring the power of the Buddha closer in time and space, making his protection accessible to both individuals and communities. These are visual markers of the safety, protection, and power of Buddhism, the Buddha's nibbana, and the possibility of nibbana. One can purchase amulets, yantra, tattoos, and Buddha statues. However, encountering relics and many famous Buddha statues requires pilgrimage. Because of their sacred nature, no one person can own such objects, but they are available to all to interact with and gain merit. Making a pilgrimage to visit the sacred sites of Myanmar, including the famous Mahamuni Buddha statue and the hair relics enshrined in the Shwedagon Pagoda, allows one to be in contact with the Buddha's presence. Going to a tattoo master to receive a sacred tattoo brings the power of Buddhism closer to one's physical body. Asking a monk to apply a yantra to one's car or front door creates a sense of protection and confidence in one's daily life. Wearing an amulet around one's neck is a widespread daily habit to protect from danger and bring in good fortune. People, especially those without much power in the world, seek protection from religion. When taking a trip, considering a new business venture, getting married, moving to a new location, or even just walking outside one's door, there are risks involved. These protective devices allow practitioners to feel that they have done what they can to protect themselves from possible threats.

PART TWO

People

CHAPTER 3

Varieties of Male Monks

The male monastic institution traces its lineage back to the Buddha when he welcomed his first disciples. This community was originally open to both men and women. However, today female ordination in the Theravada tradition is a complex topic, which will be discussed in the next chapter.

Theravada Buddhist monastic life is predicated on the difference between the renunciant, who leaves behind the life of a regular person in society, and the householder, who has a job and family. This distinction is marked visually by the robes monks wear, their shaved head, and their residence in the temple. Historians of religion question whether the monastic life was ever so clear-cut or ideal as an isolated monk wandering alone or meditating in caves. Instead, premodern and present-day monastic institutions offer much diversity and possibilities within renunciation. This chapter will explain the varieties of male monks and how they fit into Theravada Buddhist societies in multiple ways.

The first male monks were ordained simply by the Buddha saying, "Come, O monk." Since that time, an elaborate ordination ritual has developed along with complex monastic hierarchies. In mainland Southeast Asia, each temple has its own abbot; and each district, province, and region has its own leading monks. These top monks can be appointed by a king, government authority, or council of senior monastics, while popularity within Buddhist communities can create recognition for other monks. In Thailand, Laos, and Cambodia, there are two sects: a majority sect and a minority reform sect, which is typically considered more disciplined. These two sects are called Mahanikai and Thammayut in Thailand and Laos; Thommakay and Thammayut in Cambodia. In Myanmar, there are nine recognized sects; the majority of monks are part of the Thudamma sect, while the Shwegyin reform sect contains the most significant minority. Monks belong to one of the sects within their nation-state and live in a temple of monks ordained within that sect.

Basics of Male Monasticism

In Theravada Buddhism, there are two levels of ordination: novice and full *bhikkhu*. *Bhikkhu* is the Pali term for a fully ordained male. Males younger than twenty have novice ordination (*pabbajja*) as their only option, which requires only one preceptor. Once ordained, novices are expected to maintain ten precepts. Often young boys will become novice monks in a large group as part of a temple program during school holidays. It is also a traditional custom in villages to ordain brothers, male relatives, and boys in the same age group to reduce costs and collectively earn merit. The ordination ceremony for young boys is focused on how the ceremony appears to the laypeople watching. It must meet a standard of appropriateness and sacredness, with the boys looking clean, tidy, and restrained. This adds to the emotional component for the parents as the boys appear like they can take care of themselves and assume their new role. In Myanmar, novice candidates are dressed up like royal princes in elaborate costumes adorned with jewelry and makeup. The display of grandeur in their procession on elephants and horses (or cars and trucks in cities) is very important to highlight the act of renunciation that follows.

Despite their lack of experience, youth play an important role in the monastic institution. Early Indian Buddhist texts show precedence for orphaned and disadvantaged youth entering the monastic life, particularly when they are placed in the care of a monastic relative. The minimum age for entry is old enough to "scare away crows," which is as young as seven years old. Young boys who are able to throw stones so that the crows do not disturb the monks' sleeping quarters can be useful and serve a purpose in the monastery. They can take on some of the ascetic life and help older monks with the daily tasks of running the monastery. The decision to ordain can be solely in the hands of the parents, both the parents and child, or a boy might make the decision on his own, even against his parents' wishes. If a young boy is having trouble in school or has a difficult family life, he might be encouraged to ordain more than other boys who are thriving in school or family. Because young novices must live without their parents, they can develop deep bonds with the senior monks in their temple. If the abbot is not an especially warm person, other senior monks may take on more of a caretaker role.

Men over twenty can choose to ordain as novices or continue to become fully ordained bhikkhus. Bhikkhus will first receive the pabbajja ordination if they are not already novices and then will receive the second ceremony for the fully ordained monk, the *upasampada*, which requires five monks, the preceptor with over ten years in the robes. A monastic candidate must have their parents' permission, and they cannot ordain if they have communicable diseases, are under government service, or are evading jail or debt. In their monastic ceremonies, men are asked if they are under any of these conditions. After ordination, monks are called by various honorific titles meaning "revered or venerable teacher," or a kinship-related term for "older brother," "father," or "grandfather," depending on their age.

Bhikkhus follow 227 rules. These rules are found in the the *Vinaya Pitaka* (Basket of Discipline), which contains the *patimokkha*, a list of the codes of conduct. Monks are reminded of these rules fortnightly at the patimokkha ceremony—the recitation and confession that monks hold together as a sangha. Monks divide into pairs and confess any wrongdoings since the last patimokkha, then they bring any large offenses to the wider group of monks. Minor offenses can be cleared up by confessing. The most important rules for monks are the Four Parajikas—these are precepts that, if broken, mean that a man cannot remain as a bhikkhu but can reordain as a novice. This will occur if a monk kills a human being, has sexual intercourse, steals an item of value, or falsely claims possession of supernormal powers. The punishment for breaking these rules is so severe because these actions defeat the purpose of ordination. Breaking these rules dismantles the distinction and trust between monks and laity and challenges the communal life of monasticism. Forcing a monk to leave because he has broken or been accused of breaking a *parajika* often does not proceed smoothly or openly. Particularly in Myanmar, during crackdowns on popular monks who dissent from the governmental ideologies, many have been disrobed without due process.

Ten Rules for Novice Monks

Refrain from:

1. Killing living beings
2. Taking what is not given
3. All sexual activity
4. False speech
5. Intoxicants that cause heedlessness
6. Eating after midday
7. Attending entertainments
8. Wearing jewelry or using perfume
9. Sleeping on luxurious beds
10. Receiving gold and silver

The monastic schedule varies according to the day, time of year, level of seniority, and temple. It often includes a predawn wake-up, morning and evening chanting, and meals before noon. The rest of this time is divided between cleaning, studying, rituals, and meditation.

Sample Schedule

4:30 a.m. Wake up
5 a.m. Morning chanting

6:30 a.m. Alms round

7:30 a.m. Breakfast

8:30 a.m. Cleaning and washing

9 a.m. Study and classes

11 a.m. Lunch

12 p.m. Rest and chores

1 p.m. Afternoon classes

4 p.m. Chores and washing

5 p.m. Evening chanting

6:30 p.m. Private time for study

10 p.m. Sleep

One of the fundamental markers of Theravada monasticism is the necessary interaction between laity and monks, illustrated by the daily morning alms round (*pindapata*) by male monks. Monks walk barefoot, alone or in a group, and make themselves available to receive food from laypeople. The distance covered by their route can be shorter or longer depending on the temple. The daily alms round builds and maintains an important relationship between the community and local monks that is at the heart of Theravada Buddhist societies. When a layperson wants to make an offering, they remove their shoes, put the food in the monk's bowl, and kneel to receive the monastic blessing, which marks the merit the giver has acquired. In Myanmar, monks and novices exit the interaction without a blessing or acknowledgment of the offerings.

Monks can eat the collected food when they return to the temple or, depending on the temple, they can add their offerings to the prepared food being made by kitchen volunteers. Most city and village monks eat twice a day, once in the early morning and once before noon. They give away leftover food to lay helpers and even feed the dogs and cats in and around the temple. Some monks follow a stricter asceticism, taking only one meal per day, usually at midmorning. Throughout the day, monks are often called upon to conduct ceremonies at the temple or to bless people's houses or businesses. These ceremonies are usually timed before or after the monks' midday meal so they can sit down to eat before noon. After this meal, Theravada monks do not eat in public until the next day's morning meal. Before eating collectively, monks chant a reminder for their consumption:

> Properly considering alms food, I use it: not playfully, nor for intoxification, nor for putting on weight, nor for beautification, but simply for the survival and continuance of this body, for ending its afflictions, for the support of the chaste life, and not create new feelings (from overeating). Thus I will maintain myself, be blameless, and live in comfort.[8]

Theravada monks are allowed to eat meat, although in Myanmar, monks avoid eating beef. Though not common, monks can choose to be vegetarian if they would like. Before it is consumed, meat must meet certain conditions: (1) the monk cannot have seen the act of killing, (2) heard the killing, or (3) suspect the animal was killed for him to eat. Despite their lean diet, because monks lack opportunities for physical exercise and are required to accept whatever food is offered to them, many have become overweight. Over the past decade, there have been several campaigns in Thailand directed toward both monks and laypeople about nutrition and healthy diets to address the issue of obesity. Thailand's National Health Commission has determined that nearly half of Thailand's monks are overweight. Although monks consume fewer calories than lay Thai men, they rely on high-sugar drinks in the afternoon and evening to satiate their hunger. Especially when consumed on an empty stomach, this can lead to serious health problems.

Along with diet, monastics are marked by their clothing. Monks only wear monastic robes, which they receive on their ordination day. Monastic robe colors can range from yellow to dark maroon but have no significant meaning. This gamut of colors represents the shades of tree barks, which monastic robes were traditionally dyed with. Novices and monks wear the same robes. The only difference is when fully ordained monks are formally eating in front of laity, they will have a third robe on their shoulder. Other than this, the color or style of tying the robe does not represent seniority in any way. A brown robe can signify a forest monk, a yellow robe is often used for a city monk in Thailand, a maroon robe is more often seen on monks from Myanmar, while in Laos monks' robes are often orange. In general, it is up to the abbots of individual temples to state a particular color preference so that laity can make appropriate offerings. Some forest monks practice traditional robes offering, where a layperson sews a white cloth, which they present to the monks; the monks then dye the robe themselves with tree bark, plants, and wood.

Monks' wardrobes today consist of three robes: the big robe (*uttarasanga*) to cover the upper part of their body, the small robe (*antaravasaka*) used like a sarong, and an extra robe (*sanghati*) worn on the outside. They also wear a shirt (*ansa*), and a belt can be used to hold the robes together. Styles of wearing the three robes vary, but usually the rectangular-shaped robe is wrapped around the body and the vertical edges are folded and rolled together. Then it is either secured with a belt or, for larger outer robes, the remaining piece is thrown over the left shoulder and held under the left arm so it will not slip off. Monks become adept at rolling and rerolling their robes over time.

Early Indian Buddhist texts cite eight possessions a monk needs to live the monastic life: three robes, an alms bowl, a belt, a sewing needle, a razor, and a water filter. A monk can also expect to be provided with the four requisites of food, clothing, lodging, and medicine from lay donations. Monks can have additional possessions, which can be anything that aids in their practice. The vagueness of this dictum can create some confusion. If monks are using their computers to watch an action movie, is this helping them learn English, or is it planting seeds of violence? If monks own cell phones, what are the appropriate ways for them to use social media? Are they posting dhamma quotes on Facebook or watching inappropriate videos on YouTube? These additional possessions and use of technology are all dependent on context.

Although monks are often portrayed as men committed to the

religious path toward nibbana, in fact, Theravada Buddhist men in Southeast Asia often ordain only temporarily. Because the ordination is for just a short time, there is not much preparation needed for this ceremony. Young men ordain temporarily to offer merit and gratitude to their parents or a person in their family who has recently died, or to fulfill a vow they made for receiving a wish, such as passing an exam or recovering from an illness. Another surprising reason for temporary ordination is an upcoming marriage. Temples train men to become good, disciplined subjects of Buddhism. If a man spends even a few days in the temple, his marriage partner can at least know that he has made merit for his family and is a good Buddhist. Temporary ordination can be for a few weeks or several months. A popular length and period is the three-month rains retreat (*vassa*). Most men do not have that amount of time, however, and might be ordained for only a few days. On the other end of the spectrum, some men plan to ordain for a short period but enjoy the monastic life so much, they never disrobe.

Men from disadvantaged backgrounds may choose to ordain for several years to take advantage of educational opportunities. These monks often move from their rural home village to an urban temple where they hope to create a pathway out of poverty for themselves and their family. Village monasteries, with their lack of education and advancement possibilities, do not have the ability to uplift young men. These village temples are necessary to fulfill the needs of the laity and provide a focal point for the local community. Although there are probably fewer temptations and material desires in the village, urban temples allow student monks access to sites of serious Buddhist learning and degrees, which confer upward mobility. Many of these monks who ordain for educational opportunities plan to disrobe after they graduate. They want to enjoy the householder life, including forming a romantic relationship and creating a family, or supporting their natal family. If a monk chooses to disrobe, they inform another person, which may or may not be the monk who conducted their ordination. Then, after the monk has changed into lay clothes, they take the Five Precepts in a short ceremony and take their leave by worshipping the remaining monks in the temple.

Monastic Education

One of the fundamental elements of the monastic institution is education. Monks engage in the study of Buddhist texts, practices, and doctrines and teach other monks and laypeople. Monastic education includes formal education in the classroom and informal apprentice education where junior monks attend to senior monks. In Theravada Buddhist countries, Buddhism and education were completely intertwined for many centuries. Under the royal patronage of Buddhist kings, monks could devote themselves to monastic learning. In the modern era, education became a more secular affair with public and private school options. Today, many monastic schools in Thailand offer secular education along with Pali language and Buddhist teachings, while secular subjects are not part of most monastic educations in Myanmar. Striking this balance between Buddhist and secular education is an important issue that is constantly debated within Theravada Buddhist monastic communities.

Monasteries are part of the social welfare system of mainland Southeast Asia. Part of the welfare they provide, through support from governments and lay communities, is free education at the elementary, middle, high school, college, and graduate levels. Without temples, children from low-income families would have more limited means for schooling. In monastic schools there will not be as much music or sports, and there will be more study of Buddhism than at a public or private school. Monastic education is also transnational. Monks from many parts of Asia travel to Thailand, India, and Sri Lanka to attend their high schools and colleges due to the quality Buddhist monastic education available. In Thailand, access to education in English with native English-speaking teachers and secular subjects is a significant draw.

Students from more privileged backgrounds would typically

ordain temporarily but not attend monastic schools. This is the two-tiered education system that can be seen especially in Thailand: monastic schools are left to low-income families who cannot afford to pay the costs of local state schools, including uniforms, books, supplies, and so forth; those who can afford it send their children to public government schools or, even better, private international schools. Monastic schools, because they are so integrated into the community, provide a sense of trust for parents. Some of these schools allow anyone to enter for free, lay boys and girls, but some only allow boys, ordained or not, and some focus just on ordained boys.

In Myanmar, issues for monastic education are linked with rural versus urban and levels of piety. For example, because almost all the important monks in Myanmar's modern history come from rural villages, these communities have been the recruiting ground and the main support base for Myanmar's monastic community. As well, many parents who are part of ethnic groups such as Shan, Karen, and Pa O prefer to send their children to monasteries rather than to local state schools.

Written exams are an important part of a Buddhist monastic education. They serve as crucial mechanisms for deciding which monks will become leaders of the sangha—abbots, regional leaders, and eventually the highest monks in the nation. Monks who want to study the Buddha's teachings in the original language of the texts are encouraged to study Pali. They do not have to learn a new alphabet because Pali can be written in any script—Thai, Burmese, Lao, or Khmer. The study of Pali in Thailand is divided into nine levels, with annual public exams overseen by expert monks. Monks who pass level three onward will receive a certificate and special fan with the number three written on it. These monks earn the title *maha*, meaning "great." If monks want to continue their study, those who pass levels three through eight will receive their fan from the supreme patriarch, and those passing level nine will receive a special fan from the king. If a novice monk passes level nine, the king will sponsor their full ordination, though it is extremely rare for a novice monk to reach this goal. Monks can take another series of tests, the dhamma exams, that assesses knowledge of the life and teachings of the Buddha, his disciples, and the rules of the monks. If they understand these topics well, they will pass the three levels of dhamma examinations and become known as an expert in dhamma. However, the Pali exams are much more important for determining future leaders of the sangha.

Scriptural exams are even more important in Myanmar, where becoming even a village abbot requires some academic qualification. Annual exams conducted by the state are called *pathamapyan* (royal exams in Burmese). After passing three levels of pathamapyan examinations, monks may sit for the *dhammacariya* exams. The title of dhammacariya ("teacher of the Dhamma" in Pali) is given to those who pass this next level of exams. These exams, while producing a performance-oriented educational culture, make it possible to rank monks and novices, knowing who to promote to leadership positions and who is a worthy field of merit for donations.

The most important activity for young monks in the temple in Mandalay, where Ward Keeler conducted research for his book *The Traffic in Hierarchy*, is studying Pali texts for the exams. All the novices are occupied with studying while the older monks are engaged in teaching. Novices have formal study sessions in the morning, afternoon, and evening, with additional study at night. They practice their memorization aloud, often shouting the Pali texts as they review what they have learned. Each day, the students have a passage of text to memorize that they will be tested on the next day. Despite all this study and memorization, the Pali exams are difficult to pass, and often students repeat their Pali grade for several years. Rote memorization is key, not understanding or analysis. After one has memorized much of the Pali Canon, having those texts at your fingertips is considered a basis from which to preach and offer insight into the doctrine for the laity.

Phaung Daw Oo school, based in Mandalay and led by Sayadaw U Nayaka, is one example of a monastic school that focuses on secular subjects instead of Pali scriptures and examination. This is the largest monastic school in Myanmar and has been a forerunner in bringing educational reform across monastic schools. The school is most interested in preparing students for college and vocational training. The international community views Phaung Daw Oo as a model monastic school, especially because of its more modern, secular approach to education. As well, their teachers receive child-centered approach training rather than relying solely on rote memorization. More conservative monks and lay Buddhists, however, find the focus on the secular to be too extreme and would rather see more Buddhist subjects in the school's curriculum.

In Cambodia, since the toppling of the Khmer Rouge in 1979, Buddhism has been gradually expanding, rebuilding monasteries and educational institutions. Hundreds of Buddhist primary schools exist in the Cambodian provinces. Their study mostly includes three years of education in Buddhist teachings so that students can pass the state examination, after which they will be qualified to sit the entrance examination for Buddhist secondary school. In the capital of Phnom Penh, there are over twenty lower and upper schools that offer certificates of Buddhist secondary education to those monks who pass the exams. Secondary-school subjects include Pali, Buddhist discipline, and the Buddha's life story, along with secular subjects. The Preah Sihanouk Raja Buddhist University, which reopened in 1999, provides higher education in Buddhism to monks who have completed Buddhist upper secondary studies. The entrance exam is competitive as only a limited number of students can be admitted each year. A challenge for Cambodia is spreading Buddhist higher education opportunities more evenly between Phnom Penh and the provinces. The Buddhist schools in the capital are at risk of becoming too crowded, causing monks to disrobe or abandon studies because they have no temple to live in.

Despite its long history, monastic education continues to face many problems. Monastic educational institutions often lack funding, do not have enough space for all monks seeking degrees, and are unable to attract quality and committed teachers. Monks who want to obtain a doctorate in Buddhist studies often head to India or Sri

Lanka. Within each country, capital cities are centers of monastic education, attracting village boys. Novices and monks frequently move from rural areas to urban centers to pursue high school and college education. Because of this trend, the temples of cities such as Vientiane, Chiang Mai, Bangkok, and Yangon are filled with rural boys and those from indigenous ethnic groups.

Areas of Monastic Pursuits

In recent decades, several monks in mainland Southeast Asia have become the object of public worship, upheld as heroes by their lay devotees. The most important qualities for such a monk to express are communication skills through preaching, academic achievements through monastic education, community involvement through selfless development work, and embodied wisdom through disciplined meditation practice.

The accomplishments of well-known monks are quite diverse, considering the wide range of the monastic institution. While there are many possible pursuits for male monks, here we'll focus on examples of scholar monks, forest monks, meditation monks, charismatic monks, activist and socially engaged monks, preacher monks, and magic monks. Not all monks are famous for their positive qualities; a few are infamous because of their inappropriate behaviors and accusations of criminal activity. Although many monks could fit into more than one category, including categories not listed here, this overview provides a general sense of the kinds of activities monks can be involved in.

Scholar Monks

Scholar monks are authoritative voices on Buddhist teachings. Whenever there is a question of doctrine or how it should be interpreted in the modern world, top scholar monks are consulted. This is especially relevant in the modern application of the Vinaya, when learned monks act as monastic arbitrators in solving problems related to questionable cases regarding monastic law. Theravada Buddhist communities listen to these monks' opinions on the state of Buddhism in their country and which monastic activities they deem to be appropriate. Monks who have expertise in the Pali language and who can convey Buddhist teachings in an accessible way are also often popular as preachers and authors. Their content is available for purchase as CDs or books in convenience stores, bookstores, and street stalls.

The anthropologist Hiroko Kawanami has studied U Tiloka Biwuntha (b. 1939), or Insein Ywama Sayadaw, a scholar monk in Myanmar who exudes the qualities of a scholarly monk. He became a novice monk in 1954 at age fifteen in his village monastery and soon after started his monastic education. He passed the state exams every year and finally the series of dhammacariya exams, making him a teacher of the dhamma. He continued to pass the Sakyadhiha Dhammacariya exam, which has even more difficult questions, to join an elite club of scholar monks. These kinds of credentials open up influential opportunities. Besides his own monastery school, he also teaches Abhidhamma at a university in Yangon, is a judge in the Sangha Court, and served as part of the committee of top monks in the Sangha Maha Nayaka Council. His textbooks are used in the national Buddhism curriculum in Myanmar. Many of U Tiloka's students have passed the dhammacariya exam, with one even becoming a *tipitakadhara*, a monk who has memorized the entire Pali Canon.

Despite all these accomplishments, what is most impressive to U Tiloka's benefactors is his humility. He lacks both pride in his achievements and obvious desire for more attainments and power. Appearing kind and down-to-earth, he considers situations impartially, not for his own gain. U Tiloka focuses his time and energy on the whole of society, giving lessons to nuns and aiding disadvantaged children in his volunteer work. Although he is in contact with his lay followers, he also incorporates some additional ascetic practices, such as eating once a day and mixing all the food in his bowl, as well as meditating in graveyards. This, along with his availability for blessings and care for his students and family members, is praised by his supporters.

Forest Monks

Another way to attract attention from laity is to practice the renunciation and discipline of a forest monk. In contrast to monks in cities and villages who are available for ceremonies, rituals, blessings, and large merit-making events for laypeople, forest monks concentrate on practice—especially meditation. When they do interact with laity, forest monks teach the dhamma and meditation from their own experience rather than performing ritual duties. Individual monks within the forest tradition sometimes opt to take additional renunciation (*dhutanga*). These practices include never lying down, remaining in the forest, living on or near a graveyard or cremation ground, and only possessing the three robes they wear without any additional ones. In Myanmar, those who practice dhutanga eat only once a day, which serves to limit interaction with laypeople. Wandering from place to place without any settled location or isolating for multiple years in a single, desolate location such as a cave is also typical of the practices of the forest monk.

The Thai forest tradition began in the north and northeast regions of the country but has since spread throughout Thailand and internationally through non-Thai male monks. Ajahn Mun (1870-1949) is the founder of the Thai forest tradition. He created this tradition in the 1920s through his wandering practices, which attracted disciples. Two of these disciples carried forth his tradition to today. Ajahn Maha Bua (1913-2011) was Ajahn Mun's attendant for eight years until he founded his own forest temple, Wat Pa Ban That, near his hometown. Many of his followers believe that Ajahn Maha Bua lived for forty years as an arahant. Ajahn Maha Bua authored several accounts of forest teachers' lives, and many of his dhamma talks have been published as books. Ajahn Chah (1918-92), as a wandering monk in his late twenties, met Ajahn Mun and received a crucial teaching: the truth of practice can be found in establishing mindfulness. After wandering as a forest monk for seven years, he founded Wat Nong Pah Pong. As word spread of Ajahn Chah, he appealed to many international monks, which eventually led to the establishment of the International Forest Monastery, Wat Pah Nanachat, in 1975. Today, the Thai forest tradition has spread further internationally through Western monks, especially Ajahn Chah's disciples, who created centers in England, North America, Australia, Switzerland, and New Zealand.

Many of the famous arahants in modern Myanmar come from ethnic minority groups, including Thamanya Sayadaw (1910-2003), a nationally revered forest monk from the Pa O ethnic group. Before being known as Thamanya Sayadaw, U Winaya attended monastic school and took full ordination at age twenty. As a monk, he was most interested in the practice of meditation and would travel to different monasteries and masters seeking guidance. Although he inherited two monasteries, he detached himself from these administrative responsibilities in the 1980s. Having left his position as abbot, he headed to an isolated hill when he was sixty-seven years old. Through visions he located Thamanya Hill as the place to undertake intensive practice for three years. Despite his vow of isolation, thousands of devotees heard of his intention, and many arrived to pay respect to him, especially ethnic Karen people who live in Myanmar's borderlands. He used his reputation and donations to restore two pagodas on the hill and to construct more buildings for those wishing to settle there. By year 2000, as the researcher Guillaume Rozenberg reports in *Renunciation and Power: The Quest for Sainthood in Contemporary Burma*, the lay population was about fifteen thousand with four hundred monks and novices in the area.

Forest monks such as Thamanya Sayadaw and the monks of the Thai forest tradition spend long stretches of time in relative meditative isolation. They take on extra ascetic practices above and beyond ordinary monks, marking them as more sacred and containing more merit. The forest evokes so much respect because monks do not just leave behind the comforts of their towns and cities, but they also face real danger. Many of their tales include encountering wild animals, spirits, and thieves. It is assumed by laity that after a period of years in the forest, a monk becomes enlightened. The forest is scary, but it's also a place of transformation and purity. Forests as spiritual habitats have been essential in fostering these ideal, renunciant, wandering monks. Through their ability to spread loving-kindness, forest monks are believed to have the ability to tame the wild forest environment, as they have their own minds. Yet due to deforestation in mainland Southeast Asia, there is less space for these forest monks to practice, and subsequently authentic forest monks are becoming rarer today.

Meditation Monks

Monks well known for their meditation practice and teaching are somewhere in between scholar monks and forest monks. They are connected to the laity through their teaching but also isolate themselves for lengthy periods of retreat. Many of these monks have studied the Buddhist texts and commentaries regarding meditation, though they do not require any academic credentials. Instead, what is valued is their deep insight. They give sermons that would impress scholar monks, and their wisdom often comes from their own experience.

Some of the most internationally known Theravada monks are meditation masters. Mahasi Sayadaw (1904-82) was a scholar and teacher, highly regarded for his legacy of developing an accessible method of *vipassana* (insight) meditation, which uses all sensations, thoughts, and emotions to ultimately understand the nature of reality and attain nibbana. The young Mahasi Sayadaw became a novice at age twelve, took full ordination at age twenty, and quickly passed all the Pali examinations administered by the Burmese government at the time. Mahasi Sayadaw then made a firm commitment to put the doctrines into practice by becoming a disciple of insight meditation teacher Mingun Jetawan Sayadaw. Mingun Sayadaw is known as an Abhidhamma scholar who had memorized the whole of the Tipitaka. Mahasi Sayadaw learned the technical language from Mingun Sayadaw to explain his meditation method systematically and logically. After intensive practice with his teacher, Mahasi Sayadaw began to teach meditation at the age of thirty-four. Afterward, he returned to his hometown and taught the practical techniques he had mastered. He managed to bridge both aspects of the Buddhist monastic lifestyle—study and practice. Mahasi Sayadaw was a teacher engaged with society as well as a renunciant who had lived away from society, practicing meditation in isolation with strict discipline.

Venerable Sam Bunthoeun (1956–2003) was one of Cambodia's most prominent teachers of vipassana meditation. He ordained at the age of twenty-three, soon after the end of the Cambodian genocide in 1980. He was a talented preacher and scholar who eventually turned to the practice of vipassana meditation. He established a center for meditation practice for both laity and monastics at Wat Ounalom, a royal temple in the capital city of Phnom Penh. As his following grew, he established the Vipassana Dhura Buddhist Meditation Center in the nearby town of Udong. By 2000 his center was thriving; he was preaching on the radio, publishing books on meditation, and attracting hundreds of students, mostly older women. Sadly, he was shot and killed in broad daylight at the entrance to Wat Langka in Phnom Penh in 2003. His killers were never identified, but the incident is assumed to have been executed by hired assassins. There are several theories as to why he may have been targeted but no clear consensus. Ideas range from a jealous husband of a female lay supporter to rivalry among other prominent monks due to his popularity. The meditation center remains an important place to practice vipassana in Cambodia today and continues to grow.

In 2016, almost fourteen years after his killing, Sam Bunthoeun was finally cremated in a three-day ceremony in his home province, attracting hundreds of thousands of his followers. His body had been lying in state until the decision was made to cremate his body. The body was a reminder that justice had not been done and neither the killers nor the motive had been satisfactorily investigated, until Sam Bunthoeun's sister decided it was time to move on.

These examples of renowned monks demonstrate the importance of monastic meditation teachers in mainland Southeast Asia today. Their centers continue to draw lay practitioners and inspire ordinations through the simple yet profound vipassana meditation instructions. These meditation monks not only practice themselves but have also studied meditation texts and developed their own methods and ways to teach the practice.

Charismatic Monks

Monks do not just meditate and study—they also build. Special monks are believed to have *parami*, accumulated over many previous lifetimes. *Parami* means "perfection" and can be compared with the idea of charisma, which for monks combines leadership abilities, influential power, and spiritual development. Charisma correlates closely with construction projects in Theravada Buddhism. Their parami gives them a special ability to establish new religious structures and renovate older ones and allows them to easily find followers and financial backing for these buildings. The building projects can focus on construction of a single sacred site or take place within a region, creating a network of sites. Buddhist structures are necessary for Buddhism to thrive and to facilitate merit-making for laypeople. Monks who are skilled in creating and managing building projects become well known to laypeople, and their work propagates Buddhism, extending its influence and life through monuments, which mark the land as belonging to Buddhism.

In northern Thailand, several charismatic monks, given the title *kruba* (great teacher), have emerged over the past decades. Kruba Siwichai (1878-1938) is considered a modern saint in northern Thailand. He was known as a *nakbun*, an expert in facilitating making merit. He was also regarded as an engineer monk because of his role in restoring and building access to temples in out-of-reach places, such as mountains. Most famously he gathered villagers to build the road to Wat Prathat Doi Suthep, the temple located on Suthep

Mountain in Chiang Mai. He organized the restoration or construction of over one hundred temples in northern Thailand. His popularity was a problem, however, for the central Bangkok authorities who were trying to annex the northern region into their centralized authority. Kruba Siwichai was accused of acting in defiance of the central authorities when he ordained novices without permission. He was arrested several times but was cleared of any charges when almost a thousand people traveled to Bangkok in support of him. Upon his return, many more thousands of worshippers greeted him. Statues of Kruba Siwichai can be found throughout northern Thailand, especially in Chiang Mai and Lamphun. The most famous statue, located on the road to Wat Prathat Doi Suthep, is often propitiated with eggs, garlic, and other items he is thought to have enjoyed in his lifetime.

Kruba Bunchum Yanasangwaror, born in Chiang Rai in 1966, is a famous Thai monk with devoted followers in Myanmar, Laos, and China. He is especially popular with ethnic minority groups of mainland Southeast Asia, such as the Lahu, Palaung, and Shan. More recently, his status has gained him wealthy Thai followers from Bangkok. He was ordained as a novice at age nine. Early rumors of supernatural abilities to cure, borne out of his interest in practicing meditation, created excitement around the young novice. He was called to a temple in Chiang Mai to be questioned on his knowledge of Buddhist doctrine, and his performance confirmed his growing regional reputation as a monk with especially charismatic qualities. After his monastic ordination in 1986, he established his base at Wat Phrathat Donrueng, becoming abbot there, but he also traveled and initiated projects in Laos, China, and Shan State in Myanmar. These projects are seen as expressions of his compassion toward laity and a confirmation of his parami.

In addition to his building projects, Kruba Bunchum is perhaps most well known for his three-year isolated meditation in a cave in northern Thailand from 2010 to 2013, the completion of which was marked by a huge celebration with his patrons. Amporn Jirattikorn, an anthropologist who attended the ceremony, estimated that twenty thousand people participated. Kruba Bunchum resided in the cave for three years, three months, and three days; and he exited the cave at 3:33 a.m. Many of his followers were there at the cave, having arrived earlier that evening, their devotion leading them to want to see his exit and collect his hair, which he did not shave while in the cave. Most recently Kruba Bunchum became known for his prediction concerning the boys' soccer team, who were eventually rescued from the Tham Luang cave in Chiang Rai, Thailand, after being trapped for nine days in July 2018. Kruba Bunchum visited the site, meditated, and foresaw that the boys were alive and would be rescued in three days. His presence and prediction provided much-needed hope, and his communication with the cave spirits turned out to prove true.

Building or restoring a pagoda is regarded as a dangerous and difficult task. Special knowledge is required to negotiate with the territorial spirits, so they are not offended. Charismatic monks must know the right date, right time, and correct offerings before they begin construction on a sacred site. Charismatic monks continue the work of weaving Buddhism more and more into the foundation of their societies.

Activist and Socially Engaged Monks

The category of "activist monk" can appear to be in tension with the otherworldly ideal of Theravada Buddhist monasticism. This otherworldliness, which focuses on nibbana, is known as *lokuttara*, while this world, or *lokiya*, is of most importance to the laity. It must be remembered that this distinction is an ideal. After all, monks live in the world, and laity can also take time to meditate and strive toward nibbana in their householder roles. There are many historical examples of monks engaging in activism, often in the political realm and certainly in worldly affairs. Very few monks today meet the unrealistic image of the renunciant who is completely separated from concerns of the world.

Debates within Buddhist societies about appropriate monastic political involvement rise to the surface especially in moments of unrest, as was seen during the Saffron Revolution. In September 2007, monks in Myanmar took to the streets, marching in defiance of military rule. Tens of thousands of Buddhist monks used their moral authority in Burmese society to protest the military's failure to support and protect its people. The government was widely seen to be extracting resources for themselves at the expense of the regular citizen's economic development. Skyrocketing living costs and extreme inflation had made it not only difficult for laypeople to survive but also for monks to receive any donations from their supporters. Because of this, monks involved in the Saffron Revolution protested the economic suffering of the Burmese people, marching in the streets to protect the laity and show solidarity. During these marches, monks overturned their alms bowls, communicating to government affiliates that they were being denied the opportunity to make merit through donations. Actions were chosen carefully to fit within their monastic purview and to avoid potential criticisms of being worldly monks. However, this revolution failed in transforming the political system at the time; the monks' efforts ended in less than a month due to a violent military crackdown.

Venerable Luon Sovath is an activist monk fighting for human rights in Cambodia. His main strategy has been to video-record human rights and land violations committed by the government against village communities. Venerable Sovath is part of a growing group of Cambodians who are taking a stand against their government, which has been led by Prime Minister Hun Sen since 1985. Unfortunately, this has led to a smear campaign against Luon Sovath perpetrated by the Cambodian government, including videos from a fake Facebook page claiming that he had violated his vow of celibacy with several women. Luon Sovath fled to Thailand, fearing arrest. The *New York Times* uncovered that the videos of Luon Sovath with women were created by government employees. The monk now lives in Switzerland, having received a humanitarian visa. Luon Sovath has been recognized internationally for his work documenting human rights abuses in Cambodia and is featured as a significant part of a 2016 documentary film called *A Cambodian Spring*.[9]

Socially engaged Buddhism is an academic term referring to Buddhists who are less involved with politics and aim their work more generally toward solving modern problems practically through Buddhist teachings. Socially engaged Buddhists engage with the social, economic, and ecological problems in their societies, seeing Buddhist practice as an expression of this engagement. The issues that Theravada Buddhist monks face are big and small, from development monks learning new farming techniques to help their local village community to country-level projects involving healing after major societal trauma.

Socially engaged monks in Thailand are known for their focus on the environment. They invented the ritual of tree ordination to promote environmental conservation and challenge capitalism. This ritual was created in the late 1980s to capture people's attention and get them to think about trees and natural resources in a new way. Of course, only humans can be ordained, so these ceremonies are not formal ordinations. Instead, tree ordinations sanctify trees and raise awareness about their vulnerability due to increased deforestation. During tree ordinations, the anthropologist Susan Darlington observed in her book *The Ordination of a Tree*, at the same time that monks consecrate community forests and make trees into sacred objects, they also illustrate the interconnection between people and nature. Phrakru Pitak Nanthakhun, a well-known ecology monk in northern Thailand, sees his work as meeting villagers where they are. Buddhist teachings are used to persuade and motivate their communities to understand the necessity of protecting the environment from further devastation.

During the Khmer Rouge period (1975-79), two million Cambodians were killed, and Buddhism was almost eliminated from the country. Cambodian Buddhist monks fled abroad, were killed, or were forced into lay life, while temples were partially or completely destroyed. Samdech Preah Maha Ghosananda (1913-2007) had been a meditation monk in Thailand until he emerged to rebuild

Cambodian Buddhism, helping the survivors through his quiet presence and peaceful example. Ghosananda was nominated for the Nobel Peace Prize for his organization of peace walks, called Dhammayietra, through the land mine-infested regions of Cambodia. These monthlong walks, with over one thousand people, were healing for monks and laity. The Dhammayietra began in 1992 as a one-time event to begin the restorative process of acknowledging individual and societal trauma. Although Maha Ghosananda has passed away, the Dhammayietra continues annually with different causes and routes each year. More recently, socially engaged monks have mobilized relief efforts after national disasters, such as the 2004 tsunami in the islands of Thailand and the 2008 cyclone Nargis in Myanmar.

Like activist monks, socially engaged monks' work can be controversial for critics who believe the monastic's role should be exclusively otherworldly. However, for the most part, socially engaged Buddhist monks' projects have become accepted because of the positive results and healing they often achieve.

Preacher Monks

In Theravada Buddhism, only a handful of monks can draw a large crowd for their ability in oration. Preacher monks are known because of their presence in media platforms such as TV and books, which showcase their teachings. Nationally known preacher monks also excel in scholarship and meditation and often act as missionaries, spreading Buddhism in a variety of institutional settings.

Phra Maha Sompong (b. 1978) is an accomplished monk who earned the highest degree of the Pali language exam at age nineteen and received a master's degree in social work from a prominent Thai university. His dhamma teachings, in print and in person, all fall under his main concept of "dhamma delivery"—or delivering dhamma in short, pithy resolutions to problems. His books focus on simple teachings for daily life. One such book, *IPhra: Dhamma 3G*, uses the formats of Facebook and computer screens to frame his message filled with advice for teenagers and young adults. Although he has many books, he is most well known as a preacher. To this end, schools, companies, and public places such as malls invite him to give sermons. His style is informal and humorous, often resembling stand-up comedy. Although younger generations enjoy this approach, more conservative Thai Buddhist sangha members criticized Phra Maha Sombong when he preached on Facebook Live in 2021 for his content not being serious enough. Partly due to this critique, in December 2021 Phra Maha Sombong disrobed, becoming a layman.

Ashin Nyanissara, commonly known as Sitagu Sayadaw, has been one of the most popular preacher monks in Myanmar for over a decade. Born in 1937, he became a novice in his hometown at age fifteen. After he passed the state monastic exams, he received a master's in Buddhist doctrine and a diploma in English from Myanmar universities. After earning their degrees, many monks go back to their hometowns and start monastery schools, but Sitagu Sayadaw was focused on missionizing. He became a disciple of the famous monk Sayadaw U Pandita (1899-1977), and he learned how to become a preacher while continuing to study English. His preaching style is very decorative, incorporating traditional moral tales while highlighting contemporary social issues. When a lay supporter donated a plot of land to him in 1979, Sitagu Sayadaw established his base for missionary projects. He started publishing and taking trips abroad, invited by Myanmar diaspora communities. Through additional donated funds generated by his sermons, Sitagu Sayadaw led social projects for improving national development. He installed a water pump for monastic residents of the Sagaing Hills outside of Mandalay, benefiting over eight hundred monasteries and many more residents of the area. He also constructed a sangha hospital for everyone in the community and established the Sitagu Buddhist Academy in 1998.

However, Sitagu Sayadaw has more recently been criticized for siding with the military junta even after their coup toppled a fledgling Burmese democracy in 2021. His previous support of the democratic movement in the late 1980s stands in stark contrast to the Buddhist nationalism he now espouses. Additionally, by allowing top military generals to make offerings to him, Sitagu Sayadaw signals his complicity with the anti-Muslim propaganda associated with their rule. His warnings of the threat of Islam are worrying for Burmese monks interested in interreligious dialogue.

Magic Monks

Magic monks are those who are believed to possess a special ability to imbue objects with extraordinary sacred power. In his book *Mediums, Monks, and Amulets*, the anthropologist Pattana Kitiarsa defines a magic monk as a monk who has knowledge or skill relating to magic or supernatural practice and provides these magical services to others. Objects such as amulets or tattoos are sacralized through magic monks' renunciation, knowledge of Buddhist sacred scriptures, and meditative mastery. They are also specialists in rituals intended to promote good luck, prevent bad luck, and produce longevity. Other services they provide include fortune-telling; physical healing; expelling bad spirits from one's body or home; setting up a spirit house or altar; blessing new homes, businesses, or cars; and providing tips on winning lottery numbers. Pattana Kitiarsa believes that there are thousands of Thai Buddhist monks who would be identified as having these qualities of magic throughout the country. The supernatural potency of such a monk is recognized by the sacred objects and rituals' effectiveness in their protection and healing.

At the same time, many of these magic monks are criticized for their engagement with the material world, specifically their connections with the accumulation of wealth by their followers. Magic monks are part of popular Buddhism rather than elite, scholarly Buddhism. The fact that aspects of Buddhism could be branded as a means to prosperity makes critics uneasy about the state of public faith in Buddhism and contributes to the idea that Buddhism is currently in crisis. Magic monks, in contrast, see themselves as firmly within monastic institutional obligations but as specialists in magic who can provide assurance and assistance to those in need.

Monastic Scandals and Crime

Monks can stir up controversy in many ways. One common way is to break the major rules, the *parajikas*, by having sexual intercourse or being involved in criminal activities. When a monk is accused of a large-scale offense, their case often dominates the news and becomes a major source of conversation within Theravada Buddhist communities. Issues regarding monastic scandals are illustrated by Wat Dhammakaya of Thailand. The leaders of this temple have been criticized for commodifying merit through direct marketing strategies, as well as financial embezzlement. Wat Dhammakaya's understanding of merit-making is closely connected to promises of wealth, so that a certain donation amount corresponds to a desirable realm in the next rebirth. In addition to the contentious merit-making and promotional activities of the temple, Phra Dham-majayo, the extremely controversial abbot of Wat Dhammakaya, was denounced in the 1990s for accepting embezzled money as donations. Eventually the case fizzled out when Phra Dhamma-jayo transferred the money into the temple account. Most recently, in 2016, the government attempted to charge Phra Dhammajayo again for the same money embezzlement scandal from the 1990s. However, after police searched through the huge temple complex for months, they were unable to find him. No one knows where Phra Dhammajayo has fled to.

Monastic scandals are big news in mainland Southeast Asia, espe-cially Thailand and Cambodia. As Cambodia is still struggling to revive Buddhism post-Khmer Rouge, there is currently a shortage of senior monks who can be leaders as scholars and teachers. This makes it difficult to manage junior monks who have been involved in many scandals. Another issue in Cambodia is the lack of laity involved in their temple's committee, which forces monks to handle money, thus compromising their renunciatory vows. Other monks become close with political leaders, which furthers their decline in legitimacy. Because monks received voting privileges under the 1993 constitution, individual monastic figures and temples have become politicized, with some temples declaring their political party preference. Their political involvement threatens the laity's perception of their asceticism.

The biggest scandals of recent years in Thailand were perpetrated by Luang Pu Nen Kham. In 2013, most Thai people knew the name of this monk, whose nickname on international media quickly became the Jet-Set Monk. First came photos of him lying with a woman. Then a YouTube clip of the now infamous monk showed him riding in a private jet, holding a Louis Vuitton bag, wearing designer sunglasses, and carrying a briefcase brimming with cash. He fled to the United States but was eventually extradited back to Thailand and was disrobed and sentenced to 114 years in jail in 2018. This kind of large-scale scandal can break the trust laypeople have in the Buddhist monastic institution.

Other major scandals monks have been accused of within the last decade are allegations of sexual abuse and rape of underage girls and boys. Monks have also been known to commit other criminal offenses worthy of jail time, such as murder and robbery. If this is discovered or confessed, the monk must disrobe, and he will be charged with a criminal offense. Monks have also been arrested for being in possession of drugs, testing positive for drug use, and selling drugs. While this criminal behavior within the monastic institution is certainly alarming, smaller scandals can also add up. Lay Thai Buddhists post pictures on social media of monks involved in luxury activities such as shopping for top-brand products at the mall, eating expensive snack items at bakeries, and drinking fancy coffee drinks at Starbucks. Although these small and large-scale scandals represent the minority of monastic-lay relations, their representation in the media can lead laity to assume that some monks ordain to receive donations rather than devotion to the spiritual life.

Male Monastic Roles Today

As we can see from all these different types of monks and debates about appropriate monastic behavior, the duties and roles of the monk are constantly being negotiated. The arahant ideal of the monk meditating in an isolated cave still resonates, but at the same time, Buddhist communities affirm that monks cannot simply be otherworldly renunciants. Monks are both religious figures and members of society. Navigating monastic renunciation from the world while living within in it to spread and maintain Buddhist teachings has been part of the monastic institution since its earliest days. Each Buddhist country in Southeast Asia presents different challenges to the monastic community, depending on the political environment and level of economic development.

Male monks have a diversity of opportunities after ordination, including study, meditation, preaching, missionizing, activism, and social development. They can amass large followings and build new Buddhist structures, and they can disappoint laity by engaging in illegal financial or sexual activity. Although monks are held to a higher moral standard, not all of them meet this target. Monks who are especially well known and popular often have more than one specialty—for example, Mahasi Sayadaw was a scholar monk as well as a meditation master; Sitagu Sayadaw is a socially engaged Buddhist monk and well-known preacher. Although not all monks can succeed in becoming effective activists or preachers, there are multiple local, regional, and national models for boys and men to follow. For women in Theravada Buddhist monasticism, there is less range of monastic opportunities and fewer role models, but their significance is still great, which is the focus of the next chapter.

CHAPTER 4

Roles for Buddhist Women

Despite the monastic institution being dominated by men, there are significant roles for women in Theravada Buddhist societies as well. Women as laity are important members of Buddhist communities. In fact, the majority of temple-goers—especially benefactors of temples and leaders within temple communities or lay associations—are female. For Theravada Buddhist societies, this is the most accepted role for a woman—a lay supporter of the sangha. Besides playing supportive roles as laity, women can become renunciants, although their ordination is often ambiguous or lacking in acceptance. Because the role of female monks is controversial in most Theravada Buddhist societies, most women are ordained instead as *precept nuns.* This is an umbrella term for women who follow more precepts than a typical layperson but do not have the rules, structure, or respect that follows from the full monastic life. In Thailand, where there are communities for *bhikkhuni* (ordained nuns), women can live as female monks if highly motivated. This is the least accepted role for women. It is currently not possible for women to live as bhikkhuni or create bhikkhuni communities in Laos, Myanmar, or Cambodia. Because ordained women are not fully embraced within the sangha, precept nuns and female monks become recognized through extraordinary achievements, such as efforts within scholarship, social engagement, meditation teaching, and even supernatural abilities. Like all marginalized groups, ordained women must be excellent to be noticed for their accomplishments. Although women have several options to engage with

Buddhism, none of them accord a similar amount of prestige as for male monks.

Early Buddhism has an ambiguous relationship with women. Some passages from the Pali Canon point to the belief that anyone can attain enlightenment, male or female, ordained or lay. The *Therigatha* is a collection of poems by the Buddha's earliest female disciples. One of these women, Soma, expresses her view of gender when the demon of samsara, Mara, doubting her abilities, taunts her by saying, "It is hard to get to the place that sages want to reach, it's not possible for a woman, especially not one with only two fingers' worth of wisdom." Soma states in reply,

> What does being a woman have to do with it?
> What counts is that the heart is settled
> And that one sees what really is.
> What you take as pleasures are not for me,
> The mass of mental darkness is split open.
> Know this, evil one, you are defeated, you are finished.[10]

Her words show the possibilities of attainment and even equality for women. Here Soma argues that gender is insignificant to her and those like her who have renounced worldly pleasures and separated themselves from ignorance. This attitude has been labeled as soteriological inclusivity by the Buddhist studies scholar Alan Sponberg. In this positive attitude, the end goal, or soteriology, of enlightenment is inclusive of all people. Womanhood, or gender, is not relevant when a person has attained insight into the dhamma.

Unfortunately, this is not the only attitude expressed in Buddhist scriptures. In contrast, in some of the teachings from the Buddha in the Pali Canon, which are spoken to male monks, we find women as impediments to male insights:

> Monks, a woman, even when going along, will stop to ensnare the heart of a man; whether standing, sitting, or lying down, laughing, talking or singing, weeping, stricken, or dying, a woman will stop to ensnare the heart of a man.[11]

Quotes like these demonstrate a particular kind of misogyny in monks, which Sponberg dubs "ascetic misogyny." Because the monastic life is celibate, women represent temptation away from the ascetic life. Instead of women being the heroes of their own journeys toward enlightenment, ascetic misogyny casts them as obstacles in the path of men. As well, instead of the responsibility being placed on the individual who feels sexual temptation, the responsibility is placed on the object of desire.

These extremes of misogyny and soteriological inclusivity resonate for Theravada women today. The attitude of misogyny can be seen in the discomfort still shown toward ordained women compared to the comfort displayed toward the supportive roles of mothers and laywomen. The assertion that women have the same potential as men does not translate into gender equality. However, the promise of nibbana and the clarity of the Buddha's teachings have always inspired women to give and learn as laywomen and to practice as ordained members of the sangha.

Laywomen

Visakha is the ultimate laywoman to many Cambodian women. Her story from the *Saddharmaratnavaliya* (*Jewel Garland of the True Doctrine*) tells of a woman who, despite her gender, was able to exhibit morality and wisdom on the Buddhist path. In one of Visakha's past lifetimes, she made a wish to become a chief female lay attendant to a Buddha and was able to enact this when she was born into a noble family. When she met the Buddha and made offerings to him, she also received his preaching and set herself on the path to nibbana. Visakha was an exemplary laywoman, daughter, wife, and mother. With her exceptional beauty and sense of duty, she made appropriate and generous offerings to the sangha, befitting a supporter of her status. Through her donations, the sangha had the resources necessary to become a refuge for renunciants and spread their beliefs and practices. She upheld the possibility of making enough merit to escape samsara, acting as a model householder and inspiring Buddhists for the next two millennia.

Generosity

Today, female householders follow the model of Visakha by supporting monastics and monasteries, making donations, organizing holiday festivals, and participating in their temple's committee. The importance of generosity in early Theravada Buddhist communities allowed women to participate in the religious community and receive rewards in this life and the next. In her book *Burma's Mass Lay Meditation Movement*, Ingrid Jordt writes about women's *dana* (generosity) cliques in Myanmar. These cliques are made up of women who share in merit-making together as part of a moral community, organized around monks whose livelihoods their community wants to support. If one is part of a prestigious dana clique, associated with a respected monk, then one can be connected to important people and associate with these moral communities. Jordt reports that women are often involved in competition to be one of the famous female lay supporters of good monks. As well, women who discover a monk and become his chief supporter when he is young occupy a highly prestigious role. If a woman has close ties with a monk who becomes famous, she can hear dhamma or learn meditation directly from him, while others have less access. Having access to a great monk is a sign of abundant merit for the lay female supporter.

Motherhood

Women support the monastic sangha through volunteering their time and offering donations—but also by producing sons, who can be future monks. The Buddha's birth mother, Queen Maya, played a significant role in perpetuating Buddhism through giving birth. Since it is not easily acceptable within Theravada Buddhist societies today for women to ordain, women connect with renunciation indirectly through being mothers. For sons, ordination is a way to pay back the debt to their mothers for their love and care. Ordination allows sons to transfer the merit they received from their renunciation to their mothers. In this way, ordination for men and support from women is built into Theravada Buddhist societies.

In early Indian Buddhism, a mother's love is characterized as the most self-sacrificing and purely compassionate love possible. As the religion scholar Reiko Ohnuma articulates in her book *Ties That Bind*, a mother's love for her only son is the one metaphor that reaches the intensity of the level of loving-kindness Buddha extends to all living beings. This might seem positive for women; however, the exclusivity and attachment of a mother's love is explicitly contrasted with the Buddha's universal love. A mother's love is necessary, but it is far from the Buddhist ideal detachment of liberation. Although mothers are good metaphors for cultivating Buddhist virtues, in the end their particular attachments have to be overcome in order for them to achieve nibbana.

The historian Barbara Watson Andaya argues that part of the reason Theravada Buddhism took root in Southeast Asia during the twelfth and thirteenth centuries was its appeal to women, through motherhood and merit-making. Although women could not be at the top of the hierarchy, the special place accorded mothers—through local sermons, folk songs, rituals, and myths in popular religion—reached the majority of women. The merit that accrues to a mother during her son's ordination is proudly heard during chants that extoll the mother's selflessness during her pregnancy and nurturing of her son.

Body Restrictions

Although women are the most important benefactors for temples, their bodies are deemed problematic and polluting at certain Theravada Buddhist sacred sites. In Chiang Mai, Thailand, at Wat Srisuphan's silver ordination hall, which women are not allowed to enter, the explanation is stated in a sign in English: "Beneath the base of Uposatha [ordination hall] in the monastic boundary, many precious things, incantations, amulets and other holy objects were buried 500 years ago. Entering inside this area may deteriorated [*sic*] the place or otherwise the lady herself. According to this Lanna [northern Thai] Belief, ladies are not allowed to enter the Uposatha." Women are excluded from several sacred sites, such as Wat Srisuphan, because menstrual blood is believed to be a source of polluting power. It is hard to say where and when these customs came to be, although it is acknowledged in this case to be a local belief rather than one stemming from Theravada Buddhist texts. Although the sites where women are not allowed are rare, their impact is significant.

At the Mahamuni shrine in Mandalay, Myanmar, the second most sacred place in the country, women cannot enter the area where the Buddha image sits. Men can go up to the image and place gold leaf on the statue, but women can only observe from below. I remember watching my son and husband go there to pay respects as I waited in the area in front of the statue. My female students from the United States are always enraged when I take them to the Spirit Pillar, called Soi Inthakin, at Wat Chedi Luang in Chiang Mai, which declares that women's menstrual blood will deteriorate and destroy the sacred area. Surely many Theravada Buddhist women do not notice or care about these prohibitions, especially if they grew up in the areas where such sites exist. However, I have spoken with several women from central Thailand, where no such restrictions are applied, and they do not take their exclusion lightly. At the same time, bhikkhuni from northern Thailand whom I have spoken with about this issue focused on the dhamma in their response, reasoning that it is better to let it go and not cling to anger.

In addition, when entering any popular temple, there are often signs letting outsiders know how to dress appropriately. Certainly, most Southeast Asian women know how to dress when entering a temple; these signs are instead meant for international tourists, especially women. Although they are addressed to everyone to "Please dress politely," the signs only portray women's bodies as a problem, with an X over drawings of women displaying cleavage, bare shoulders, shorts or skirts above the knees, or a bare midriff. I have never seen pictures of a man with his shirt off or short shorts.

Because of these issues with the female body, older women, who are outside of the period of menstrual pollution and sexual desire for most male monks, are an essential part of temple communities. Especially in Shan communities, an ethnic group in which the majority practices Theravada Buddhism, women in their elder years stay at the temple on special Buddhist holy days. They participate in ascetic practices and incorporate aspects of the renunciant lifestyle. During this time, they wear white robes and take the Eight Precepts, sometimes staying up all night listening to sermons and meditating.

Besides more structured roles in society as mothers and supporters of Buddhism without ordination status, there are, of course, many regular lay Buddhist women too. They might travel to temples while on vacation in a new city or different Theravada Buddhist country, offer food to monks on their birthdays, make merit at the temple on Buddhist holidays, or attend a short meditation retreat for a few days.

History of Female Ordination

Unlike his birth mother, Queen Maya, the Buddha's stepmother, Mahaprajapati, had a complex relationship with her son. This friction emerged when she asked to follow her son into the monastic life after her husband, King Suddhodana, had died. In premodern India, it would be natural for Mahaprajapati to want to be under the care and protection of her son in her elder, widow years. However, the Buddha initially was reluctant and refused the request. The monastic life is a celibate order, making it difficult for both men and women to be ordained together. The Buddha did not deny women the ability to practice, but he did deny, at first, the possibility to live a celibate, homeless life in the male monastic environment. Eventually the Buddha was convinced by his attendant and cousin Ananda, who reminded the Buddha that Mahaprajapati raised him and that all people can attain nibbana, and Mahaprajapati and five hundred women of her clan formed the first bhikkhuni order.

In the process of allowing ordination for his stepmother and her clan of women, the Buddha also set up the institution of the female monastic order. Bhikkhuni were given 311 precepts (men have 227) and eight *garudhammas* (heavy rules). These rules include not criticizing a monk or punishing him in any way and obligating a female monk to pay respect to a male monk, no matter how much more senior she is. These rules clearly create a hierarchy where female monks are lower in status than their monastic brothers. Yet some of these garudhammas make male monks responsible as teachers to and protectors of the female monks. These rules include female monks not being allowed to spend the rains retreat alone in an area without male monks, and male monks offering a teaching to bhikkhuni communities on a bimonthly basis. These visits were meant to help the women understand the doctrine and discipline by competent, wise monks, who were enjoined to impart their understanding.

The fact that women were allowed to be ordained shows the possibilities for women in Buddhism but also the difficulties they have historically faced. It was revolutionary at the time for women to be allowed to join the monastic order and for the Buddha to declare that women have equal capability to attain enlightenment. Together, the four elements of the sangha—bhikkhus, bhikkhuni, laywomen, and laymen—establish a firm Buddhist social order, with each serving as one pillar of the foundation. Because of this, bhikkhuni were considered by the Buddha to be an essential element of his institution. At the same time, women will always remain lower than men in the Buddhist monastic hierarchy. Although many women are dedicated to and have achieved liberation, they are still influenced by the gendered social constraints of religion and society, which includes educational opportunities, family obligations, and even their confidence levels.

As this early community developed, more rules were put into place so that higher ordination for women had to be conferred by both male and female sides of the community. This was because when female ordination candidates were asked monastic interview questions—Do you lack genitals? Are your genitals incomplete? Are you without menstruation?—they became shy to answer in front of male monks.[12] For this reason, bhikkhuni managed this initial part of determining the viability of the candidate, and the male monks handled the ordination ceremony. This process eventually transformed into a training period of two years following six precepts for female monastic candidates. During this period, the candidate is called a *sikkhamana*. The six precepts they follow include the basic five precepts, with the third precept being celibacy, along with abstaining from food after mid-day.

In the 200s B.C.E., the bhikkhuni order spread to modern-day Sri Lanka and China. In the tenth century C.E., the bhikkhuni order died out in Sri Lanka after war with the Colas from South India, which decimated Buddhist institutions. The male monastic lineage was revived from the Theravada monastic lineage in mainland Southeast Asia; however, since there were no or possibly very few female monks available in Southeast Asia, the female monastic lineage was not revived in Sri Lanka. Because of the rules established in the early bhikkhuni communities that both sanghas be involved in the full ordination of women, no new candidates could enter the female monastic sangha.

The female monastic lineage continued, however, in East Asia, where the Mahayana sect of Buddhism is practiced. With help from female monks of the Mahayana monastic lineage, the possibility for monastic ordination for Theravada women was first revived in 1996 in Sarnath, India, with the help of Korean bhikkhunis, and then again in 1998 in Bodh Gaya, India, supported by Taiwanese bhikkhunis. The German Theravada scholar monk Bhikkhu Analayo has concluded that the bhikkhuni ordination in Bodh Gaya stands on firm legal ground to restore the lineage and aligns with the precedent of the law set down by the Buddha.

Conservative-leaning senior monks judged this ordination invalid, while bhikkhuni and some bhikkhus and lay allies asserted it was legitimate. The conservative bhikkhus argue that they cannot authorize what has not been authorized by the Buddha. Since there is no explicit rule about how to revive a lineage, they believe it is not possible. Since the female monks in the revival ordination originated from the Mahayana lineage, conservative Theravada bhikkhus argue that these female monks use a different Vinaya and rituals and therefore cannot be considered Theravada bhikkhuni. The inflexibility of the ability to revive the order comes from the self-identity of Theravada, which claims to have a kind of purity that is believed to have been corrupted in Mahayana forms.

Despite these objections, bhikkhuni communities continue to grow, with thousands of female monks living in Sri Lanka and hundreds of women ordained each year there from various countries. For many, the bhikkhuni ordination is still controversial and the more acceptable option is a lower category of ordained women called precept nuns.

Precept Nuns

Precept nun is a category of female renunciants in Theravada Buddhism that does not originate from the Buddha or his time. There is little historical evidence revealing when, where, or why precept nuns developed in Theravada Buddhism. Their status is ambiguous, sometimes resembling an ordained person and sometimes a layperson. Precept nuns typically keep the Eight Precepts, the same amount for a layperson staying temporarily at a temple. But unlike a layperson, they live within a temple's religious community, shave their hair, wear robes, and have an ordination ceremony.

In Thailand, Laos, and Cambodia, precept nuns wear white robes, while in Myanmar, precept nuns wear a light-pink robe. They are called different names in each country: *mae chi* in Thailand, *don chi* or *yay chi* in Cambodia, *mae khao* in Laos, and *thilashin* in Myanmar. The terms in the first three countries listed all have relational meanings like "mother" or "grandmother." *Chi* is a descriptive term for any kind of religious ascetic, so *mae chi* refers to a female or mother who is an ascetic. *Khao* means "white," so the Laotian *mae khao* is the mother in white. Myanmar's *thilashin*, in contrast, means "upholder of virtue." Because a thilashin's robes are not white but pink, and therefore closer to the male monk's maroon, visually they are closer to a renunciant status equal to male monks than those precept nuns who wear white. However, none of these precept nuns is given the same kind of respect or status as a male monk.

Precept nuns' living conditions greatly vary, from those who feel inspired by their male monk companions in the same temple, to those who have little community around them and are treated poorly by male monks. Others live in their own communities—some well funded, some barely surviving. Educational institutions for precept nuns remain minimal in Thailand and are almost nonexistent in Laos and Cambodia. Comparatively, in Myanmar, there is a well-developed system of education for thilashin. Precept nuns who have some purpose to their monastic life—such as education, meditation practice, teaching, or helping to run the temple's affairs—would most likely describe themselves as fulfilled.

Mae Chi of Thailand

In Thailand, mae chi are thought to have existed as a category of renunciation for centuries. They receive little support socially or institutionally for their renunciation since they are considered laypeople by the Thai government. For instance, they do not receive benefits of subsidized transportation, medical care, or education. For the same reason, they are not part of the census for religious persons, so it is hard to estimate exactly how many there are, although recent estimates number them between twenty to thirty thousand. At the same time, precept nuns fall under the category of ordained people when it comes to political activity, so they are not allowed to vote.

In her research article "Becoming *Bhikkhunī? Mae Chis* and the Global Women's Ordination Movement," Lisa Battaglia, a scholar of Thai Buddhism, found that many mae chi are not interested in becoming fully ordained female monks. These mae chi are unwilling to be seen as fighting for equality and would rather demonstrate their acceptance of hierarchy as a natural part of life. Mae chi worry that people might see them as trying to attain something rather than having the proper spiritual motivation. They are also concerned that the revived Theravada bhikkhuni lineage is impure, sharing the opinion of conservative monastics. Similarly, the anthropologist Joanna Cook notes in her book *Meditation in Modern Buddhism*, based on her research in a meditation temple in northern Thailand, mae chis' ultimate aim is the realization of nibbana, which they perceive as transcending gender.

Since becoming a precept nun is not the typical path for a woman—and often comes at high social cost, especially for young, healthy, unmarried women—mae chi usually have strong spiritual motives for their ordination. As identified by the researcher Monica Lindberg Falk in her book *Making Fields of Merit*, the lay life, for mae chi, is depicted as filled with problems of familial suffering, unfulfilling work, abusive or alcoholic husbands, and poverty. The life of the mae chi is certainly not easy, so these women are not simply trying to drop out; instead, they hope to realize the Buddhist truth of suffering and seek a path toward liberation in the safe and calming temple environment. They seek a life with more meaning than lay life, which they consider as lacking purpose.

It can be difficult to get permission from family members and parents, but eventually as the women persist, refuse to marry, and sometimes run away, their parents relent. In other families, women are encouraged to ordain. This would usually be the case for a family with some means who has other daughters and sons and who are supporters of Buddhism. Within Thai cultural values, daughters care for their parents in old age. Even if a woman does not marry, she can still be there to support her parents. Ordination disrupts this expectation. Because of this, some women are only able to ordain later in life after their children are grown and their parents are deceased. Since the Thai public prefers to make merit with monks, mae chi face financial hardships and must find ways to support themselves.

Hierarchy is a noticeable part of life in the Buddhist temple as mae chi physically mark themselves as inferior by waiting for monks to pass, serving monks, waiting for them to start eating before they begin, and sitting below monks. Mae chi choose to show their subordination because cultivating these virtues of humility is part of monastic practice. One mae chi from a temple in Chiang Mai told me that for her, the temple environment is like a frame—she is happy in this frame because she is protected and cared for by the rules of the temple and by the abbot. Despite the drawbacks to their situation, outsiders should not assume that all or most mae chi are being suppressed and should resist their oppression. It is important not to place the value of equality on the highest pedestal but instead to recognize the perspectives of the precept nuns themselves. Although they lack access to much of what monks take for granted, they do not consider themselves pitiable or oppressed. Because their goal is liberation, precept nuns feel lucky to be able to devote themselves to this pursuit to whatever extent they can.

Don Chi of Cambodia

In the article "Shades of Gender and Security in Cambodia," the researcher Alexandra Kent reports that there were approximately ten thousand Cambodian precept nuns in 2000. However, it is difficult to estimate the number of nuns in the country today because of the group's diversity and the absence of formal living arrangements. Don chi are often perceived in Cambodian society as pious female devotees at the end of their lives, pitied as social outcastes and widows without familial connections. However, don chi can earn respect as teachers within temples. In field research undertaken in the early 2010s, Lara Schubert found that don chi in local wats in Phnom Penh have several leadership positions, including receiving and collecting donations and teaching vipassana meditation and Buddhist scriptures to laywomen and some laymen. These don chi are especially respected because of their spiritual knowledge and practice. At the same time, Schubert discovered a less respected position for ultra-poor don chi, who engage in much manual labor.

While some elder nuns may use the temple as their only refuge, others are middle-aged and supported by their children. These women may not be officially ordained but spend most of their time at the temple while living at home with their children.

Cambodian precept nuns have been seen as mediums to spread development within local communities. The United States Agency for International Development (USAID) funded the Nuns and Wat Grannies program, which grew into a Cambodian non-governmental organization (NGO) called Reproductive and Child Health Alliance (RACHA). RACHA provided training in newborn and child health as well as family planning for nuns to counsel community members. RACHA decided to focus on nuns for this training because the Buddhist temple is ubiquitous in Cambodia, and topics such as breastfeeding were embarrassing for new mothers and male monks to discuss with each other. In 2011, RACHA trained over 2,500 nuns in nine Cambodian provinces and has helped to increase positive breastfeeding practices. International organizations from North America and Europe have also provided aid for these women to be used as resources for community healing. The Association of Nuns and Laywomen of Cambodia (ANLWC) holds conferences, with its mission to improve the status of women in Cambodian society. Instead of advocating for female monk ordination, Cambodian nuns have been working toward what Peou Vanna, the president of the ANLWC, called "a quiet movement of Buddhist women."

Besides being part of development work in their villages, communities of don chi in Cambodia live fulfilled lives in other ways. As the researcher Elizabeth Guthrie notes in "Khmer Buddhism, Female Asceticism, and Salvation," one community that illustrates this is Wat Mangalavan, in Phnom Penh. Precept nuns in this community are engaged in a spiritual pursuit toward nibbana. There were over seventy nuns there in the 1990s, providing a powerful presence in the daily routine of the temple. These precept nuns follow the schedule of the monks, eating the same food prepared by laity. They assist laypeople who come to see the abbot of the temple, but they also spend much time in study and meditation. These nuns seek out spaces and teachers for their own goal of spiritual freedom. This goal is at odds with the goals of international NGOs who see the appropriate roles of female ascetics as being part of secular society, caring for others.

Mae Khao of Laos

In Laos, mae khao share a similar situation with Cambodian don chi. Mae khao do not have access to education and do not have many resources to support themselves or garner support from others. Their dress and lifestyle are like mae chi of Thailand but with fewer opportunities for social mobility. Precept nuns in Laos do not have their own temples or educational facilities, living instead in hidden corners of some temples, as the scholar Karma Lekshe Tsomo has found in her research into their situation. They live off the surplus food monks collect in exchange for cooking and cleaning in the temple. They renounced to live a full Buddhist life and improve their morality but are given very little access to the benefits of renunciation—they lack education, adequate accommodations, nutrition, and health care, which does not bode well for them to achieve their spiritual goals or to be seen as exemplars within Lao society. However, mae khao do receive identification cards that categorize them as Buddhist nuns. Although these nuns have some autonomy in that they can handle money and cook for themselves in their discrete part of the temple, their lives remain tenuous and economically dependent on others. Their precarity is seen in the fact that they are vulnerable to instability and might be forced to move if the abbot that supports them moves or passes away.

Thilashin of Myanmar

Thilashin of Myanmar have more opportunities than their neighbors in mainland Southeast Asia. In 2010, there were over forty-three thousand of these precept nuns. Thilashin are recognized as an official part of the monastic community by the Department of Religious Affairs in Myanmar, and they manage independent nunneries. However, instead of walking silently on a daily morning alms round like male monks, thilashin spend the whole day once a week or month stopping in front of houses and businesses repeating a chant encouraging generosity. In exchange, thilashin receive uncooked rice instead of the cooked, hot meals monks receive.

Their vocations consist of two tracks—one of study for virgins who were never married, and the other of meditation for the older women who already were married and had children. Unlike in Cambodia and Laos, young women and girls have educational opportunities as precept nuns in Myanmar. Although the education of nuns was initially not supported by the state, and getting an education is certainly challenging, thilashin have been able to use their knowledge and scholarship to enhance their support and standing in Myanmar.

Not until the early 1900s were nuns allowed to take part in the pathamapyan, or royal exams for monastics in Myanmar, and nuns had to wait until after World War II to sit for the scriptural exams conducted by lay associations. In 1942, the dhammacariya degree was instituted for nuns, and the first nun passed in 1943. Nuns needed male monk allies to teach them the pedagogical methods needed to pass the exam, which involves much complex information and memorization. These sympathetic and open-minded male monks were crucial for nuns' education in this early period. Even when nuns found a teacher, it was difficult to enter a male-dominated classroom and environment. As the scholar Hiroko Kawanami describes in *Renunciation and Empowerment of Buddhist Nuns in Myanmar-Burma*, some nuns stood at the back of the lecture halls or hid behind curtains so they could listen without being seen. Despite these disadvantages, nuns worked diligently and passed their exams. Now the exam system has created an upwardly mobile arena for thilashin to garner support and become respected scholars and teachers of dhamma.

Besides scholarship, meditation is also an important part of spiritual fulfillment for thilashin. In her study of the Mahasi Meditation

Center in Yangon, the anthropologist Ingrid Jordt found that the meditation movement has helped thilashin get recognition beyond their gender, because of its emphasis on nibbana. The institution of the meditation center has allowed women to have a place for their practice, where they can achieve the highest goals. Instead of ordaining a son or giving material support, women can attain insights for themselves, which takes them outside of the hierarchies within their societies. At the same time, only a male monk can unequivocally be seen by Theravada societies as someone who renounces the world and is able to transcend their gender.

Ambiguity is the key word for precept nuns. Although individual nuns can gain prestige and support, there is still a large disparity between male and female renunciation in Theravada Buddhism. Male ordination is much more openly celebrated, while women's renunciation is more likely to be questioned and not praised. Many nuns cannot fully renounce and often remain obliged to their families, having to go home and take care of sick relatives and look after their patrons in a way that male monks are not subject to. Despite some instances of equality and leadership roles, several researchers in Cambodia, Myanmar, Thailand, and Laos have interviewed precept nuns who have declared that women have less merit than men and that women's bodily sufferings during menstruation and childbirth were the result of lower karma. Because of this perceived deficit, they are working to store up enough merit to be reborn as males in their next lives.

Revival of Bhikkhuni Ordination

The Theravada bhikkhuni lineage was revived in 1998, and ordination became available for women. Sri Lanka has been the host for mainland Southeast Asian women to take ordination. Although having this option is an important step, ordaining in Sri Lanka poses its challenges too. It is difficult for female monastic candidates to have the support necessary to travel to Sri Lanka, and the

Sri Lankan annual training and ordination only has the capacity to ordain a limited number of women each year. The bhikkhuni ordination is also more complex than a bhikkhu ordination. Unlike male ordination where only five male monastics in good standing are necessary, ordination for women requires ten—five each from both the male and female sides.

In Thailand, the Theravada bhikkhuni revival movement began in 1928 when the social critic and layman Narin Klueng had his daughters ordained. They were soon arrested and forced out of the robes as the head monk of Thailand, the Sangharaja, forbade female ordination and decreed it a monastic offense for a bhikkhu to ordain women. This rule is upheld today. In 2003, the Thai Senate Select Committee advised that the 1928 ruling was invalid because it contravenes the Thai constitution's freedom of religion and nondiscrimination of women, but the Sangha Supreme Council's position has remained unrelenting. The Sangha Supreme Council has declared that higher ordination for female monks must have the participation of both male and female monks. Since there are no Theravada bhikkhuni that the Sangha Supreme Council would recognize as legitimate, the ordination of women is not possible in Thailand.

Because Theravada bhikkhuni ordination in Thailand is impossible, women who seek ordination beyond the precept nun category must find alternative methods. Voramai Kabilsingh was ordained in the Mahayana monastic lineage in Taiwan in 1971 and began a temple for women, Wat Songdhammakalyani, outside of Bangkok. She was not accepted as part of the Thai Theravada Buddhist sangha, but she was accepted as a Mahayana bhikkhuni who lives and practices in Thailand. Eventually, Voramai's daughter, Chatsumarn, after a successful career as a professor and public intellectual, traveled to Sri Lanka to receive novice ordination in 2001 and again in 2003 to receive full ordination, becoming the first bhikkhuni in Thailand within the Theravada tradition. Now known as Dhammananda Bhikkhuni (b. 1944), she continues to be an outspoken advocate for bhikkhuni ordination in Thailand and abroad, and she continues to lead Wat Songdhammakalyani temple.

Bhikkhuni Nanthayani (1954–2022) is another prominent Thai bhikkhuni. She received novice ordination in 2006 and full ordination in 2008. Bhikkhuni Nanthayani has two branch centers in northern Thailand and over a hundred disciples, all ordained in Sri Lanka. She was well known as Mae Chi Rongduan for twenty-six years before ordaining and establishing her first community, Nirotharam, in 1995. Her second community, Suttajit, was established in 2003. Nirotharam is focused on training in the monastic life while Suttajit residents concentrate their time on meditation practice. These bhikkhuni go on alms rounds regularly in their local communities. They are also supported by Thai people outside of these local areas, with international visitors and Thai Buddhists from Bangkok arriving on a regular basis. Instead of advocacy and discussion of issues surrounding women and ordination, these bhikkhuni focus on their monastic performance, the study and spread of Buddhist teachings, and meditation practice.

In contrast to Thailand, there are no bhikkhuni communities in Cambodia, Myanmar, or Laos. Saccavadi, a Burmese woman, returned to Myanmar from Sri Lanka, where she had ordained as a bhikkhuni, and she was subject to severe punishment because of her choice. Saccavadi had been a thilashin for sixteen years before she moved to Sri Lanka to attend a monastic university. While in contact with Sri Lankan bhikkhuni, she was inspired to follow the same path, even though Burmese monks strongly advised her not to. When she returned to Yangon to visit her ailing father in 2005, the State Sangha Maha Nayaka Council summoned her to a religious court hearing and charged her with impersonating a monk. Saccavadi recounted the humiliating hearing, recorded by the journalist Christine Toomey, where senior monks demanded that she put on the pink robes of a thilashin and admit that she was foolish for having ordained as a female monk. Being confused and scared, she changed into lay clothes instead of the thilashin robes but could not bring herself to read a statement of guilt aloud. Because of this, she was sentenced to five years in prison. Not being able to handle prison life, she decided to confess after a few months. She returned to Sri Lanka and then traveled to the United States to practice with a small group of female monks in California, but she could not cope with the trauma of her experience. She then went on a solitary retreat in a cabin and fell in love with its owner, whom she soon married.

While Myanmar has a long wait for bhikkhuni acceptance, Thai bhikkhuni have created an innovation for female monks—the possibility for temporary novice ordination. Both communities of Dhammananda Bhikkhuni and Nanthayani Bhikkhuni regularly hold a mass ordination of women who would like to try on the monastic life and learn more about Buddhism. Temporary ordination is a longstanding and culturally significant practice for young males, but not until 2009 did temporary ordination become available for female novices. Dhammananda Bhikkhuni has offered temporary ordination twice per year since that time. The monasteries in northern Thailand also regularly offer this opportunity. Upward of one hundred women are ordained at one time during these ceremonies. They stay as novices in the temple for about two weeks, learning how to wear their robes, collect alms, and meditate. For young boys, temporary ordination is considered a rite of passage into manhood and is a way to repay one's mother who brought them into the world and cared for them. Now daughters can fulfill this role and repay their mothers too. This is an important way for women to feel they have some ability to honor their mothers and is undoubtedly empowering and affirming for Thai women.

Just like men, women are inspired by the Theravada Buddhist teachings and want to follow the monastic rules to help them along this path. That they are denied these rules and the structure of the monastic life is unsurprisingly upsetting and disappointing for many women. These women do not want to live as mae chi or laywomen; they want the structure that the Buddha laid out for them. "This is my ticket to freedom. Stop trying to take it away from me!" one American bhikkhuni exclaims in the documentary *Buddha's Forgotten Nuns*.[13]

No matter their status within Buddhism, women are a vibrant and necessary part of the traditions and institutions—as supporters and leaders, teachers and students. Lay, ordained, and women somewhere in between have contributed to Buddhism in their meditation practice, social engagement, support, and scholarship. Because women do not have clearly defined roles, they have diverse possibilities. Women face more challenges and struggles, however, and must be particularly focused and driven to accomplish their goals.

Notable Female Figures

Because women are not recognized as full monastics, they must create their own roles, finding niches within their Buddhist societies. Below are examples of individual laywomen, precept nuns, and bhikkhuni who have successfully become meditation masters, socially engaged leaders, and healers with supernatural abilities.

Meditation Masters

Because of the high status accorded to scholasticism as a pursuit for Buddhist monks historically, meditation practice has been more available to women than educational opportunities. Despite it being difficult for women to gain access to education through the monastic institution, some women have become well known and respected in their countries for their knowledge of Buddhist texts and doctrines. Since the late nineteenth century, during the rise of the institution of the meditation center, vipassana meditation has become a significant avenue for women to become leaders. While full participation in monastic institutions is difficult for Theravada women, female participation in meditation is not. Because the meditation center creates possibilities for national and international audiences to learn meditation in an intensive retreat environment, more teachers are needed to meet this demand. If there are not enough monks, or if the monks are not as skilled as ordained and laywomen, Buddhist women are able to create spaces of authority for themselves. Below I discuss some exceptional women who are considered meditation masters.

LOAK KRUU. One don chi, whom the scholar Alexandra Kent interviewed, is referred to as Loak Kruu. *Loak* is an honorific that shows respect, and *Loak Kruu* is typically how one addresses a male teacher. Loak Kruu follows the Eight Precepts and lives permanently at her meditation center, while some of her children live with their father. She decided to become a don chi after attending a conference of the Association of Nuns and Laywomen of Cambodia and started studying meditation. Her knowledge of meditation is what allowed her to acquire a form of Buddhist expertise recognized by her local community. She teaches to monks and laypeople on a piece of temple land donated to her by a head monk. Her pathway to recognition is not part of the monastic institution. Rather, Loak Kruu had to construct this empowering pathway to autonomy on her own.

UPASIKA KEE NANAYON. Upasika Kee Nanayon (1901-78) did not want to be a mae chi. Instead, she became an *upasika*, a nonordained woman who takes more Buddhist precepts than a layperson, and usually wears a white shirt and black bottoms. Growing up in a large family, she felt an aversion to marriage and childbirth, so she worked hard to save money to devote herself to practice. After becoming a successful businesswoman, and following her parents' death in 1945, Kee was able to pursue a renunciant lifestyle without relying on offerings from others. She enacted this vision by living in her aunt and uncle's small home that was to become Upasika Kee Nanayon's women's practice center. This is significant since, at the time, mae chi were assumed to be brokenhearted widows or deficient women who could not make it in the world. She developed followers through meeting with students every day for group meditation, discussion, and chanting. Many of her talks have been published, which in turn attracted more followers. One of her books, *Pure and Simple*, has been translated into English. The women at her center continue to listen to her speeches and make her teachings known through continued printing and publishing of her books for widespread and free distribution.

MAE CHI KAEW (also spelled Mae Chee Kaew). Mae Chi Kaew (1901–91) is considered to be an arahant by the well-known Thai monk Ajahn Maha Bua. She grew up in rural northeast Thailand and faced many challenges in her life before ordination. She was married and had an adopted daughter before she finally persuaded her husband to let her become a mae chi. After her husband remarried and her child had a new family, Mae Chi Kaew finally had an opportunity to pursue her quest for enlightenment. At first, Mae Chi Kaew was too entranced by her meditative abilities in concentration, which sent her into cosmological realms and offered her many fascinating visions. However, this type of meditation was not helpful on the path to liberation. Maha Bua's stern council shifted her practice to the point where she was able to attain nibbana by focusing on her internal mental states exclusively. Until her death, she guided and taught many nuns and laypeople about the Buddhist path and meditation. Her life demonstrates the possible achievements of female meditators and provides a strong model of a female meditation teacher. The Mae Chi Kaew Memorial Stupa was built in her honor in 2006 in her hometown in Mukdahan Province. Her bones are believed to have turned into relics as the final proof of her attainment.

Socially Engaged Women

Theravada monastics have always engaged with society rather than being concerned solely with their own spiritual development. Modern Theravada women are no exception, and they have generated several Buddhist-inspired social projects, NGOs, temples, and organizations to fill needs in their societies. Observing the suffering faced by women, children, and families within their communities, they have created workshops, teachings, spaces for discussion, and refuges for women and families in need of aid.

MAE CHI SANSANEE STHIRASUTA (also spelled Mae Chee Sansanee Sthirasuta). Mae Chi Sansanee (1953–2021), a former fashion model, was known for her social activities and creative methods of teaching meditation and dhamma. She bought land outside of Bangkok, which became the beautiful meditation center Sathira Dhammasathan. Through the donations of her generous family, she was able to create her center and maintain several socially engaged activities. Mae Chi Sansanee was concerned with education and women in the domestic sphere. She began by providing preschool education to handicapped children and then offered training in Buddhist teachings and meditation to high school and university students. Her center has become a rehabilitation home for sexually abused women and is also used to run programs for mae chi, deepening their practice and understanding so that they can apply Buddhist teachings to development issues in their communities. She even supported a group of young boxers to earn money fighting while developing their spiritual lives. Like other female monastic and nun communities, she focused on applying Buddhist teachings for women, families, and youth. Interestingly, in her teachings and work, she was not interested in discussing gender or gender equality within Buddhism.

KETU MALA. Ketu Mala is a Burmese thilashin who acknowledges Buddhism's deep-rooted patriarchy in her country. She has received the title of "Feminist Buddhist Nun" by the journalist Jennifer Rigby. Ketu Mala aligns with Western feminist ideals because she is working toward equality within the Burmese monastic institution. In her youth, she remembers feeling deeply wounded by gender discrimination when she could not enter the ordination hall when her male family members were being ordained. Today she lives at Pa-Auk Forest Monastery where her teacher, Pa-Auk Sayadaw, supports women monastics. Many other male monks in Burmese society are not allies, however. Ketu Mala must choose her words and actions carefully so monks do not think she is trying to compete with them. Even discussing the possibility of creating the bhikkhuni sangha in Myanmar right now is impossible. Most male monks are uncomfortable when she is in the spotlight, giving a speech on a stage, and they are seated below as part of the audience. To them, this situation appears to reverse the gender hierarchy. Because of this, she is working to raise the prestige and perception of thilashin. She founded the Dhamma School Foundation to bring Buddhist teachings into mainstream education. Her network of thousands of schools has helped to educate more than half a million children in Myanmar.

OUYPORN KHUANKAEW. Ouyporn Khuankaew grew up as a "traditional Buddhist," with male monks at the head of her temple and men leaders in the village families. Suffering from a violent childhood and abuse from her father, she found relief in feminism. Once she understood the causes of structural violence against women, she developed deeper understanding and healing techniques through Buddhist teachings and practices. Since she made this connection between feminism and Buddhism, Ouyporn has worked to mix feminist empowerment with Buddhist healing in her activism. In Chiang Mai, Thailand, through her organization the International Women's Partnership for Peace and Justice, she leads women's retreats, workshops against domestic violence, and offers leadership training for precept nuns. She has developed programs for Buddhist peace building, nonviolent resistance, and social change for women. Her organization emphasizes empowerment of women through working with female activists, refugees, and abuse survivors throughout Asia.

Supernatural Abilities

Another historically important avenue of support for women is supernatural abilities. Exemplary females with these powers have been able to establish their authority as religious teachers and healers. Buddhist communities are eager and open to the possibility of Buddhist practitioners exhibiting supernatural powers obtained through their morality and meditation practice. Although this is a rare feat, it is possible for women to display these healing qualities and become well known for their supernatural powers.

MAE CHI THOTSAPHON. Mae Chi Thotsaphon is a best-selling author and popular television personality who is believed to be able to help people heal the bad kamma they have created in the past. On a weekend day, she might have over one thousand people visit her to listen to teachings and consult with her on how to resolve their kamma. This kind of practice would be seen as inappropriate for male monks, but as a mae chi, Thotsaphon has more freedom to heal, as she is not confined by the monastic rules. Monks are not allowed to boast about their skills or talk about them, which might be regarded as claiming to have extraordinary spiritual achievements. Although she is not seen to be enlightened, Mae Chi Thotsaphon has achieved a highly regarded status among the Thai Buddhist community, with many devoted and influential devotees.

However, some monks are critical of Mae Chi Thotsaphon's ability to resolve other peoples' kamma. The scholar monk Phra Maha Vajiramedhi has argued that the services she provides fall outside of Buddhism. He labels this as a form of Buddhist commercialism because lay Buddhists offer money in exchange for receiving advice on how to resolve their kamma. In his orthodox view, Vajiramedhi asserts that the only way to resolve kamma is by yourself, noting there is no place in the foundational Buddhist teachings that states that one person can know and resolve the kamma of another person. Instead of focusing on ways to resolve kamma from past lives, Vajiramedhi advises Thai Buddhists to focus on this life and how they are living right now.

MAE BUNRUEAN TONGBUNTOEM. Another female Buddhist who exemplifies spiritual abilities is Mae Bunruean Tongbuntoem (1895– 1964), whose powers are described by Martin Seeger, a scholar of Thai Buddhism. She learned meditation from her uncle, who was a famous meditation monk. Mae Bunruean married and lived as a wife, and later a widow, without ordaining permanently, although she was a mae chi for short periods. Throughout her life, many supernatural occurrences were reported to have happened to her. For example, one night in her home, she made a vow to enter a pavilion in her local temple, and somehow, without leaving her house, she appeared in her local temple just as she had wished. She was able to heal ailments through massage and endow medicines with positive energies. Her spiritual attainments have been made tangible through the amulets she produced and remains of her body, which became crystallized relics. Mae Bunruean's amulets and other objects related to her magically protective powers continue to be venerated decades after her death.

Triumphs and Challenges

There is a broad range of roles for women within Buddhism, both as laity and ordained members. Ordination for women is more complicated than for males because of the decline of the Theravada bhikkhuni lineage. However, the plight of women in Buddhism is not simply one of patriarchal domination and feminist resistance. Some women love supporting and serving the monks as laywomen and precept nuns. Other women desire to be fully a part of the monastic institution as bhikkhuni.

For Theravada men, ordination and the celibate life of a monk are rites of passage through which they realize their masculinity and become seen as men in their communities. Men gain maturity and the ability to transfer merit to their parents. Their celibacy proves their maturity, discipline, and control over their sexuality. For Theravada women, celibacy does not prove maturity or female identity—femininity is achieved through marriage and motherhood. Women fundamentally violate these social norms when they practice celibacy and reject the domestic, maternal realm.

In the end, women are inspired by the same spiritual ideals as men. Many of the women surveyed in this chapter are not concerned with gender but instead with Buddhist doctrines dealing with human birth and how to get out of the cycle of rebirth. Within patriarchal systems, women face particular challenges. However, through Buddhism's universal teachings of liberation from suffering, women have worked within these challenges and achieved their goals. Many of the women who succeed are especially strong-willed and determined. However, it is impossible to know the number of women who were not able to overcome the challenges faced due to societal constraints on their paths toward nibbana.

CHAPTER 5

Theravada's Relationship with Other Religions

Buddhism is often considered to be a tolerant and peaceful religion, with many adherents declaring that not a drop of blood has been spilled in the name of the Buddha. That is actually impossible to measure since most group conflicts involve a number of factors including political, ethnic, cultural, linguistic, and ideological, as well as religious difference. Of course, Buddhists espouse a doctrine of nonviolence, just like all religions in ideal situations. The most important and first precept for all Buddhists is to refrain from harming living beings. However, a doctrine of nonviolence does not make a cultural group immune to intolerance and violence. Religions exist in distinct social situations and have the capacity to inflame or dampen potential sites of conflict. Religion, in this case Theravada Buddhism, is not necessarily a force for good or bad but a set of beliefs and practices that are used in specific contexts and within particular societal dynamics.

During the premodern period of kingdoms in mainland Southeast Asia, Buddhist ideas, temples, and monks were used as tools for royal legitimation. The colonial period saw Buddhism as a source of refuge, a binding force, and an institution in need of protection from foreign rulers. After colonialism, Buddhism was a key component of bringing communities together to create a sense of nationalism in new nation-states. Today, in mainland Southeast Asia, where Theravada Buddhism is the majority religion, state governments align themselves with Buddhism more than other religions. Because of this, minority religious groups have not always felt welcomed by their Buddhist compatriots. In fact, in some regions, history records more exclusion than inclusion, and this has indeed resulted in violence.

Theravada Buddhism has unique relationships with spirit religions, Hinduism, and Chinese gods, which have all become incorporated into one popular religious culture. Theravada Buddhism, from its ordination lineages to the purity of its texts, is interested in maintaining the boundaries between what is inside and what is outside of orthodoxy. At the same time, Theravada Buddhism accommodates and integrates alternate religious elements through iconography, shrines, mythology, and art. This is in part because spirits and deities are just that—religious elements. These elements are not whole systems of knowledge, which would compete with or diverge from Theravada teachings aimed toward nibbana. Statues to Ganesh, amulets depicting deities, or shrines to local spirits fall within Theravada cosmology; they just are not part of the ultimate teachings that would lead one to nibbana.

This chapter explores Theravada relationships with indigenous, Indian, and Chinese religions, and then Buddhist attitudes toward Christianity and Islam, which cannot be assimilated into Buddhist societies as easily. But first we survey the ways Theravada Buddhism is spread to other religious and cultural groups.

Buddhist Missionaries

Along with Christianity and Islam, Buddhism is one of three missionary religions. The model for many people, when imagining a missionary, would most likely be a Christian going door to door actively proselytizing to convert people to their faith. However, this is not the only way to be a missionary. Buddhists do not actively proselytize by going out to talk to people who may not be interested in their religion. Instead, Buddhists act as missionaries by spreading their teachings to those who are curious. Every Theravada monk's duty is to make their doctrines and values available to the world as much as possible so that those who are curious have resources to study, practice, and feel comfortable visiting a temple to learn more. Compared with Christian missionaries, Buddhists have much lower stakes. Buddhists are not interested in conversion because within the Buddhist cosmological view of kamma and rebirth, there are many chances to learn and apply Buddhist teachings. For Christians, the single-lifetime view necessitates an urgency for others to hear about Jesus and convert so they can be closer to reaching heaven upon death. For Buddhists, becoming a member of a Buddhist community is not the goal of spreading the teachings. Many Buddhist monks I have spoken to state that identifying oneself as a Buddhist, although it might be helpful, is unnecessary. Buddhists themselves are aware of the Christian proselytizing efforts and how they can appear aggressive. Because of this, I have found that Theravada Buddhist monks seek to distance themselves from being called missionaries. "We are ones who show, not ones who know," one monk expressed to me, meaning that they show the path through their actions but do not express certainty of the only way to nibbana. Although Buddhists do not fit proselytizing practices of Christianity, they are missionizing in ways that use practices and ideas from their own tradition, demonstrating their faith in the dhamma.

Theravada Buddhists are typically eager to discuss their religion, for the most part, with anyone who shows an interest. This excitement comes from the idea that it is important to spread the dhamma to all who are interested, as expressed in Buddhist scripture:

Walk, monks, on tour for the blessings of the manyfolk, for the happiness of the manyfolk, out of compassion for the world, for the welfare, the blessing, and the happiness of devas and men. Let not two (of you) go by one (way). Monks, teach dhamma that is lovely at the beginning, lovely at the middle, and lovely at the end...There are beings with little dust in their eyes, who, not hearing dhamma, are decaying, (but) if they are learners of dhamma, they will grow.[14]

Monks should teach out of compassion for those who could learn the dhamma, those with only a little dust in their eyes. Yet, Buddhist teachings are not permanent and will eventually even disappear. Not only is the dhamma impermanent, but it is also perceived in various times and places to be slowly on the decline. This belief introduces some urgency to Buddhist missionizing. Within Pali texts there are several timelines associated with Buddhism's end, a popular number being five thousand years from the time of the Buddha's death. The exact timing is not fixed, however, and can be extended if Buddhist communities maintain their religiosity.

Theravada Buddhist sanghas seek to spread Buddhism deeper within Buddhist societies but also to introduce practices and beliefs to non-Buddhist audiences. Although there are historical examples of missionary monks leaving their homelands to teach others, and currently Theravada temples established abroad, most monks are missionaries in their home temples, spreading Buddhism further into their local communities. Monks who live in urban, international centers of the Theravada world have the additional opportunity to spread Buddhism to foreigners and tourists who visit their temples.

Although contemporary monks do not advise conversion to Buddhism for foreign travelers, there have been instances of political motivation for active proselytization and conversion within Theravada nation-states. Missionizing practices in Thailand occurred in the 1960s when Buddhist monks, as part of a program created by the Thai Sangha and supported by the government, sought to convert indigenous peoples and villages in the northern highlands. The Dhammacarik (wandering dhamma) Bhikkhu Program (DBP) began in 1964 with the aim to convert indigenous groups who adhere to practices propitiating the indigenous spirits. The purpose of the DBP was to integrate indigenous people into the Thai nation-state through teaching the dhamma and following a Buddhist way of life.

In contrast to the intentional proselytization of the DBP, the author Kamala Tiyavanich notes in her book *Forest Recollections* that in the early 1900s, monks within the Thai forest tradition wandered among similar groups of indigenous people. The forest monks had a sympathetic and overall positive view of these non-Buddhists. Although the indigenous communities did not know at first the proper ways to interact with monks, the villagers were endearing and honestly curious about the monks' way of life. After the forest monks became friendly with the villagers, the monks taught them simple meditation practices. These individual forest monks made no attempt to change these people's beliefs or convert them to Buddhism but rather attracted followers through simply showing the Buddhist way of life.

In Myanmar, the International Theravada Buddhist Missionary University was established in Yangon in 1998 as an institution for any Buddhist scholar to learn Buddhist texts and practice. The university provides free tuition through government support so that their graduates can propagate Buddhism to the world. Part of the objectives of this university are to share the teachings of Theravada Buddhism and train missionaries well versed in morality, Buddhist study, and practice. One of the departments of this university is the Faculty of Religious and Missionary Works, which offers classes on Buddhist missionary practices. This university, like the DBP in Thailand, demonstrates how state involvement uses Buddhism as a civilizing force to draw ethnic, religious, and racial outsiders further into the nation-state.

Although monks have missionized to convert indigenous people, Theravada Buddhists have also incorporated indigenous spirit practices into their broader religious system. In similar ways to how Theravada Buddhists assimilated indigenous spirits, deities from India and China have also mixed fluidly with the majority religion. In contrast, Theravada Buddhism is unable to integrate other world religious systems such as Christianity and Islam, which contain alternative and competing systems of knowledge.

Indigenous Spirit Religions

Theravada Buddhism in mainland Southeast Asia contains deep roots of culture and an indigenous layer of spirit religions, which are extremely persistent. Propitiation of spirits has proved impenetrable amid centuries of social and political changes. Interactions with spirits are, for the most part, individual and private, relying on ritual specialists to imbue a shrine with the nearby spirits. Once Theravada Buddhism became the dominant cultural force in mainland Southeast Asia, spirit beliefs and practices were not absorbed completely into this new religion. Instead, Buddhism and the spirits entered a hierarchical relationship. Buddhism, as a world religion, is seen as superior by most Theravada Buddhists because it has otherworldly (*lokuttara*) practices, including asceticism and renunciation, that lead to nibbana, whereas the worship of spirits is considered lower because their power is limited to this-worldly (*lokiya*) domain. However, the powerful new ideas of Buddhism did not demean the power of spirits but generated a symbiosis between the two religious systems. Village communities of indigenous, ethnic minority people remain, including the Akha, Hmong, and Karen people, who practice spirit religions exclusively. However, Theravada Buddhists mainly see spirit religions as providing extra support and reassurance along with their formal religious affiliation, adding to the options available for apotropaic or protective practices.

In his research on Laos in *Spirits of the Place: Buddhism and Lao Religious Culture*, John Holt, a religious studies scholar, has found that Buddhism did not penetrate completely through to the worship of spirits. In Laos, the spirits do not fall underneath Buddhist ways of understanding the world, which includes rebirth and kamma. From Holt's investigations into Lao Buddhism, he finds that the spirits, or *phi*, are not bound by the ethical constraints of kamma. Phi are believed to have a separate origin than Buddhist cosmology, and spirit folk cosmology does not attempt to reconcile spirits with Buddhism. In fact, Holt believes that Buddhism is seen through the lens of spirits, instead of the other way around. Because the spirits are the original owners of the land, they maintain their own domain of authority outside of Buddhism. In Laos, Buddhism is inspirited, as Buddhist statues are believed to contain an active spirit, which can be propitiated for protection.

In Thailand, Theravada Buddhism has been placed by researchers and scholars at the top of a hierarchy, with spirit religions underneath, combined into one system. However, if we consider forms of popular religion, spirits have been highly visible despite their placement under the framework of Buddhism. Some scholars, such as Pattana Kitiarsa, see official Theravada Buddhism losing ground to unofficial forms of popular religion, drawn indiscriminately from spirit traditions and increased by mass media and the wish for prosperity. Urban centers such as Bangkok with its rural migrants arriving for work have also increased the need for religious practices that provide agency and meaning to marginalized groups.

Myanmar contains the most standardized system of national spirits, the Thirty-Seven Lords, or *nats*. Because Theravada Buddhism clearly has a superior status within Myanmar, spirit mediums draw upon the ethical values of the Buddhist precepts to signal to others they are moral forces acting within a Buddhist framework. Most of these spirit mediums and those who use their services identify as Buddhist. At the same time as followers of the spirits aim to draw on Buddhism's higher power, Buddhist institutions seek to separate themselves from the spirits. For example, no spirit ritual would take place inside a pagoda. Monks can bless these kinds of rituals before they begin, but they cannot take part in the rituals. Monks cannot worship nats because monks maintain a higher status. Through this separation, Buddhism maintains its status as pure and superior to the spirits in Myanmar.

In Cambodia, for the Khmers, the land first belonged to the spirits of the ancestors, the *neak ta*. But once Buddhism arrived, the spirits played complementary functions. Local spirits cannot help in the afterlife, but they can be asked, in exchange for some offering, to aid in the here and now. Cambodian spirits have been assimilated into Buddhist spaces with shrines to neak ta at the perimeters of temples. Other indigenous spirits of Cambodia, known as *anak ta*, are often located in the northeast corner of the temple. These spirits protect the monastic space while receiving offerings from the temple community.

These circumstances reveal that spirit religions and Theravada Buddhism are in constant dialogue and dynamic relationship. Within each country of mainland Southeast Asia, there are varying levels of separation and closeness. In Laos, the Buddhist temple and pagoda are necessary as a frame for the spirit. In Cambodia, spirits can live in the temple, drawing from its morality to become good, tamed spirits whose power can be used for beneficial ends. In Thailand, an explosion of popular spirits might become more important than merit-making in the temple for vulnerable and marginalized populations looking for security. Myanmar is most interested in separating Buddhism from spirits, causing spirits and their mediums to explicitly draw on the ethics and power of Buddhism.

Hinduism

The process of Indianization, or the expansion of Indian culture into Southeast Asia, began around 300 B.C.E. Indian culture was regarded as signifying power, royalty, and nobility. An early manifestation of Hinduism, called Brahminism, arrived in Southeast Asia as part of the Indianization process. Indianization occurred in cultural waves, with Southeast Asian kings and elites selecting parts of Indian culture and religion that helped to legitimate their power. Brahminism provided the template for royal ceremonies as well as the idea of a god-king, or *devaraja*.

Most recently the god-king ideal was portrayed by Thailand's Rama IX, King Bhumibol Adulyadej, who died in 2016. Rama IX, through his parami (charismatic authority), is increasingly becoming considered sacred and semi-divine, even possessing magical and supernatural powers. Before King Bhumibol, King Chulalongkorn (Rama V, 1853-1910) also reached close to the level of god-king. Because of King Chulalongkorn's great merit and deeds of leadership, he is thought to have been reborn as a divine being who helps humans and looks after those who worship him. Buddhist kingship creates an identity of protection from a patriarchal, strong paternal figure, counterbalancing the isolating effects of urban globalization.

This idea of the benevolent, uniting, sustaining, and caring king continues to inspire.

Theravada Buddhists today would be familiar with the Brahmanical layer of Indianization through Indian deities, including Ganesha. Evidence of Ganesha statues begins in fifth-century-C.E. Cambodia. Today, commercial buildings, especially large shopping complexes, contain elaborate shrines to Ganesha. Ganesha statues are prominent and popular in some Buddhist temples, such as Chiang Mai's silver temple, Wat Srisuphan. Theravada Buddhists may possess Ganesha statues displayed on altars below Buddha images in their homes and businesses. Practitioners turn to Ganesha as they do any other powerful figure—for safety and protection, a particular wish to obtain one's desires, or general help with wealth, health, and prosperity.

Theravada Buddhists who purchase Ganesha statues are not changing their identity or claiming Hindu religious affiliation. At the same time, these gods from India are an alternative source of power from the indigenous spirits of the land and should be treated differently. During performances for Ganesha in Thailand, Indian music and dance demonstrate an interest in connecting with contemporary cultural aspects associated with India. The older ways of propitiating Ganesha with Thai- or Khmer-style music is being replaced with modern Indian music in popular worship. Worship of Hindu gods like Ganesha responds to people's immediate and worldly needs more effectively than Buddhism, which is perceived as more serious and connected with leaving this world than everyday concerns. Most Theravada Buddhists, then, do not encounter Hinduism but Hindu deities, which are thought to offer protection in similar ways to the indigenous spirits.

Hindu temples are present in urban areas, established by diaspora communities of South Asian descent. These temples are frequented, for the most part, by Indian migrant communities and are largely unknown to Theravada Buddhists. These temples are part of modern Hinduism, which incorporates rituals, chanting, and devotion to the variety of gods inside. Whether as Hindu deities depicted in statues or as symbols of royal power that remain from early Indianization, elements of Hinduism have been incorporated under the Theravada Buddhist umbrella. These powerful deities and ideas have remained, under the hierarchy of Buddhism but higher than the indigenous layer of spirits. The Chinese deities from Mahayana Buddhism and Taoism fall in the middle of this hierarchy.

Chinese Religions

Chinese deities, like Hindu ones, have blended into the Theravada Buddhist complex. Chinese religious influences began in mainland Southeast Asia in the nineteenth century with the establishment of temples associated with family clans. The migration of populations from southern Chinese ethnic groups such as Hakka, Teochew, and Cantonese were the first to establish themselves and integrate into the Theravada Buddhist world. Researchers have found that Thai Chinese have both assimilated and integrated into Thai society while also maintaining distinct cultural and language practices. The assimilation of Chinese religions has worked both ways as people of Chinese descent became supporters of Buddhist temples while establishing Chinese iconography and practices in their local temples. Though Chinese popular religious elements of Taoism and Mahayana Buddhist practices have differences from Theravada Buddhism, they are not irreconcilable. There are several Chinese temples in the Chinatowns of Bangkok and Yangon. The Chinese New Year and Moon Festival continue to be important holidays for Southeast Asians of Chinese descent, where they pay respect to their ancestors. At the same time, some Chinese descendants also perform rituals at and donate to Thai temples.

Chinese religious practitioners from island Southeast Asia, including Malaysia and Singapore, have had an impact on Buddhist temples and communities. Chinese tourists often visit sacred sites, participate in festivals, and visit Buddhist monks with a reputation for magical powers. Sacred objects, such as amulets, are seen as powerful because they are considered older than Chinese objects, and their foreignness allows for more power. Chinese communities are also conspicuous in the island of Phuket, in southern Thailand, through their Vegetarian Festival, celebrated for nine days usually between late September and early October. This festival is observed by Chinese diaspora communities, southern Thai, and other visitors who join in the activities devoted to Taoist divinities, mostly the Nine Emperor Gods, along with the well-known goddess figure from Mahayana Buddhism, Kuan Yin. The Vegetarian Festival is known for its spirit mediums, whose self-mutilation—usually sticking needles, spikes, swords, and other objects through their cheeks—contrasts with the more aesthetically pleasing Thai Buddhist ceremonies and performances. Chinese folk traditions are also mixed in southern Thailand during Songkran, the Thai New Year, where Thai monks are carried on palanquins like Chinese deities. This mixing offers a sense of familiarity and newness to Thai Buddhists as well as ethnic Chinese Malaysian and Singapore tourists.

While ethnic Chinese tourists from parts of East and Southeast Asia have seen Thailand as a tourist destination for many decades, only recently have tourists from mainland China visited in large numbers. Following the huge success in China of the 2012 blockbuster comedy *Lost in Thailand*, coupled with eased visa restrictions, Thailand has seen a rapid increase in Chinese tourism. The Chinese middle class has expanded and thus the number of Chinese tourists has expanded. However, some of these tourists' interactions with Theravada religious sites have caused controversy. When blurry photographic evidence surfaced of a man kicking a temple bell at Wat Prathat Doi Suthep, an important temple in Chiang Mai, Thailand, Thai authorities assumed it was a Chinese man, indicating the possibility of stereotyping and racial bias. Chinese people were nearly banned from the tourist temple Wat Rong Khun in Chiang Rai after the artist and owner Chalermchai Kositpipat complained about the state of the bathrooms after a visit by a Chinese tour group. Monks I have spoken with in Chiang Mai about the increase of Chinese tourism noted that many of the Chinese tourists they encountered appeared to be uninterested in the sacredness of the site, treating the temple as any other tourist attraction. Occasionally the monks noticed that Chinese men wanted to discuss Buddhism with them, though the language barrier made this difficult. In general, Chiang Mai monks believe that Chinese people are not as interested in Buddhism because they are used to temples and monks from their country. Chinese Buddhists understand how to pay respect to the Buddha statues and engage in devotional activities but do so in their own way, bowing three times from the hips while standing, rather than the kneeling prostration of Theravada Buddhists.

Chinese and Hindu immigrants contribute to the religious diversity of mainland Southeast Asia, especially urban centers. Chinese religious elements, like Hindu ones, mix freely with Theravada Buddhism. Although this mixing would not be accepted by reformist monks representing orthodox Buddhism, Chinese deities, such as Kuan Yin, have moved further into the mainstream, developing first within marginal communities and outside of official Theravada Buddhism as expressions of popular devotion.

Some monks and laypeople promote and participate in deity and spirit worship readily, while others hold fast to the ideal of nibbana as the ultimate goal, which is beyond the purview of any spirit or god. Critics label spirit worship as a form of superstition and a way of taking advantage of the undereducated through commercialism, selling services and products related to the worship of illegitimate figures. As well, the extent to which people discuss, show off, and promote their popular religious practices will depend on how comfortable they feel sharing that information. In some circles, those practices might be judged as naïve and gullible, but in other groups, friends and colleagues might be excited to learn of a new source of power and good luck.

In a complete Theravada Buddhist altar, the Buddha statue is placed on the highest shelf, representing its most prominent position in the spiritual world. Images of famous monks known for their power and proximity to nibbana would be next. Figures from Mahayana Buddhism are below them, along with Indian gods.

Below this would be Chinese Taoist and folk deities. Finally, at the bottom shelf of the altar would be royal spirits and then local indigenous spirits of the land. All of these figures can fit together in one religious space. However, monotheistic world religions do not fit within this hierarchy, and this separation can make for an uneasy relationship.

Christianity

Buddhism is the dominant religion of the majority lowland populations of mainland Southeast Asia: Thai, Burmese, Lao, and Khmer. However, for ethnic minorities who are outside of these majority lowland groups, Christianity is a significant option, offering the prestige of a world religion while resisting the religious authority of the state.

Christianity represents subjugation through colonialism and aggressive conversion tactics of missionaries but also the modern, developed Western world. The idea of a Christian missionary, with their work of conversion, seems to be in competition with Buddhism. Theravada Buddhists sought to shield their communities from Christian missionaries during the colonial period by founding Buddhist schools for lay boys and girls and increasing opportunities for Buddhist study and meditation for everyone. Whereas Buddhists find themselves to be open-minded and accommodating, some monks, such as Phra Sobhon Ganabhorn of Thailand in the 1980s, declared Christian missionaries insulting toward Buddhism and aggressive in their conversion tactics. In part because of these issues, Christianity has failed to take root in the region dominated by Theravada Buddhism.

Christians make up about 5 percent of the Myanmar population— compared to less than 2 percent in Thailand, Laos, and Cambodia. In mainland Southeast Asia, Christianity appealed to ethnic minority groups in part because the indigenous spirit religions were becoming too costly in time and resources. Anthropologists of Hmong and Akha groups in Thailand have found that many converts were motivated by economic advantage. This kind of practical appeal has worked for Christian missionaries. Missionaries also provided schools, medicines, and help with businesses. Some of the Karen in Myanmar converted to Christianity to obtain the knowledge, power, and protection that Christian missionaries provided. Today the Karen are one of the biggest Christian groups with Baptists, Catholics, and other Protestant denominations. They have access to international networks and a sacred text in the Bible, which, for them, represents the ultimate truth. These ethnic minority converts, instead of assimilating into the dominant Buddhist culture, chose Christianity partly to oppose the domination they feel by the majority group of Theravada Buddhists.

In mainland Southeast Asia, Christianity has made the most impact in Myanmar. This can be attributed to the role of the British colonial government. Although not actively attempting to propagate Christianity, they created a conducive environment for missionary movements and activities. The lowland Burmese were the first to receive these missionaries, but the Burmese Buddhists—whose everyday life was so interconnected with the temple—expressed an apathetic if not hostile reception. Missionaries were much more welcomed by the highland people who were often in conflict with the Burmese majority. Many ethnic minority groups such as Chins, Kachins, Lisu, and Lahu today are predominantly Christian due to the colonial missionary period that began in 1826. After Burmese independence in 1948, conflicts between the ethnic minority groups, many of whom had converted to Christianity, and the majority Burmese, who identified as Buddhist, had a religious dimension. Today, the government seeks to marginalize Christian communities by restricting their missionary activities.

The rest of mainland Southeast Asia has proven even more resistant to Christian missionaries. Although Christians opened schools, hospitals, and other kinds of charity and relief work in Thailand, most of the converts have been ethnic minority groups such as Karen and Lahu. For Cambodians, Christianity was halted during the communist Khmer Rouge regime, which denied all forms of religious practice. Since 1990, Christians have been practicing in Cambodia and the country has been open to missionaries. Although Buddhism was eventually embraced in communist Laos, Christianity remains distrusted, especially because of its association with ethnic minority groups who are rebellious toward the state, such as the Hmong.

Theologically, it is not easy to incorporate Christianity into a Theravada Buddhist framework, but some thinkers have tried to do just that. Theravada Buddhist monastic scholars, like Buddhadasa Bhikkhu, have sought to understand and analyze how Buddhism and Christianity are compatible. His comparison between the two religions is documented in his book *Christianity and Buddhism*. Buddhadasa Bhikkhu understands the highest knowledge of God in Christianity to be equivalent to the deepest Buddhist teachings. For him, Christianity fits into Buddhist cosmology, including kamma and nibbana. He places Jesus and Buddha on the same level as enlightened beings leading others on the path to universal truth. In another example of interpreting Christianity through a Buddhist lens, the Thai Buddhist studies scholar Saeng Chand-ngarm finds many similarities between Buddhism and Christianity in his booklet *A Buddhist Looks at Christianity*. From his perspective, all religions originate from suffering, and Buddha and Jesus each sought paths to alleviate the suffering of humanity. He argues that the central core of Christianity is purity of heart, which he locates in Buddhism as freedom from mental defilements of greed, hatred, and delusion.

Activism is another point of connection between the two religions. Sulak Sivaraksa, a well-known socially engaged Buddhist of Thailand, has invited Christian activists for his Spirit in Education (SEM) conferences. SEM's approach is to insert Buddhist teachings of contemplation into the learning process of mainstream education. Christians have been invited as experts in training sessions, and the movement has led courses in development training for Christian groups in Myanmar. Although there was initial suspicion on both sides, eventually SEM expanded in Myanmar to support a wide range of educational institutions in the country.

This is a rare example of how building trust among Christian and Buddhist groups generates possibilities for mutual development. However, SEM is based on social activism, not finding common ground through theological concepts. Development and social justice movements can create cooperation, but interreligious dialogue is much more difficult. Because Buddhism is seen as the cornerstone of identity for much of mainland Southeast Asia, conservative members of the sangha have a negative assessment of Christians, who they perceive as seeking to undermine this close connection.

One prevailing representation of Christian converts among Theravada Buddhists is that they are only interested in this religion because of the worldly gains and bribes they were offered by missionaries. Many of the monks I have spoken with in Thailand considered Christian converts as not true practitioners of the religion. Non-Buddhist indigenous people, they believe, became Christian because of the material benefits, not because of anything superior about the religion. Whether or not converts are interested in the material rewards from Christian missionaries, one important reason for choosing Christianity is rejection of the dominant culture of Theravada Buddhism.

Islam

Like Christianity, Islam is regarded as a distant religion, outside of the system of Theravada Buddhism. Unlike Christianity, Buddhist interactions with Islam do not bring up associations with missionaries or colonial subjugation. Yet Muslims are perpetually viewed as foreigners in mainland Southeast Asia, despite their deep roots—in some cases, many centuries—in the region. Though an interest in interreligious dialogue has begun in conflict areas of Myanmar and Thailand, in other areas Muslims are already seen as part of the community, contributing as neighbors and village members.

Islam is mainland Southeast Asia's largest minority religion, comprising about 5 percent of the populations in Thailand and Myanmar. Pockets of Thai, Chinese, and Middle Eastern Muslims have integrated into Theravada societies. This is not the case for the greatest numbers of Muslims, located in southern Thailand, which borders Malaysia, and in the Rakhine State of Myanmar, which also borders a majority Muslim country, Bangladesh. This conflict emerged in southern Thailand due to the history of the region, which was previously the Islamic kingdom of Pattani. The people in this region are still 85 percent Malay Muslim. These communities retain a strong social memory of once belonging to an Islamic sultanate and resent that the Thai state seeks to replace Muslim schools with Thai government schools, and the language of instruction is Thai instead of Malay and Arabic. The tension lies in the distinctive identity of the Malay Muslims compared with Thai Buddhists. They have struggled to gain any kind of political autonomy from their government, resulting in Malay Muslims' hostility toward Thai rule. Malay Muslim separatists claim that state authorities do not respect their religion or language, resulting in human rights violations. This conflict between Malay Muslim insurgent groups and the Thai state in the provinces of Pattani, Narathiwat, and Yala has been ongoing since 2004, when the region began martial law, which resulted in thousands of deaths on both sides, the majority being Muslim civilians. These deaths have occurred through sporadic bombings, random shootings, and other flashpoints of mass violence.

Buddhist nationalist groups such as the Buddhism Protection Center of Thailand (BPCT) have existed since 2001. The BPCT, consisting of about three thousand Buddhists, both laity and monks, devote their time to "defending Buddhism," mostly through political means and dispensing information to people about threats to Buddhism. The group portrays Islam as a violent religion with a long history of aggression toward Buddhism and claims that Malay Muslims want to take over the area and force out Buddhist communities. The unrest in southern Thailand coupled with global discourses about Muslim terrorism has contributed to feelings of distance and otherness.

Thai Buddhists feel that their religion's presence is necessary in southern Thailand to protect the nation, its order and morality.

For example, in 2015, the Venerable Apichat Promjan, a lecturer at the royal Bangkok temple Benjamabophit, posted on Facebook that the government should burn a mosque for every Buddhist monk killed. He asserted that monks in the south are defenseless against the Muslims, whom he labeled as Malay bandits. Venerable Apichat Promjan is not interested in mercy for Muslims who harmed and killed Buddhist monks because he believes Muslims have no mercy for Buddhists. Instead of compassion, he seeks revenge and to awaken all Thai Buddhists to what he believes is the fact that Muslims are trying to take over the whole country. Because of this ideology, in 2017 he was forced to disrobe due to his anti-Muslim rhetoric.

Buddhist-inspired violence, as Michael Jerryson researched in his book *Buddhist Fury*, requires there to be a space of conflict—a politicized Buddhist representation and an attack on that representation. The murder of a monk creates intense reactions among Thai Buddhists, including violent retaliations at Islamic schools. The power of the monk's body in Thailand is due to the state and its alignment with the Buddhist institution; when someone attacks a Thai monk, they are perceived as attacking Thai Buddhism and the Thai nation as a whole. Queen Sirikit of the Thai royal family created the Volunteer Monk Program in order to increase the number of monks in southern Thailand and protect Buddhism in that area. Much like missionary monks sent to expose Buddhism to the indigenous hill tribe people in the north, monks were sent by the government to promote links between central and southern Thailand.

Temples in this area have become bases of operations for police and soldiers, who are supported by the local communities. This creates a clear identification of the Thai state as a Buddhist state rather than a government that protects all people. According to Jerryson, some soldiers have even been known to ordain and be stationed in temples that were lacking monks. Although violence and the monastic institution do not ideally mix, the military found this necessary in these circumstances and rationalize their actions by asserting that monastic rules allow for monks to defend themselves. Military monks exist to ensure that the monastic institution is maintained in southern Thailand and monks are available to teach the dhamma. However, no such support is given to mosques. The activist monk Phra Paisal Visalo believes that neither Buddhism nor Islam promote injustice or violence but instead were created to help people live with peace and compassion. Both Buddhists and Muslims, he finds, are taught to strive not for their own happiness but for happiness in their societies. Instead, Buddhists and Muslims have created divisions and enemies. A proper view, as Phra Paisal understands, would be for Buddhists and Muslims to feel equally upset when Muslim demonstrators die as when Buddhist temples and monks are harmed. He would like to see religious leaders of both sides condemn the killing of people of both faiths without fearing retaliation.

Because of this ongoing conflict in the south, feelings of threat and defensiveness permeate throughout the country. In March 2015, in the northern province of Nan, a mosque proposal stimulated disagreement and conflict between Buddhists and Muslims. The mosque was proposed to be built next to Wat Bupharam, a central Buddhist temple. For the Buddhist residents of this small town, the mosque would invite the same problems occurring in the southern provinces. A protest at a central temple, Wat Phrathat Chae Haeng, of over one thousand people, including Buddhist monks, demonstrated against the mosque with signs that read "Nan people do not want the mosque" and "Nan is the city of Buddhism." A report from the Patani Forum titled "Understanding Anti-Islam Sentiment in Thailand" reveals that Nan Buddhist groups feel their communities are less at risk without a mosque. They hope to remain totally Buddhist in the area, in what villagers claim is in continuity with hundreds of years of their ancestral history. Concern over more Muslims moving to Nan because of the mosque and increasing the Muslim population were also cited as reasons for the protest. Currently there is still no mosque in Nan Province, distinguishing it as one of just two provinces in all of Thailand that does not have a mosque.

In Myanmar, the rhetoric of Buddhist violence is also present, linked with notions of Buddhist nationalism, the fragility of

Buddhism, and the need to protect it from outside threats. This image of Buddhism as frail—despite its majority numbers of adherents, monks, temples, and state support—comes from the idea of impermanence and decline. Signs of decline have been felt at various points in Burmese Buddhist history, especially the colonial period when the British exiled King Thibaw and there was no one to protect Buddhism, sponsor rituals, or promote reform. One of the ways to decrease the rate of decline is to protect Buddhism from what can be perceived as external enemy forces. The belief that Muslims are by and large a violent group of people has made Buddhists express defensiveness.

Today in Myanmar, this defense of Buddhism is especially apparent in the Rakhine State, one of the poorest regions of the country. The ethnic Rohingya, who have lived in Myanmar for centuries, hit a flashpoint in 2012 when a Buddhist woman was allegedly raped by Muslim men. When news of this spread, violence ensued as well as laws regulating conversion, citizenship, and marriage between Muslims and Buddhists. Rumors of forced conversion and sexual abuse perpetrated by Muslim men are readily accepted as facts. When monks who speak out against Muslim hatred face risk and threats of their own, a recipe for communal conflict is complete. Although some high-ranking and well-respected senior monks are able to speak out to defend Buddhism's stance on compassion, these voices are often drowned out by more forceful ones.

Venerable U Wirathu, a Burmese monk, is one of the most infamous of these forceful voices. In *Time* magazine, the journalist Hannah Beech named U Wirathu as "the face of Buddhist terror." This article as well as a 2018 documentary *The Venerable W.*, which features him, have contributed to his international infamy. In response, U Wirathu expresses the view that he and the Rakhine Buddhists are victims, especially of the Western media, who he believes favors the Muslims and only reports news unfavorable to Buddhists.

U Wirathu incites violence against Muslims through his sermons. In his preaching, instead of Buddhist doctrine, he references Burmese Buddhist identity when framing hatred of Muslims. As the

Burmese scholar Nyi Nyi Kyaw asserts in "The Role of Myth in Anti-Muslim Buddhist Nationalism in Myanmar," U Wirathu has accused Muslims of engaging in "wombfare"; because of perceptions of Muslim males as polygamous and hyper-fertile, U Wirathu believes that Muslims are slowly taking over the population by breeding more quickly. This myth is taken seriously because it threatens the survival of Buddhism. U Wirathu is respected despite his violent and discriminatory rhetoric, because of his position in society and the ways lay Buddhists are raised to listen to monks and pay attention to their sermons. As explored in chapter 3, in Theravada Buddhist society, monks are viewed higher in social and moral hierarchies than laypeople because of their lifestyle, rules, and renunciation of a typical worldly life of a householder. Because of this, when U Wirathu declares Muslims as a threat to Buddhism under siege, his sentiments are enthusiastically endorsed by many of his followers.

U Wirathu first began his anti-Muslim rhetoric in 2001, along with other monks promoting Buddhist nationalism at the time. However, this earlier wave resulted in U Wirathu being jailed from 2003 to 2012. He was released early from his twenty-five-year sentence in an amnesty for political prisoners. He immediately returned to his monastery in Mandalay and urged a boycott of Muslim-owned businesses. During 2012–2013, U Wirathu's movement, 969, was highly visible around the country. The numerology signifies traits of the Triple Gem and is meant to counter the numbers 786, which South Asian Muslim business owners use to indicate their establishment is owned by Muslims.

Since 2013, a larger and more structured movement has become more widespread and influential: the Association for Protection of Race and Religion, or Ma Ba Tha, where U Wirathu is a central committee member. Ma Ba Tha has lobbied for laws on race and religion meant to control and limit the Muslim population. Members of Ma Ba Tha believe that the Rohingya are playing a long game seeking to transform Myanmar into an Islamic nation. Yet in reality, Rohingya in the Rakhine State have been forced to live in refugee camps with little food or access to educational opportunities. Many have tried to flee in refugee boats but die in transit due to the risky nature of their vulnerable position. U Wirathu and other Buddhist nationalist monks multiply the perception of Islam as a distant religion that seeks to overwhelm and undermine the Buddhist majority population.

Buddhist Incorporations and Exclusions

Although Theravada Buddhists accept that non-Buddhists can get to nibbana without Buddhism, they believe that the Buddha's teachings supersede all other systems by pointing to the way most directly. The ethical orientations of other religions could certainly help humans enact good kamma and gain a good rebirth. Like the Buddha, any person could theoretically find the path to liberation from suffering. The truth of reality is out there for anyone to find, but the Buddha already points the way, so it makes sense to Buddhists to follow him as their teacher rather than waste time through another religion or discovering the way on their own.

Theravada Buddhists incorporate indigenous spirits as well as Indian and Chinese deities into their broader religious culture. This system has worked for Theravada Buddhism for centuries; however, it is not without critique or debate. Many elite monks would like to strip away extra-Buddhist influences and the need for popular practices altogether, denigrating them as superstitious practices. However, these elements are becoming more and more accepted in the mainstream. Ganesha festivals are becoming more popular as well as the Chinese Vegetarian Festival in Phuket. Kuan Yin statues along with spirit shrines can be found in temples across the region so that Theravada Buddhist laity have a variety of resources to take advantage of when in need of protection. Because of this, there is no attitude of defensiveness regarding these elements that originated outside of Buddhism.

To varying extents, Theravada monks have engaged in dialogue and cooperation with representatives of other religions, notably

Christianity. However, Christianity and Islam are seen through the lens of difference and exclusivism. These world religions are not separated into elements, nor can their worldview be integrated within Buddhist cosmology. Because these monotheistic religions represent a totally different way of perceiving the world and the afterlife and therefore cannot be incorporated or assimilated into Theravada Buddhism, there will always be tension and competition. In some cases, unfortunately, this has contributed to violence, especially when mixed with Buddhist nationalism and the religion's inevitable decline and need for protection.

PART THREE

Practices

CHAPTER 6

Lay Buddhist Practices and Beliefs

Theravada Buddhism intersects intimately with the lives of ordinary people in mainland Southeast Asia. However, it is also easy to observe the influence of religious phenomena such as indigenous spirit cults and Indian deities in the popular religious practices of lay Buddhists. Popular religion here does not imply practices that are less serious or worthy of attention. Instead, they are the practices commonly enacted by the ordinary laypeople of mainland Southeast Asia. Popular religion, as defined by the anthropologist Robert Winzeler in his book *Popular Religion in Southeast Asia*, is applied to practitioners of world religions, such as Buddhism, and describes practices oriented toward satisfying everyday needs, including protection, health, love, fertility, and economic success. With an abundance of resources to petition, Buddhists can feel protected and proactive against life's uncertainties. When teaching about popular lay practices to primarily North American students, I have often observed a bias toward the ultimate goal of nibbana through the monastic lifestyle. Shouldn't all Buddhists be striving to attain enlightenment? Why are there even malls in Southeast Asia when Buddhism emphasizes simplicity over consumerism? Why are there advertisements for cosmetic products when beauty does not matter on the path? These kinds of questions are quickly answered with some perspective. Maybe eventually all beings will be able to achieve enlightenment. However, the goal has never been for every human to reach nibbana in this lifetime. Buddhism needs laypeople and householders to support the religion and make offerings to those who are closer to the monastic ideal in this life. Being a householder is important and necessary for Buddhism to thrive. It is possible for lay Buddhists to aim their efforts toward nibbana in this life, but more likely they are interested in a good rebirth in their next life through making merit. They also can be interested in the protective powers of Buddhism. Although the popular orientation toward Buddhism offers a multitude of practices, this chapter provides general frameworks for ways of thinking about lay practice today.

Moral Practices

The ideal morality of lay Buddhists is encapsulated in the Five Precepts. These precepts are found in the Pali Canon of the early Theravada tradition as part of the way a new disciple would demonstrate their adherence to the Buddha's teachings. However, in Southeast Asia, after Buddhism became the majority religion, Theravada Buddhists did not need to affirm their adherence to the precepts to show their affiliation. Instead, it's customary to receive the Five Precepts as part of any ceremony or ritual.

If laypeople feel they cannot take all five, they might remain silent during parts of the recitation. For example, someone might not recite the fifth precept if they plan to go out drinking later or the first precept if killing is a part of their job, such as a farmer or fisher. Yet, laypeople often take these precepts as an aspiration or training, not as a strict obligation, and so would not necessarily feel deep regret if they break them in small ways, such as killing a bug or having a single alcoholic drink one night. The fourth precept, which calls for honest speech, is especially easily broken in small ways. Full adherence, it is acknowledged, is not always possible in people's daily lives. However, in the temple environment, practitioners will make every effort not to break the precepts, even warning others to step over a line of ants so they do not inadvertently kill them. I have known monks in some temples to emphasize that those who practice the Five Precepts strictly will be guaranteed rebirth as a human, something very desirable considering the alternatives of unfortunate births as animals, hell beings, or demons.

When laypeople stay overnight at a temple, as part of either a meditation retreat or a merit-making effort, they will be asked to take the Eight Precepts. As the anthropologist Nancy Eberhardt notes in her book *Imagining the Course of Life*, elderly people in Shan Buddhist communities leave their homes every week on the Buddhist holy day to take the Eight Precepts and stay overnight worshipping at the temple. When thinking back on their past, older people may feel regret over bad actions, which resulted in bad kamma. This may lead people in such positions to focus their effort on making merit and increasing their store of good kamma to increase their chances at a better rebirth. One way to do this is through personal sacrifice and increased religiosity, such as those outlined in the Eight Precepts. The extra three precepts add additional renunciation. For the sixth precept, the practitioner avoids untimely meals, which translates to not eating after noon. The seventh precept asks practitioners to refrain from beautifying the self or participating in or viewing any kind of entertainment. The eighth precept mandates followers to sleep on a thin mattress provided by the temple. The third precept is also changed from avoiding sexual misconduct to avoiding any sexual activity, which would be extremely inappropriate while staying in a temple. Laypeople can keep these precepts in their own homes, but it is considered easier to attend to while following the temple's routine. After departing the temple, laity will usually take the Five Precepts again.

Eight Precepts

I undertake the rule of training to refrain from killing living creatures.

I undertake the rule of training to refrain from taking what is not given.

I undertake the rule of training to refrain from sexual activity.

I undertake the rule of training to refrain from false speech.

I undertake the rule of training to refrain from consuming intoxicating drinks (and drugs) that lead to carelessness.

I undertake the rule of training to refrain from taking untimely meals.

I undertake the rule of training to refrain from dancing, singing, music, and other entertainment, use of garlands, perfumes, and personal adornment.

I undertake the rule of training to refrain from high beds and seats.

Donation

Generosity is the cardinal virtue of Buddhist laity. Without donations, the temple and monastic institution could not exist. Giving can be material or nonmaterial and is especially part of the purview of lay Buddhist women, as described in chapter 4. Laypeople support the sangha in many ways, fluctuating depending on the individual, their time of life, or their community. It's possible to give food to monks every day, go to the temple weekly to pay respect to the Buddha image, make merit by giving donations annually, or visit the temple on most Buddhist holidays and try to observe the Five Precepts. Yet lay Buddhists might also go to the temple a few times a year and only make merit when something is going wrong in their lives.

Lay Buddhists give money and supplies such as cooked foods, kitchen supplies, toilet paper, and toothbrushes, and their time for cooking meals, cleaning and decorating, or helping with renovation and construction work in the temple. Laity make these offerings in the temple but can also do so outside the temple in the daily ritual of alms giving. During these morning rituals, laypeople wait outside their homes or in markets, with food ready to put directly into monastic alms bowls. This interaction will last a few minutes or less but helps the giver feel good, especially on an important day, such as a birthday. In Myanmar, this practice is usually maintained by an elderly or unmarried female in the household, as observed by Hiroko Kawanami in *The Culture of Giving in Myanmar: Buddhist Offerings, Reciprocity, and Interdependence*. This daily interaction is so important that someone else must be found to take over if this household member goes on vacation.

Donation boxes are ubiquitous around temples. Contributions to these boxes can be used for medical care for monks, renovating the temple, water and electricity bills, maintenance of the temple school, and more. Depending on the temple, donation boxes might have specific purposes written on them so the donor can choose which project they would like to support. Other Buddhist donor practices can be found in shops inside or outside the temple, which sell offerings and other devotional items. These items often include offering trays, baskets filled with necessities for monks, candles, and robes to offer at a temple. If a temple is home to a famous statue or magic monk, they may not use all the offerings they receive. Other temples without such support might use all the food and material items they receive for their necessities each day.

Some popular donatory practices inside the temple involve a short activity. One of these practices is to write your name on a cloth that will wrap around the pagoda. Another activity is to pour water over a sacred item in the temple, which can be done by filling a cup with water and sending it to the top of a pagoda with a pulley, paying respect to the relic in the stupa. If someone is having bad luck, they can purchase a candle of their birth date and burn it to generate positive luck instead. There is usually a recommended donation for these items and activities, but donating follows the honor code; no one watches to see how much is given.

Although the sangha is the recipient of first choice, Buddhists also support charitable organizations. Some do this in addition to their sangha offerings, and others to show their disapproval of the sangha. This has occurred in Thailand where monastic scandals have led some laypeople to believe orphanages and schools are worthier of support. The best of both worlds is to donate to a monastic project, which is organized to give to a community in need. For example, at Wat Suan Dok, the Monk Chat program often organizes a fundraising drive to help low-income communities of the minority ethnic indigenous groups. Those who donate get the merit from donating to the sangha as well as helping communities in desperate need.

Making Merit

Merit is the boon or benefit from doing good. Contributing in any way to the livelihood of monastics and the institution of Buddhism or bettering oneself through practice creates merit for the individual. Merit is related to good kamma. When Theravada lay Buddhists say they are going to a temple, the point of the visit is usually not the same as for tourists—to take pictures and admire the ancient architecture. Although this may be part of the trip, one of the primary purposes would be to make merit in some way. The temple is set up so that it is easy to make merit. In some temples, a monk's duty will be to sit inside one of the main halls and wait until the laity comes to facilitate their merit-making.

Monks represent a field of merit, while laity plant seeds into this field through their support and reap merit. This making of merit is believed to negate the effect of past evils in the present life and the next. This is called the "Buddhist moral economy," or the economy of merit. This exchange binds monks and laity together. Monks, at the top of the Buddhist social hierarchy, are considered to have the most merit. Through their disciplined lifestyles and dedication to study and practice, they are considered worthy recipients of gifts and offerings. Depending on the status of an ordained person, this field of merit can be large or relatively small. Donating or offering to a person with a large field of merit allows the giver to receive a larger amount of merit than if they donated to a person with a smaller field of merit. Theravada Buddhists judge a field of merit to be large or small based on the monastic's lifestyle, discipline, and monastic years. At the same time, it is often said that laity should make merit by offering to the robes, or the institution of monasticism, rather than considering individual monks.

People with lower fields of merit include novice monks, precept nuns, and lay meditators. Because they follow fewer rules, these groups are less worthy of merit and therefore usually receive less alms. Lay meditators can also be considered a field of merit because, although they are not ordained, they still adhere to renunciatory practices and work hard to meditate all day long, which is worthy of support.

An important feature of merit is that it can be transferred. When the monk chants a blessing after receiving an offering, the layperson typically pours water, evoking the water that the earth goddess used to defeat Mara's army in the life story of the Buddha, and thinks where they would like the merit to be directed: A recently deceased relative? A sick friend? A coworker who needs a change of luck? Theravada Buddhists are taught that one owes a large debt of gratitude to their parents because of their sacrifice in raising them as children. Simply by stating that they wish this merit to be spread to their parents or other loved ones, these people will receive that merit made. After the death of a relative, formal ceremonies will take place over several days to transfer merit to the recently deceased, including at the funeral and first anniversary of death.

This transfer of merit allows the practice to be communal. After all, merit is not a commodity to be selfishly hoarded. In fact, one gains merit by transferring it to others. Merit is an exponential source of spiritual well-being. Merit-making is done for oneself and for others, and it is intended to create a feeling of lightness and happiness. Buddhists cannot know how or when the merit they make will come back to benefit them or others, but making merit is a significant aspect of Theravada Buddhist lay life, nonetheless.

Major Ways of Making Merit

1. Contributing to the construction of a temple
2. Ordaining or having a son ordained
3. Repairing a temple
4. Offering robes at a kathina ceremony
5. Offering food to monks on alms round and in the temple
6. Observing Buddhist holidays at the temple
7. Observing the Five Precepts strictly
8. Making excursions to sacred temples

All Buddhist holidays include some aspect of merit-making. From lunar weekly holy days to the Buddha's birthday, all these events mark an auspicious and appropriate time to make merit. At these special times there will be even more merit-making activities, such as donating a money tree. Families, coworkers, or other groups gather to make a decorative tree, with bills of money representing the leaves. Pious older men who are former monks usually lead rituals for laity during these merit-making occasions.

At different times throughout the year, temples host fundraising events to receive donations for a particular project. Building new accommodations, acquiring a new temple building, or establishing a new meditation center all require donations from the laity. For these events, the temple advertises a certain date for laity to come and make merit to help with the project. Often amulets are made for these occasions so that each person who donates a certain amount receives a protective amulet. These fundraising projects might be organized to coincide with a Buddhist holiday and include volunteer laity giving away food and drinks.

Kathina is the most important merit-making holiday in the Buddhist year for lay Buddhists. As mentioned in chapter 1, kathina is the formal annual ritual of giving robes to the monks at the end of the vassa, or rains retreat season. Monks need new robes during this time as the Buddha had observed some monks' attire had become unkempt during the vassa, so he allowed laity to give new cloth in order that monks would be fit to go out for alms and be seen in public. Kathina is a most festive occasion with many people joining from the region. To act as one of the principal sponsors of a kathina ceremony is a goal for some Buddhists and requires considerable disposable income. Sometimes wealthy donors from a big city will sponsor a kathina at a rural temple they believe to need funding or to be particularly sacred. The ceremony concludes with a preaching by the senior monk motivating people to continue their meritorious deeds.

In Myanmar, the Buddhist studies scholar John Holt, in the book *Theravada Traditions*, has observed donations of household items, along with robes and money trees, left out in frequented urban areas so that others would see and be inspired to give. On the morning of the kathina, a procession of vehicles picks up the goods to bring to the temple with much music and celebration. During the kathina celebration, the famous Shwedagon Pagoda of Yangon is open all day and night as dozens of lay religious associations set up festivities for the tens of thousands of patrons.

In Luang Prabang, monthslong planning results in a three-day-long merit-making festival in the historic temple Wat Xieng Thong for *Boun Phravet*. *Boun Phravet* is a celebration of the Vessantara Jataka, the longest and most detailed of the previous birth stories of the Buddha for Theravada Buddhists, illustrating the bodhisatta's perfection of generosity. The festivalgoers earn merit by listening to this story of giving. One monk might recite the entire jataka in one day. Alternatively, ten hours of recitation can be broken up into two days with monks taking turns each hour.

In Cambodia, *pchum ben* is the most important ritual period of the year, taking place near the end of the rains retreat. This fifteen-day celebration is focused on attending to the dead, to help them make a successful transition to their next rebirth. Merit is transferred to the dead by offering food to monks. Many Cambodians who have moved to the city of Phnom Penh for work return to their natal villages for this holiday. During this festival, the king of hell, Yamaraja, allows all *preta* (ghosts) to return to their villages. The ghosts search for gifts of food from their relatives at Buddhist temples. If in their searching at seven temples they find food, the preta will grant their blessings on the relatives. If they find nothing, when they return to hell, they will likely curse their descendants.

Merit needed for health and longevity can be received through special rituals. In northern Thailand the life extension ritual (*suep chata*) may be held at any time, but the fifth life cycle or the sixtieth birthday, is considered an auspicious time, or, alternatively, when one has had bad luck or has an illness. During this ritual, the person sits underneath a temporary structure of bamboo poles in front of an altar while absorbing the Pali chanting of the monks present.

In some temples, one option for merit-making is animal release. Birds trapped in a cage or small aquatic animals in buckets of water are sold in these temples for the opportunity to set them free. The idea is that by liberating an animal, you will make merit. However, a bird might be caught again or trained to go back into the cage, so it might not actually be freed. Similarly, an aquatic animal may be released into a part of a river in which they will not survive for long. Someone interested in making merit by liberating an animal might be better off heading to a market to purchase a live animal and set it free in a proper environment. At the same time, the people selling this merit-making service of freeing the animals are clearly in need of income, so it could also be a viable ethical choice to help them. Stalls selling caged animals for release are becoming less frequent but still can be found at popular temples and tourist spots.

Protection and Wish Fulfillment

Within Theravada Buddhism, there are many options for those seeking protection and wish fulfillment in an uncertain world. Spirits, deities, and figures from local legends all fall under the umbrella of Theravada Buddhism and relate to practices that lay practitioners can perform.

Calling on the Spirits

The belief in and management of local spirits of a region are present throughout mainland Southeast Asia. Belief in the spirits is manifest in a multitude of spirit shrines. These shrines can range from formal structures made from teakwood or concrete located outside of businesses and malls to informal ones consisting of makeshift tables and wooden shelves situated beside trees or on the side of the road. Once I even saw a spirit shrine made of recycled materials affixed to an electricity pole. One scholar, who had recently left Thailand after living there for several years, described to me what he missed about the country: the enchantment. When I saw that pair of spirit figurines attached to the pole on a busy street, I thought there might be something to this observation.

Individuals interact with the spirits when needed or at an annual ritual in honor of the spirits of the village. Because local spirits are unpredictable, Buddhist practitioners seek to make sure the spirits are in their corner, providing aid. If one neglects to maintain the spirit shrine, the spirit may be more harmful than helpful. If someone is having money or health problems and does not have a spirit shrine, the solution may be to erect one. Perhaps the spirit is upset because they are lost and do not have a home, or they feel neglected, therefore they wreak havoc on people's lives. A shrine and daily offerings contain them and direct their power as a force for good. The spirits can also be tricked. To avoid a car accident caused by a malevolent spirit, for instance, the color of one's car is important. The color should match one's astrological chart. If, however, a car is the wrong color, all that is needed to correct this is a bumper sticker informing the spirits "This car is red" or whatever color is recommended by an expert in astrology.

Most formal spirit shrines have little figures inside them. These figures, along with the shrine, are bought and made into homes for spirits. Through the help of a ritual specialist, the spirits are called to reside within these spirit shrines. In Laos, however, the spirits are not represented through figures. Their spirit houses and shrines are empty, or the spirits are represented by a pole or pillar at the center. Spirits are brought daily offerings of bright-colored food and drinks, such as bananas and red fruity soda, and often decorated with yellow garlands or jasmine flowers. These bright colors appeal to the spirits; the color yellow especially attracts gold or riches.

There are many different types of spirits—evil spirits, celestial spirits, field spirits, forest spirits, sky spirits, tree spirits, village guardian spirits, spirits of ancestors, dangerous spirits of those who died violently, among many other types. Many cities in Thailand have a central pillar (*lak muang*), which contains the highest and most powerful spirit of the city and from which the spirit watches over and protects the residents. This pillar can be propitiated in the same way as a spirit shrine, except it is shaped as a pillar instead of a house. In Chiang Mai, the city pillar is called Sao Inthakin, and it is located within a Buddhist temple, indicating Buddhism's power over the spirits. Each year the city pillar has an eight-day celebration beginning on the twelfth day of the sixth lunar month. There is a procession on the first and last days around the city to promote prosperity for all the inhabitants. Women are not allowed to go inside the structure containing the pillar. As mentioned in chapter 4, some sites are off-limits to women because menstruation is thought to be impure.

But while human women are seen as harmful to the city pillar, there are many female spirits who are propitiated by all. In Thailand, these female spirits are the rice goddess (*mae posop*), who protects the rice fields and is a symbol of the Department of Agriculture, and the goddess of wealth (*nang kwak*, meaning "the beckoning woman"), who is seated in a kneeling position with a bundle of riches on her left and her right hand raised in a gesture of calling forth. This image is thought to bring in customers and improve business. Devotees can ask these female spirits, in statue form, for success in their harvest or business.

The various qualities of the spirits are considered in offerings of exchange. For child spirits, such as the recent Ai Khai (egg child) or more ancient Kuman Thong (golden child) spirits of Thailand, soda drinks and toy trucks are considered appropriate. For the spirits of the land, boiled chicken or eggs are often given. Older spirits are thought to appreciate betel nut and other old-fashioned products. King Naresuan (1590–1605) is associated with roosters and can be seen with many small concrete rooster statues propitiating him. King Chulalongkorn (1853–1910) was known as a king with worldly tastes, so he is offered cigars and cognac bottles. These spirits and gods are all from different places and times, and so having these familiar objects will help to accommodate and emplace them while ingratiating them to curry favor.

One pervasive theme within Theravada Buddhism is taming wild spirits to side with Buddhism. Theravada Buddhism is believed to have the power to transform untamed spirits into caretakers and guardians of the religion. In a legendary story from Chiang Mai, Thailand, two giants, Grandmother and Grandfather Sae, are terrorizing the region by eating the villagers. Miraculously the Buddha appears and manages, through his presence and power, to persuade the giants to stop eating people. Even though the giants agree to adhere to this rule, just in case, the villagers allow the giants to eat buffalo meat once a year. This legendary moment is enacted annually at the base of Doi Kham Mountain, where spirit mediums ceremoniously eat the raw flesh and blood of a buffalo. Then the giant spirits are taken to pay respect to a banner depicting the Buddha. Because the banner is hung from a tree and moves in the wind, the spirits of the giants are tricked into believing that the Buddha is still watching over their actions. Buddhist monks also preside over this ceremony by chanting and receiving offerings before the spirit medium show begins.

Another example of spirit practices is the boat race festivals of Luang Prabang, Laos, which take place in the ninth month of the lunar calendar. These races propitiate the naga, dragon-like mythical creatures who are believed to control the water necessary for rice agriculture. Before the race, each village takes their boat to the village temple for the monk to bless the boat. Before the race begins, the boat racers listen to a sermon by a monk, receive holy water, and circumambulate the pagoda. Offerings are made to the naga and the spirits of the boat. Through celebrating the naga on this day, villagers feel more secure that these guardians of Buddhism will help make the land fertile.

Nats (spirit lords) are male and female spirits specific to Myanmar who relate to Buddhism in complementary and subordinate ways. King Anawrahta (r. 1044–77 C.E.) attempted to purify Buddhism by destroying nat shrines and forbidding practices related to them. But this attempt failed, showing their persistent nature and compatibility with Buddhism. King Anawrahta instead installed a king of nats, named Thagyamin, to rule the nat pantheon while being attendant to Buddhism. Nats are complementary to Buddhism by allowing for emotions that Buddhist practice discourages, such as hatred, greed, desire, and jealousy. Spirit festivals sanction practices not allowed in Buddhist ritual environments, such as drinking and gambling. The main nat festival takes place near Mandalay over three days on Mount Popa.

Even more related to Buddhism than nats within the Burmese pantheon are *thaik* and *bobogyi* because they are seen as part of the project of maintaining Buddhism in Burmese society. Many pagodas in Myanmar contain a chamber filled with gems, jewels, and other sacred items intended for the next Buddha. Thaik, the treasure guardians of the pagoda, are depicted as beautiful young women dressed in green. Statues of these spirits began to be displayed within pagoda compounds in the 1990s. Bobogyi are grandfatherly old men dressed in white who point toward the pagoda they are protecting. The main function of the bobogyi is to make wishes come true, always acting as benevolent figures. However, because bobogyi are extremely old, they are seen to be attached to the worldly realm. In Yangon, the Sule Bobogyi is one of the most famous for granting wishes, and more recently the Botataung Bobogyi has grown popular among Thai tourists. The economic market caters to this popularity with bobogyi-related merchandise including amulets in the Thai style and T-shirts in Thai language. In Thai these figures are known as *thep thanjai*, or the gods who can grant wishes instantly. Anthropologist Neeranooch Malangpoo has researched this transnational phenomenon and found that dozens of thep thanjai statues have been erected in Thai temples in Thailand. The rise of these kinds of popular statues reflects the increasing demand for practices related to spirits—including travel, wishes, offerings, and purchasing souvenirs—to produce magical speed in response to the quickened pace of life in modern Southeast Asia.

In Myanmar, another spiritual figure even closer to Buddhism is the *weizza*. Weizza have escaped the karmic cycle through their achievements and are believed to be able to return to this world when the future Buddha Maitreya is born. Becoming a weizza requires years of training in alchemy, meditation, sacred spells, and magical diagrams. Weizza have the morality of serious lay Buddhist practitioners and aim for enlightenment, like Buddhist monks. However, they are still spirits who can act in this world, which separates their practices from official forms of Buddhism. Lay followers install shrine rooms and even a bed for a weizza master "guest" to appear. The most famous weizza master is Bo Min Gaung. He was a layman who is believed to have entered weizza-hood upon his death in 1952. In his book *The Buddha's Wizards*, Thomas Patton, a scholar of Burmese Buddhism, researched how devotees of Bo Ming Gaung felt they could discuss their lives with this weizza in a way they can't with the Buddha. To them, the Buddha feels remote, whereas Bo Min Gaung is immediately present, which followers demonstrate by lighting cigarettes and placing them into the statue's hands.

In Cambodia, village ceremonies take place by first extending an invitation and asking for permission from the neak ta, spirits of the ancestors. Neak ta shrines may contain stones representing the spirits, but they can also be depicted in statues anthropomorphically. When interacting with a neak ta, people can conduct a small ritual vow to gain a blessing for a small and immediate problem or host a more formal ceremony to ask for aid in serious difficulties that might affect the whole village, such as a drought. The most famous neak ta in the country is a protector of the nation, Khleang Moeung. He was an army general who helped to defeat Thai invaders. Performances of his exploits take place at the National Theater, and an annual celebration takes place at his statue. This ceremony celebrates his sacrifice for his people, which included self-immolation and spreading cholera among the enemy as a ghost.

Bray and *boramei* are a category of Cambodian spirits that demonstrate the power of Buddhism. Bray are dangerous female spirits of virgins or women who died in childbirth. In Cambodia, bray are filled with impurity because of the violent way they died. However, this violence and impurity can be harnessed as magical power. In Cambodian temples, bray are usually emplaced within the columns of buildings. This transformation of the spirit from an untamed force into a tamed spirit who stays within the temple makes bray guardians of Buddhism. Buddhist monks also ritually encourage this type of spirit to reside in the pedestal of the main Buddha image or in statues of famous kings or monastic figures. Once a bray has become pacified in this way, it is known as a boramei. When Cambodians make an offering to a Buddha statue, the boramei will receive the offering.

A surprising example of taming a powerful spirit from contemporary Cambodia is the perpetrator of the Khmer Rouge genocide, Pol Pot. Since his death, he has been transformed into an ambivalent ancestor of the land figure. As part of the Buddhist ideal of compassion for all beings, the inhabitants of the area where Pol Pot died held a funeral and dedicated the merit to Pol Pot, as it was believed that his murderous acts would lead to an unfortunate birth. However, when the media heard this story, the villagers did not want to be taken for followers of Pol Pot and so stopped. This left the figure of Pol Pot open to the cult of spirits within the Khmer religious system. People in the area make offerings of food to the altar and tomb where Pol Pot's spirit is believed to inhabit. In this case, Pol Pot is a lower spirit, called anak ta. Although he is an extremely malevolent person, he is also powerful. Because the contemporary Khmer share this land with ancestors, previous powerful inhabitants must be honored.

The persistence of spirits and necessity of ritual practices surrounding them demonstrate that Indianization never fully enveloped Southeast Asia. Even the body itself is imagined through the lens of the spirits. In Cambodia, the *braling* and in northern Thailand the *khwan* are spirits or souls that animate the human body, and they must be in harmony. Spirits can separate from the body during periods of fright, travel, or illness, and they need to be called back through a ritual specialist. Practices related to spirits draw on their power—persuading them to fulfill one's desires, transforming their power into protection, or if unable to be tamed, to take their malevolence elsewhere.

Calling on the Deities

Brahminism, an ancient form of Hinduism, arrived in the early king-doms of Southeast Asia before Buddhism. Today, early Indian dei-ties, such as Vishnu, fall under the cosmology of Buddhism and are depicted as attendants to the Buddha and guardians of the temples. Vishnu rides on a half-man, half-bird called Garuda. One of Vishnu's roles is to guard openings to temple doors. He is more commonly represented by his avatar Rama in the depictions of the Ramayana epic. Scenes from the Ramayana can be seen in temple murals, along with the half-monkey god Hanuman. Toward the end of World War II, early Indian gods such as Brahma, the god of creation, became especially popular in Thailand, with many hotels having a shrine for Brahma instead of a spirit. Brahma occupies a central role in Bang-kok's Erawan Shrine, which is thought to be extremely powerful in wish-granting. The Erawan Shrine has also been a flashpoint for conflict, as seen in 2006 when a young mentally ill man smashed the deity with a hammer and was subsequently killed by an angry mob, and in 2015 during an unresolved bombing that killed twenty people. Even though this is a stand-alone shrine in the middle of an urban area, it is meaningful enough to create violence.

Southeast Asia also received religious elements from China and incorporates these into temple environments. Some Theravada temples feature divination methods from Chinese religions. The sticks of fortune, or wooden numbered sticks placed inside a can-ister, are popular as fortune-telling devices. The practitioner gently shakes the canister, tipping it forward. One can hear the "clink" of these fortune sticks hitting each other until one falls out. When the first stick drops, the person seeking to determine their luck records the number, which corresponds to a fortune located nearby. Many temples also display the animals of the Chinese twelve-year-cycle zodiac. The Fat Buddha, or Budai, originating from China and thought to be an incarnation of Maitreya, can be found in Theravada temples where Thai Buddhists of Chinese descent have made dona-tions. Theravada Buddhists have not paid as much attention to this

Mahayana Buddhist figure as to the goddess of compassion, Kuan Yin. A manifestation of the Indian figure, Avalokitesvara, Kuan Yin is depicted with a vase from which her compassionate dew flows. She is known for her kindness and ability to increase prosperity in business and the home. Because she is a female figure, she can be propitiated for issues related to romance and fertility as well. This eclecticism within her own cult of worship fits in very well with the eclecticism related to Theravada popular lay practices. There are several large and sacred statues of Kuan Yin in the urban centers of Thailand's Bangkok and Chiang Mai.

Popular Buddhist practices, similar to the practices for spirits, include making offerings to these deities and asking for assistance. The major difference from spirits is that these deities are not ambiguous or amoral—they are always morally good and therefore higher than spirits in the hierarchy.

Calling on the Local Legends

In 2014, the professional cyclist Jutatip Maneephan won a gold medal for Thailand in the Asian Games. Before the competition, Jutatip asked the statue of the nineteenth-century populist monk Kruba Siwichai to grant her wish for good luck in the race. Because of her win, she returned to the statue to fulfill her vow. She had promised to run up the road to the top of the nearby mountain, Doi Suthep, three times as thanks and reciprocity toward Kruba Siwichai. Kruba Siwichai was born in 1878, and even as a young monk he developed a reputation for meditation and magical powers, which earned him his title of kruba, or revered teacher. Today at his shrine at the foot of this mountain, laity offer eggs, because he was a vegetarian monk, in exchange for wishes received, along with wreaths of marigolds and incense.

In Thailand, many national heroes and regional monks become resources for wish fulfillment. Rama V, or King Chulalongkorn (1853-1910), who is believed to have saved the nation from colonialism, is propitiated at his statue in Bangkok. As well, his portrait can often be seen in businesses, hung near an altar with other religious resources. This is also the case with the more recently deceased King Bhumibol, Rama IX (1927–2016), whose pictures as a young man ordained or in full king regalia as an older man are found in most temples in Thailand. Portraits of these kings act as protection and aid for businesses.

Legends of Queen Camadevi are also prevalent in northern Thailand, where she saved her kingdom from a demon and brought civilization, through the power of Buddhism. In *The Legend of Queen Cama*, Queen Cama, or Chamadewi, rules over the walled city Haripunchai. Chamadewi represents Buddhist civilization, which must triumph over the wild forces of the forest-dwelling animists and their King Wilangkha. Wilangkha, from the forests of Doi Kham, courts the city-dwelling Chamadewi with gifts but also spears, showing his crude form of power. Chamadewi defeats Wilangkha with her cleverness, sending him a gift of a turban, which is secretly made from her menstrual undergarments. This polluting substance, when placed on Wilangkha's head, causes him to lose his powers, ultimately leading to his downfall. Just like the Buddha, Chamadewi cleverly compromises with these untamed forces to bring them into Buddhism's orbit. Today her statue is propitiated in the town of Lamphun with marigold and jasmine garlands, banana-leaf decorations, and colorful fruits such as oranges and bananas.

Queen Suriyothai and Ya Mo or Thao Suranari are also worshipped because of their sacrifice of personal happiness to save Thai kingdoms from Burmese and Lao enemies, respectively. Queen Suriyothai fought bravely against the Burmese and even sacrificed her life for her husband, the king. She also sacrificed by marrying the man she needed to, instead of the man she loved, in order create the proper royal alliances in the Ayutthaya kingdom. Queen Suriyothai can be worshipped at many statues in central Thailand but most famously outside of Ayutthaya city, where she is riding her battle elephant. Ya Mo is a heroine honored at the Suranari memorial in Khorat, a city in the northeast region. She is worshipped because of her efforts to stop the army invading from present-day Laos. She is a warrior and a guardian who, depicted as an aged grandmother, conveys protection and loving-kindness. Because these women protected their communities, they are believed to continue to care about their people.

In Cambodia, the story of the Leper King from the Angkor civilization dates from the thirteenth century, with his legend found in Cambodian chronicles by the mid-nineteenth century. His statue is associated with the Bayon temple near Siem Reap, but it has been transferred to Phnom Penh's National Museum. Although it is not known exactly which king of Angkor is being referred to or if he did in fact have leprosy, today the statue of the Leper King is worshipped for its wish-granting powers. The museum waives fees for individuals wishing to worship the statue. The Leper King, just like the previous local legends, only makes sense to people who are part of that local community. However, all these local legends are propitiated by Theravada Buddhists as part of the larger corpus of deities and spirits that can offer assistance in this world.

Although there is a basic hierarchy in place of Buddhism above the deities, and deities above the local spirits, in practice Theravada Buddhists do not always divide the spiritual world so neatly. They make offerings and ask for worldly desires to any spirit or deity who might offer assistance. Maybe a layperson would ask the same local spirit shrine that has brought them success before or maybe they heard that another deity, such as Ganesha, is effective and accommodating. However, the closer connection to Buddhism and its morality spirits and deities possess, the more powerful they are imagined to be.

Calling on the Spirit Mediums

Lay Buddhist practitioners have access to spirits and deities through not only statues but also spirit mediums. Spirit mediums are individuals believed to be chosen by supernatural beings who allow spirits and deities to move and speak through them via possession. Spirit mediums can be called on to heal the sick, predict the future, and offer advice on an upcoming decision, along with other counseling and ritual duties. It would be quite controversial, and extremely rare within Theravada Buddhism, to claim that the Buddha could act as a spirit able to possess a human. However, the spirits, gods, famous monks, and figures of national origin discussed are all possibilities. In Thailand, even figures from contemporary popular culture have possessed mediums.

In Myanmar, nat mediums are called *natkadaw* (one who is married to a nat). Their initiation ceremony is referred to as a wedding. Afterward, the medium can develop a connection to other nats and create their own nat troupe. Mediums perform dances that narrate the nats' lives and personalities through costumes and distinct behaviors. In addition to performances, spirit mediums also meet with clients individually. Devotees are instructed to make offerings—fruit, flowers, liquor, and boiled eggs, among other goods—to particular nats who will be helpful in resolving their issue. Mediums are usually at the social margins, portrayed physically through effeminate gender performance for males and masculine performance for females. These gender-nonconforming members of society transform this difference into validation and income through their careers as spirit mediums. The nats are part of an elaborate system of exchange between these spirits, mediums, clients, and community members who offer adjacent services, including costume designers, beauticians, and musicians hired during performances and festivals.

In contrast to nats, the rituals of possession for Burmese bobogyi, thaik, and weizza are ethicized under Buddhist morality. For example, alcohol consumption would not be appropriate for a medium possessed by these more Buddhist-type spirits. Moral spirits connected to Buddhism fulfill the needs of the urban middle class who are interested in following Buddhist norms but also want to draw on some of the alternative power of possession cults. Bobogyi, thaik, and weizza mediums distinctly differentiate themselves from spirit mediums who channel the nats, often offering their services free of charge and not taking part in dance or entertainment, enhancing their claim of being closer to mainstream Buddhism.

Rup arak are female mediums in Cambodia who speak to *arak* (a class of benign and malevolent spirits) during spirit medium ceremonies. The researcher Alexandra Kent offers the example of a female spirit medium named Thida. Thida is a low-income rice farmer in a village of northwest Cambodia. She is the medium of six spirits of deceased elderly monks and renunciant women who had attained the Buddhist perfections. She was initially resistant to the possession because, as a farmer working hard to make ends meet, she needed to focus on making money for her family. But once her neighbor's child was ill, she realized she knew how to heal them. Since this time, she agreed to receive the spirits and help her community. Whenever Thida receives money for her services, instead of keeping it for herself, her spirits remind her to donate it to the temple. Monks in Thida's nearby temple are also mediums, which is possible in Cambodia. However, monks cannot go into trances or treat cases related to the female body. In these cases, Thida is called on to help.

In Thailand, a variety of spirits possess mediums, including Thai kings from previous dynasties and kingdoms, Hindu deities, and sacred spirits from local legends and myths. The researcher Pipad Krajaejun has chronicled contemporary spirit mediums who are possessed by contemporary celebrities and fictional characters from Thai soap operas and Hollywood films such as Brian O'Conner from the *Fast and Furious* movie franchise, deceased singer Bob Marley, and other characters such as Doraemon, the Japanese cartoon cat from the future. These figures are attractive through their violent or unexpected death, ideals of world peace, and ability to predict the future, respectively. Well-known deceased magic monks or forest monks are possible channels for spirit mediums because these monks are believed to reside in one of the heaven realms and so are available to help humans. Great kings from Siamese history, as well as prominent princes and princesses, who are widely known through national monuments and public-school curriculum have also been incorporated into spirit medium cults.

These mediums are the personification of the spirit and deity cults, bringing this abundance of religious resources to life. Spirit mediums, along with propitiation of statues and shrines, offer a wide diversity to lay Buddhist practice. Theravada Buddhist monks, for the most part, would not participate as laity do in this popular worship. Since their ideal is otherworldliness and autonomy, reliance on spirit shrines or spirit mediums would be considered inappropriate.

Thai Horror Films

Thai horror films illustrate lay Buddhist practices within a Theravada society in a popular and scary format. This movie genre demonstrates complex ways for negotiating death and the fear of death within Theravada cultural and religious contexts. Thai horror films often depict a recently deceased person centering revenge upon someone or a group of people who have wronged them. This type of ghost, known in Thai as the *phi tai hong*, is the most frightening and dangerous of all spirits. The phi tai hong is frequently a vengeful woman who has met an untimely death either directly or indirectly caused by a man who was not treating her well. She might also seek revenge because she had to separate from a man she loved unexpectedly. From these movies one can glean that women within Thai society are depicted as having more worldly attachment than men. Indeed, these movies often feature male monks who have cultivated, through the power of Buddhist training, a detachment from worldly desire. There are many Thai horror films that display popular lay practices related to Buddhist morality and spirit worship. Characters who are depicted as respecting the spirits through making offerings and maintaining the Five Precepts have a better chance of surviving to the end of the movie. I have selected a few well-known and well-regarded films as examples out of many possibilities.

Nang Nak

Nang Nak is a legendary story that has been popular for centuries and continues to be with movies, comic books, and TV shows based on the tale. The now-classic version of this film is called *Nang Nak* from 1999, directed by Nonzee Nimibutr. Nak is a pregnant woman whose husband, Mak, must leave to serve in the army. After she dies in childbirth, it appears as if she and her baby are still alive to Mak, when he returns. Because the villagers all know she has died, they are fearful of Nak and Mak. Whenever anyone tries to tell Mak about his wife, Nak allegedly harms or kills them. When Mak is finally convinced of the truth, Nak's anger is difficult to contain. In the 1999 version, a hermit priest is seen attempting to quell Nak's untamed spirit. However, she just laughs at him and throws him quite a distance, presumably killing him. A high-ranking monk is needed to come and pacify Nak's spirit through the power of his presence and Pali chanting. His sacred words calm Nak and allow her to accept her death and depart from Mak.

In the 2013 comedic film version of this story, called *Pee Mak Phra Khanong*, directed by Banjong Pisanthanakun, the ending of the 1999 version is turned on its head. In this version, rather than accepting the statement "Ghosts and humans cannot live together," the movie asks, why not? Instead of accepting her death, Nak and Mak continue to live together as they had been before the discovery of her death. The film also reveals that Nak never hurt anyone and so is not really a violent spirit. She is just a woman who wants to continue to love her husband. In this version, she is allowed to do that.

Today Nang Nak's shrine at Wat Mahabut in the Phra Khanong district in Bangkok is popular for those wishing for lottery numbers. The popularity of her shrine, connected with this well-known tale, demonstrates the Buddhist power of domestication over a malevolent phi tai hong and the interest of Theravada Buddhists in entering an exchange relationship with such spirits.

Phobia 2

Phobia 2 is a 2009 film that contains a series of five morality tales, all relating to ghosts and kamma. The ghosts have all violated one or several of the Five Precepts, leading to an unfortunate rebirth. In the first story, "The Novice," Pey is a teenager living a troubled home life with divorced parents. While vandalizing cars and throwing rocks to steal goods, he accidentally hits and kills his father. After the accident, his mother and her new partner send Pey to the monastery to hide out. Although the killing was not intentional, Pey was breaking the precepts against causing harm and stealing. Pey's experience as a novice monk is unsuccessful in calming his anger at his mother and overcoming the guilt of killing his father. Pey is offered many opportunities to make up for his past, but he remains frantic and aggressive, the opposite of the calm demeanor expected and aspired to in a temple. He violates monastic rules by eating at night and local taboos by eating food offerings for the ghosts. Because he does not allow the protective power of Buddhism to envelop him, his punishment is portrayed as being stoned to death by a ghost. In the end, he becomes a ghost himself.

Laddaland

In 2011, Sopon Sukdapisit's *Laddaland* received unprecedented success. Its surprising popularity arose from its concern with the middle class, modernization, and globalization. In this devastating movie, a father desires to create a new life for his family in a new housing complex called Laddaland. However, his attachment to this lifestyle becomes completely undone. The ghosts perpetrating the haunting are not the typical phi tai hong, steeped in angry revenge over some obvious immoral act. Instead, the ghosts are of the present, trapped in their own attachment to social mobility and economic success, symbolized by the father at the heart of the movie. The modern man who is unable to make it in the globalized world is the source of fear and horror in this movie.

None of these movies are explicitly about Buddhism. However, from Thai horror movies it is easy to understand the pervasive nature of Buddhism in the imagination. These movies offer vivid depictions of the place of Buddhism in Theravada societies, with its teachings on kamma and attachment alongside its superior powers of protection. These movies, which feature lay Buddhist characters facing the consequences of their actions, also demonstrate the significance of proper moral actions.

Popular Practices as Spiritual Support

Much of lay Buddhist practice involves the uncertainty of life and the certainty of death. Many ghost stories are derived from legends of corpses who have not yet accepted their death. This is a real cause for fear because these ghosts are powerful and confused, a bad combination for the living. Buddhism helps to alleviate this fear through its powers of taming spirits, ghosts, and recently deceased beings. A Buddhist funeral will usually, but not always, be enough to persuade the dead to realize they are no longer alive.

The uncertainty of life—need for protection and aspiration to flourish—impels Theravada Buddhists to seek out and try an abundant amount of possible spiritual support. Word of mouth as well as mass media have allowed popular practices to spread beyond local communities. Newspapers, magazines, television shows, and books that include content on famous monks, spirit mediums, Buddha statues, and amulets all encourage this kind of eclecticism toward the various outlets and resources Theravada Buddhists have at their disposal. Of course, monks who deny the efficacy of popular practices see worshipping this mixture of deities and spirits as a waste of time. These elite, reform-minded monks and laypeople believe that only through one's own effort can one rid the mind of greed, anger, and delusion. They would consider pleas to supernatural powers as a weak and misguided dependency.

However, most Buddhist practitioners are not oriented toward nibbana and are interested in taking advantage of the resources surrounding Theravada Buddhism to make their lives a little more certain and comfortable in the here and now. Spiritual resources within the broader complex of Theravada Buddhism provide agency for dealing with the anxieties of globalization while supporting the opportunities found in capitalism.

CHAPTER 7

Meditation

Although meditation is not the primary Buddhist activity for most monks and laypeople, it is a crucial part of the Eightfold Path leading to nibbana. As one progresses on the path, the three components of morality, concentration, and wisdom mutually reinforce one another and continually develop. Morality provides the framework for a contemplative life, while mindfulness, concentration, and insight meditation practice create purity of mind. Especially insight meditation, known as vipassana, results in deep understanding of Buddhist truths, or training in wisdom. Through this meditation practice, one learns how to see things "as they really are."

Contrary to popular ideas of meditation outside of Asia, meditation is not a secular practice that involves no belief or understanding of the tradition surrounding it. Rather, Buddhist meditation teachers who teach the practice to non-Buddhists often believe that the practice itself can create a kind of faith in people—that meditation will allow anyone to naturally arrive at the truths of Buddhism. These Buddhist truths are, from a Buddhist perspective, the universal truths for all humankind for all times. Non-Buddhists are often motivated to practice because they perceive meditation to increase productivity and alleviate stress. Buddhists could certainly be interested in these moderate goals too; however, faith in the Buddha and the eventual possibility of enlightenment are also important motivating factors. Theravada Buddhists believe that meditation is a meritorious activity, helping them not only to ultimately leave the cycle of rebirth but also to accumulate merit and good kamma along the way—in this life and future ones.

Meditation within Theravada Buddhism can be practiced by anyone anywhere. The important part, meditation teachers often emphasize, is to simply begin the practice and to keep doing it. Usually, beginning meditators receive simple instructions. Meditation practices are intellectually straightforward yet challenging to continually follow. Over time, practitioners can experiment with different teachers and different techniques. However, the simplest way often taught today within mainland Southeast Asia is to follow one's breath at the nostrils as an anchoring object to calm the mind. Aside from formal sitting or walking meditation, a significant daily meditative practice for Theravada Buddhists is chanting. At temples, stupas, or personal shrines in the mornings or evenings, Buddhist monks and laity read from a chanting book or recite from memory praises to the Buddha, Dhamma, and Sangha.

Concentration and Insight

Buddhist scriptures describe the mind as distractible and wild. However, it can be controlled and tamed, as seen in this selection of sayings of the Buddha from the Dhammapada, one of the most well known of the Buddhist scriptures from the Pali Canon:

Whatever foe may do to foe, or haters those they hate, the ill-directed mind indeed can do one greater harm. (chapter 3, verse 42)[15]

The mind is very hard to check and swift, it falls on what it wants. The training of the mind is good, a mind so tamed brings happiness. (chapter 3, verse 35)[16]

The mind's swiftness and ill-direction can be calmed by the practice of meditation. Formal meditation is typically taught in four positions: seated, standing, walking, and lying down. Most Theravada meditation practices vary between seated and walking meditation. During seated meditation, the legs can be crossed one over the other or in half-lotus or full-lotus position, and the back is straight but relaxed. Walking meditation can be practiced extremely slowly, following each movement of the foot as it travels through space, or less slowly, pacing back and forth on a walking path. Standing meditation is an option if one gets too sleepy during seated meditation and can be incorporated into walking meditation. Lying meditation is mostly used as relaxation before sleep.

Theravada Buddhism has two basic kinds of meditation practice: concentration and insight. Concentration, or *samatha* (calm, tranquility, unification of the mind; a state of undistractedness), is when one focuses exclusively on one object of concentration. This kind of focus is, of course, difficult for most people; our minds are used to having multiple thoughts every minute with a constant rotation of stimulating images. However, over time, one object, such as the in-and-out breath, can become exciting and peaceful, like a gentle, interesting movie. During this process, patience develops, along with mental purity. The quality of mind, which is important for attention, is best when not too sleepy or restless. Meditation is not a way to space out, and sleeping is not helpful toward the goal of stable attention.

When the meditator locks onto the object, they transition from a low level of concentration to a deeper level, which consists of varying degrees, referred to generally as *samadhi*. When one is in samadhi, the five hindrances—sense desire, ill will, sleepiness, restlessness and remorse, and doubt—to concentration are temporarily eradicated. When these hindrances are absent, meditators experience deep absorptive concentration states (*jhanas*). The Pali Canon discusses the importance of the four jhanas. The first jhana contains five qualities: applied and sustained attention, joy and bliss, and one-pointedness of mind. The second, third, and fourth jhanas take one deeper into absorption by decreasing qualities, until the fourth jhana only consists of the quality of equanimity. There are four more jhanas higher than this, which are known as the formless absorptions. During these absorptive states, one detaches from one's normal perception of stable reality altogether as the mind draws more and more away from worldly experience, culminating in the cessation of conception and feeling. These stages are believed to be purifying through temporarily eliminating content from the mind and allowing one to detach from one's thoughts and feelings.

Some lay Buddhists speak in hushed, frightened tones about concentration meditation because it can lead to visions from other realms of the Buddhist cosmology. Tales of meditators encountering images of malevolent spirits are well known, leading Buddhist friends to ask me when I came back from a meditation retreat, "Did you see anything?" Here they are referring to any unusual visions that might have appeared in my mind. Higher jhanas can lead to developing supernatural powers (*iddhis*). However, meditation teachers would consider this a distraction from the real task of meditation—to "see things as they truly are" through insight meditation.

Insight (*vipassana*) is the main form of meditation practiced in Theravada Buddhism today. During this type of meditation, one maintains an anchor on one object, such as the breath, but also opens the field of awareness to many objects, including anything that comes into the six sense doors—mind, touch, hearing, sight, smell, or taste.

The aim of vipassana is to root out all traces of the three defilements of greed, anger, and delusion while cultivating a deep recognition of the veracity of the Three Marks of Existence—impermanence, suffering, and non-self. Vipassana practice allows one to observe the nature of impermanence in one's own body and experience as well as one's lack of control and lack of an inherent, stable self. These insights lead to the recognition that anything without substance is inherently filled with suffering. Vipassana aids in realizing this through investigation and deconstruction of the cognitive processes of one's own mind. Gradually the practice moves the meditator away from grand narratives, a sense of wholeness and concepts of space and time, to a much more granular and disaggregated experience of reality. Rather than our ordinary understanding of reality, which conceives of one's subjective experience in consistent ways, vipassana aims to break this down into discrete, impermanent units. For example, the meditator can disaggregate the intention to move one's leg and the actual movement of the leg, or the intention to pick up the spoon and the actual movement of the arm to pick up the spoon and begin eating.

The benefits achieved through vipassana meditation are believed to be transformative and irreversible. Anyone can reach this understanding, whether they have studied Buddhism, grown up Buddhist, or never heard of Buddhism. Those who reach the end of the path of vipassana become known as the Noble Ones. They follow four stages leading to nibbana. Each attainment is achieved in succession and is accompanied by distinct transformations. The first stage is the stream-enterer (*sotapanna*), who will take a maximum of seven lifetimes to attain nibbana. The second stage is known as the once-returner (*sakadagamin*), who will be reborn only one more time before reaching liberation. The non-returner (*anagamin*), the third stage of the noble path, will not be reborn as a human but will either attain nibbana in this lifetime or be reborn in one of the highest heavens and become enlightened there. The arahant, the fourth noble person, has "done what needs to be done" and reached the culminating experience of the Buddhist path—the complete cultivation of morality, concentration, and wisdom.

Although these two types of meditation work in tandem to allow one to progress along the Buddhist path of practice, contemporary Theravada meditation teachers debate the relationship between samatha and vipassana. Some teachers assert that moment-to-moment forms of concentration are sufficient, while others have students practice concentration for a third of the retreat before introducing vipassana. Yet other techniques advise students to master all jhana states first before moving to vipassana. No matter the amount, both concentration and insight are necessary and incorporated to varying degrees into contemporary meditation retreats.

Meditation in Theravada Buddhist Scriptures

Buddhist meditation methods are derived from the Pali Canon. One place to look for the role of meditation in the path to nibbana is the Buddha's life story. After the bodhisatta who became Gotama Buddha renounced the palace life, he studied the practice of concentration meditation from two teachers, Alada Kalama and Uddaka Ramaputta. Under their guidance he attained the highest levels of formless jhanas and was offered positions of leadership within these communities. However, he knew that these states were impermanent, creating removal from the sensory world but not the end of suffering. After he left these early teachers, the Buddha lived in extreme asceticism so that he was just eating a few drops of soup per day. He experienced much pain in his body, which he realized was not conducive to enlightenment.

At this time, the bodhisatta had a memory from his childhood when he spontaneously entered a jhana state. He remembered his first meditation experience when he sat under a rose apple tree to watch his father and the royal court participating in the royal plowing ceremony. During the ceremony, as everyone was working and celebrating, the young child cultivated stillness and peace. Upon reflection he realized there is nothing wrong with this wholesome kind of pleasure he received from the calmness and joy he felt from concentrating his mind. This spurred him to formulate the Middle Way, the path between luxurious indulgence and extreme self-denial. Upon the night of his enlightenment, the Buddha entered the fourth level of jhana and had three knowledges, which constitute the realization of Buddhahood. Two of these knowledges were the recollection of his own former existences and the divine eye, with which he could see beings passing away and taking rebirth in accordance with their karma, thus having complete understanding of the cosmos and how karma and samsara work together. In the last of these knowledges, he realized the Four Noble Truths and the doctrine of causation, which keeps sentient beings in samsara. Upon this moment of awakening, he knew he would not be reborn into another existence.

Along with the Buddha's own meditative path, Theravada Buddhist scriptures record the Buddha's teachings about the practice taught to his disciples. Modern Theravada Buddhist meditative practices draw mainly from three authoritative texts: the *Satipatthana Sutta* and the *Anapanasati Sutta*, two suttas of the Pali Canon that are treated by Buddhists as direct teachings of the Buddha; and the *Visuddhimagga*, the fifth-century treatise by Buddhaghosa.

The Satipatthana Sutta

If you ask a Theravada meditation instructor where their method of vipassana is derived from, they will most likely say they teach based on the four foundations of mindfulness as described in the *Satipatthana Sutta*: body (*kaya*), feelings (*vedana*), mind (*citta*), and mind objects (*dhamma*). Each foundation delineates a set of practices to follow.

The Four Foundations of Mindfulness

1. *Mindfulness of the body*: One contemplates one's own body through fourteen different applications. These basic practices form the basis for more abstract objects, such as feelings and states of the mind.

2. *Mindfulness of feelings*: One notes three types of feelings—pleasant, unpleasant, and neutral—that make up their experiences in the present moment. These practices emphasize the changing, impersonal, and impermanent nature of feelings.

3. *Mindfulness of the mind*: This includes being aware of the state of the mind, if it is concentrated or distracted, and whether the qualities of greed, hatred, and delusion are present or absent. Like mindfulness of feelings, the practice of mindfulness of the mind facilitates the perception of mental states as impermanent and not belonging to a self.

4. *Mindfulness of mind objects, or dhammas*: This entails contemplating Buddhist lists like the five hindrances and the Four Noble Truths. The *Satipatthana Sutta* concludes with an

assurance that through these practices successful meditators can expect to reach the level of *anagamin* or *arahant*.

The Anapanasati Sutta

A few teachers prefer the *Anapanasati Sutta*, which focuses its instructions more closely on mindfulness of breathing. The instructions in this sutta have been used as preparatory practices in developing the practices put forth in the *Satipatthana Sutta*, although the sutta itself claims that mindfulness of breathing alone can encompass all four foundations. Here mindfulness of breathing is detailed in sixteen steps that follow a similar pattern to that of the *Satipatthana Sutta*. Each of the four foundations of mindfulness in the *Anapanasati Sutta* is practiced through the awareness of breath. It begins with understanding that the duration of breath can vary. The next steps describe how, as one deepens in concentration, one trains the mind in experiencing the pleasant feelings that accompany this. In the final steps, the meditator directs this level of purification of the mind toward insight practice.

The Visuddhimagga

Both meditation suttas in the Pali Canon are open to a range of interpretations by contemporary teachers. In contrast to the Pali Canon suttas, the *Visuddhimagga* (The Path of Purification) is a systematic presentation of the stages leading to nibbana, with detailed instructions on how to reach liberation. Buddhaghosa, an Indian monk who lived in Sri Lanka, wrote the Visuddhimagga in the fifth century. Since this is a large commentarial text, it is much more comprehensive than a short sutta could be. Instead of using samatha and vipassana practices within one discourse, as in the Pali suttas, the Visuddhimagga creates two distinct paths. The first path envisions cultivation of concentration to a high degree before the meditator turns to insight. Here, forty objects of concentration are recommended as possible *kammatthana* (places of work) to reach samatha. The second path focuses almost exclusively on insight, with very little cultivation of concentration. Buddhaghosa called vipassana practice without jhana "dry insight" because there is no "moisture" from the jhanas on this path. Since Buddhaghosa's interpretation neatly divides meditation into two categories of concentration and insight, meditation teachers have learned and thought about meditation in these terms.

The Metta Sutta

While you are likely to encounter a mix of concentration and insight instruction in vipassana meditation retreats today, you may also encounter the concept of *metta* meditation, which derives from the *Metta Sutta*. These teachings of the Buddha exhort the good and wise to spread loving-kindness by making these wishes:

> In gladness and in safety,
>   May all beings be at ease.
> Whatever living beings there may be;
>   Whether they are weak or strong, omitting none,
> The great or the mighty, medium, short or small,
>   The seen and the unseen,
> Those living near and far away,
>   Those born and to-be-born—
> May all beings be at ease![17]

After a meditation session, participants might be reminded to spread the merit of their practice by wishing loving-kindness to others. I use this time after meditation sessions to reflect on the people in my life and wish them well in their current pursuits, repeating simple phrases based on the *Metta Sutta*:

> May we all be happy.
> May we all be safe.
> May we all be healthy.
> May we all live with ease.

Following the tiring work of training one's attention on one object in concentration or on every moment of one's experience, as in insight, the work of metta meditation feels like a pleasant bonus activity. These phrases can also be introduced at the end of retreats to express gratitude and spread the merit of one's effort to others. These meditative practices have been adapted from Theravada Buddhist scriptures to fit the lifestyles of modern lay audiences who cannot dedicate their lives to meditation. Few monks can dedicate themselves solely to meditation, as many have academic or administrative duties. Just as monks can incorporate some meditation into their day, laity can visit temples to practice the basics of meditation on a regular basis or they can attend an intensive retreat at a meditation center.

Meditation in Temples

Merit-making is the central activity of most temples. These meritorious deeds are divided into generosity (*dana*), following ethical precepts (*sila*), and mental development (*bhavana*). All three of these meritorious actions work together, with generosity and ethics acting as firm bases from which to concentrate the mind. Bhavana encompasses the meditation practices of vipassana and samatha while also aiding in generally cultivating and uplifting the mind.

At temples without specific meditation centers, meditation is often practiced among the monks—from five to twenty minutes spent in collective silence—after the morning and evening chanting recitations. These sessions do not include formal meditation instruction but are more a gesture toward the goal of attaining a calm and stable mind. Of course, monks can practice meditation in their rooms during their free time as much as they would like. Student monks enrolled in degree programs at monastic colleges often have a period set aside each academic year for a collective meditation retreat. Even though degrees center on Buddhist and sometimes secular subjects, a meditation retreat of ten or more days is deemed important enough to be a mandatory requirement in some monastic universities. Forest temples have much more time set aside for meditation than temples in the city.

However, some city temples might have meditation sessions for monks and outsiders. For example, Wat Langka in downtown Phnom Penh, Cambodia, hosts hour-long meditation sittings four times a week. When the session begins and ends, the leading monk rings a bell. In between, everyone sits silently and attempts to focus on their breath as best they can. The only instruction is a monk asking if anyone needs a rundown of the basic technique before the session starts. Since participants are expected to have some familiarity with the practice, the point of the group meditation is to use the community for support and motivation.

The Vipassana Retreat at Meditation Centers

Before vipassana meditation retreats became popular, meditation practice was, for the most part, undertaken by a minority of monks with individual teachers. The few monks who would become well known for their teaching ability and knowledge would accept a few disciples, to whom they would give personalized instruction based on those students' temperaments and past experiences. In her book *Esoteric Theravada*, Kate Crosby researched the premodern Theravada meditation practice known as *boran kammathan*. This ancient meditation approach was established by high-ranking monks and kings dating back to the sixteenth century and was the dominant form in Cambodia, Laos, and Thailand by the eighteenth century. This practice became marginalized and labeled as "unorthodox" during the reform movements of Buddhism in mainland Southeast Asia during the nineteenth century. Because of sectarian rivalry and shifting royal sponsorship, traditional meditation was downplayed and discouraged especially during the rise of the Burmese vipassana technique and communism in Laos and Cambodia, which eliminated religious practices.

The shift to modern techniques occurred under the backdrop of the British colonization of Burma (1824-1948) and the threat of colonization by Britain and France to Siam. The response to colonialism and threats against Buddhism was a kind of Buddhist nationalism, which manifested in part as the mass lay meditation movement. Because of this need to preserve and uphold Buddhism, Myanmar was the first country to create opportunities for laypeople to study Buddhism and practice meditation intensively. During the 1950s, meditation became a popular activity, especially among the urban middle class of Thailand and Myanmar. The middle class, especially those who had completed a Western-style education, sought to align their national culture with the standards of the international community. As the practice opened further beyond lay Buddhists, non-Buddhist foreigners also became part of the target audience for meditation centers.

These accessible, modern meditation techniques were taught in a unique institution within the history of Buddhism: the meditation center. Unlike the Buddhist temple, a meditation center's daily schedule is packed with periods of meditation. Every moment should be spent in mindfulness of every action, along with periods of formal walking or sitting meditation. Some meditation centers are located in idyllic forest environments with forest monk teachers and room for hundreds of people. Other centers might be in urban areas, such as Bangkok, with mostly lay teachers and space for only twenty people in their courses. Yet meditation centers all have a systematized and formalized program and schedule that practitioners must follow individually or in group periods of meditation. Many meditation centers ask retreatants to wear white and follow the Eight Precepts. However, some centers frequented mostly by foreigners allow them to wear any modest outfits and to abide by the Five Precepts.

Sample Meditation Schedule for Vipassana Retreats

4 a.m. Wake up and begin mindful walking and sitting practice
6 a.m.-7 a.m. Breakfast
7 a.m.-8 a.m. Cleaning, washing, bathing
8 a.m.-10:30 a.m. Mindful walking and sitting practice

10:30 a.m.–11:30 a.m. Lunch

11:30 a.m.–1:00 p.m. Cleaning, washing, bathing

1 p.m.–2 p.m. Mindful walking and sitting practice

2 p.m.–3 p.m. Interview with teacher

3 p.m.–5:30 p.m. Mindful walking and sitting practice

5:30 p.m.–6 p.m. Optional evening drink

6 p.m.–7 p.m. Optional chanting with monks and/or nuns

7 p.m.–10 p.m. Mindful walking and sitting

10 p.m. Sleep

Most meditation centers alternate their meditation activities between sitting and walking meditation. Each vipassana meditation technique and center will have instructions for what to do with one's mind while practicing sitting meditation, such as following the breath at the nostrils or abdomen, focusing the mind on different points of the body, or scanning the body for sensations. Different centers might also vary the timing of the meditation sessions. Some meditation centers start off practitioners at fifteen minutes of sitting and then gradually extend this to longer amounts of time until one hour is reached. Other meditation centers begin and end with the one hour of sitting. In some centers, walking meditation can be done in a somewhat brisk way, like a normal walk, where attention should be focused on one's feet touching the ground. Other techniques break down walking into its parts of lifting the foot, moving it forward, and placing the foot back on the floor. This is done in a defined space of a couple yards so that the practice looks more like a tedious form of pacing than walking.

A highlight in the schedule for most practitioners is the interview with the teacher. The interview is crucial for advancing one's practice and is the only time of day when meditators are officially allowed to talk. In some centers, the interview may only occur two or three times during the retreat, or it could be optional, while in many centers a short daily interview is expected. In the beginning, it can be challenging to maintain continuity and stay focused. However, once meditators are more established in mindfulness and concentration, they can more easily maintain double-digit hours of meditation per day. If a student complains of mental distraction or physical pain, the teacher will advise the meditator to notice, acknowledge the difficulty, and resume maintaining awareness. The teacher directs the student from attaching meaning to their thoughts; instead, the goal is to be aware and mindful of the sensations and feelings arising without judgment.

For a monastic or layperson who has been on many retreats, meditation can have a transformative effect. This possibility of transformation is not how meditation is promoted to international audiences, however. The Tourism Authority of Thailand advertises meditation as an escape to a timeless practice where one can better deal with a busy modern life. Meditation teachers, a selection of whom are discussed below, created their retreat formats with deep transformation in mind.

Mahasi Sayadaw Retreats in Yangon

The institution of the meditation center began in Burma with the Mahasi Thathana Yeiktha (MTY) founded by Mahasi Sayadaw (1904–82) in 1947. MTY was the first institution of its kind, formed under sponsorship from the Burmese government and lay supporters. Mahasi Sayadaw was a well-known scholar monk, meditator, and meditation teacher. He kept a record of his interviews with thousands of meditators and analyzed their progress. After refining and standardizing his teaching, Mahasi Sayadaw believed that he had determined the most direct way toward nibbana. His method is based on the idea that it would take the average person two months of intense practice to achieve the first stage of enlightenment. The declaration that a regular person could reach the first path of enlightenment within this short time span was a revolutionary idea at the time.

MTY became the main hub of the mass meditation movement with over a million meditators certified to have made attainments toward nibbana. Every day at MTY, hundreds of people sit in long rows with eyes shut and in silence. A bell clangs to signal the end of each hour-long meditation session. Meditators rise and move slowly to their next session of walking meditation. Every aspect of daily activity becomes the practice. The four hours of sleep become less and less necessary as one slows down their movements and mental chatter. Meditators are asked to try to notice the last breath before sleeping and first breath upon waking. There is one brief interview with a teacher every day. Otherwise, the focus is internal, with no speech or communication with others unless necessary.

In her book *Burma's Mass Lay Meditation Movement*, Ingrid Jordt reported on the retreats at MTY through her own experience as a meditator and researcher. Jordt found that meditation teachers must discern between students who narrate an authentic meditation experience and those who relate conceptual knowledge about attainments they learned from reading or listening to others. The meditation teacher must be able to give the correct instruction so that the meditator does not believe they are at a higher stage than they are. At the same time, the teacher can never know for certain. That is why some students, who are thought by their teachers to have reached higher stages of insight, are invited to listen to a tape of Mahasi Sayadaw explaining the progress of insight meditation. This way each meditator can know their level of attainment for themselves. This leads to laity asking one another playful questions such as "Did you listen to the tape?" "Did you pass the course?" "Did you get the insurance policy?" These questions relate to the idea that the course is designed for the meditator to reach the first path of enlightenment, which comes with a guarantee that one will never be reborn in the lower unfortunate realms of samsara once one has reached this level of attainment.

Mahasi Sayadaw's teaching on meditation begins with purifying one's conduct, which is accomplished by observing the Eight Precepts. Mahasi Sayadaw also recommends placing trust in the Buddha as the Enlightened One and one's meditation teacher, which highlights the important role of faith. After this preparation, the basic technique consists of a single exercise for seated meditation—

making continuous mental notes of the rising and falling of the abdomen as you breathe, being aware of all bodily sensations. If one becomes distracted from the awareness of this sensation, then the meditator should make a mental note of the thought and come back to the rising and falling. Meditators can note mental states such as imagining, thinking, reflecting, wandering, and the like. In addition to sitting meditation, Mahasi Sayadaw recommends that meditators note every physical movement, such as bending the neck, straightening the back, moving the foot, and so forth; and the sensations of the body, such as itchy, stiff, tired, painful, aching. In this way the object of concentration is every changing movement and thought. If there is nothing else to note, then the mind can rest on the rising and falling of the abdomen. The constant noting practice is meant to remind the meditator to maintain awareness but not to become interested in the content of their experiences.

Mahasi's method described above is "dry" vipassana practice, without samatha meditation as preparation. Through this technique, as described by Mahasi Sayadaw in his *The Progress of Insight*, the meditator eventually attains the four paths to nibbana. Today in Myanmar there are over three hundred meditation centers affiliated with Mahasi Sayadaw, though his influence can be seen in every vipassana meditation retreat. Basic retreat formats and the belief that anyone can make real progress through intensive practice comes from Mahasi Sayadaw and the establishment of MTY.

U Ba Khin and S. N. Goenka.

U Ba Khin (1899-1971), a government official under Prime Minister U Nu and a lay Buddhist teacher, founded the International Meditation Centre in Yangon in 1952. Because of U Ba Khin's Christian school education and government job, he could teach in English and to international students. He developed a system of sweeping the body, performed by paying attention to the body part by part, noticing impermanence of all sensations. As one progresses, energy flows in the body become unblocked and the sweeping becomes more rapid. This develops until the experience of one's mind, body, and the world consists of a series of vibrations. While Mahasi Sayadaw focuses on mindfulness of the body, U Ba Khin's approach draws more from the mindfulness of feelings and advocates practicing his vipassana technique after developing a level of concentration by focusing on the breath at the upper lip. For both, the initial focus on the body or feelings implies that all four foundations of mindfulness will develop alongside.

U Ba Khin's most famous disciple was S. N. Goenka (1924–2013). Goenka was born in Myanmar in a family of Indian heritage. Because of this and his commitment to Hinduism, he was at first reticent about practicing Buddhist meditation. However, Goenka, a high-ranking business leader in his community, was afflicted by migraines and U Ba Khin's approach to meditation practice quickly cured him. U Ba Khin continued to teach Goenka vipassana for the next fourteen years. Goenka became one of U Ba Khin's most important students and was responsible for returning vipassana to India.

After becoming a teacher himself, Goenka set up retreats and retreat centers in India in 1969. After finding success in his native land, he expanded his method to retreat centers throughout the world. Goenka streamlined U Ba Khin's method into a ten-day course. The first three days of the retreat focus on mindfulness of breathing and developing concentration. During the fourth through ninth days, retreatants practice observing sensations throughout the body, while the tenth day is dedicated to loving-kindness meditation. These courses are popular in Thailand and Cambodia, where this method is well respected for its quality of instruction and intensity.

In the Goenka method, sweeping and scanning the body is taught in a systematic and careful way, emphasizing the importance of equanimity toward pleasant and unpleasant sensations. Progress in the practice is noticed when meditators can mentally scan from head to feet without obstruction. Goenka explains these obstructions as *sankhara*, which are all the reactions we have to our experiences, both positive and negative, that build up over time. Through vipassana meditation, sankhara rise to the surface, release their sensation, and then disappear. If we can stop reacting to future experiences, then we can attain equanimity and prevent new sankhara from arising.

Goenka is known for promoting the dhamma as nonsectarian and universally accessible to all kinds of people. Goenka taught more than three hundred courses in India and worldwide. In 1982 he appointed assistant teachers and volunteers to facilitate the courses, aided by videos of Goenka's teachings and talks. Currently thousands of assistant teachers and volunteers conduct courses globally, and the courses are always offered free. By the time of Goenka's death in 2013, he and his students had established more than 150 centers around the world.

Ajahn Tong Meditation Retreats in Northern Thailand

In Thailand, interest in meditation centers and lay meditation began in the late 1940s. Phra Phimonlatham (1903-89), the abbot of Wat Mahathat, a royal temple in Bangkok, selected monks from every region of Thailand to study meditation techniques in depth. These monks studied at Wat Mahathat, and some were sent directly to Burma to study with Burmese teachers such as Mahasi Sayadaw. One of these Thai monks was Ajahn Tong Sirimangalo (1923-2019), who developed his own method after studying the techniques of vipassana in Burma. When he returned to Thailand, he quickly began spreading vipassana throughout the northern region. Upon his death, many of his followers considered him to be an arahant.

Practitioners of Ajahn Tong's technique prepare themselves with two sets of white clothing to wear, toiletries, and a personal timer, which is used to track each meditation session. Lay students approximate the life of a renunciant through eating only twice a day, limiting sleep, and wearing white clothing, which marks them as meditators. As the retreat days pass, participants are expected to complete increasing hours of meditation. For example, after a week or so, meditators might be asked to do twelve hours of meditation a day and limit sleep to four hours a night. Toward the end of the retreat, students sit and walk for an hour each, meditating for fourteen to eighteen hours a day. The final three nights and four days of a beginner retreat are spent without sleep, meditating continuously to get the most out of this intensive experience and make a breakthrough toward nibbana.

Ajahn Tong retreats can last from ten days to twenty-six days. The retreat style contains no group activities. Instead, everyone meditates individually in one of the meditation halls, outside, or in their room, aided by a timer. They begin with fifteen-minute sitting and walking meditation periods and gradually increase to an hour. Each meditation session consists of three parts: prostration, walking, and sitting meditation. The slow, mindful prostration allows meditators to focus their minds and bodies, in preparation for their periods of walking and sitting meditation. Walking meditation progresses from a basic two-step movement to awareness of six parts of each step. The meditators walk in this slow way for a few yards across a small room. When they reach the end of the path, meditators mentally note when they are stopping, standing, intending to turn, turning, standing, intending to walk, and beginning the walk again.

The sitting meditation practice consists of a complex awareness. The meditator first focuses on the breath rising and falling in the abdomen. Meditators progress by labeling "sitting" after the rising and falling. Then the meditator focuses on the mind touching different parts of the body. These touch points are increased as the retreat goes on, with a total of twenty-eight points given in fourteen pairs. This exercise is meant to keep the mind focused on vipassana, not to get into any deep level of concentration. In between meditation sessions, meditators are encouraged to remain aware of all their movements when going to the restroom, eating, or washing. The interviews each day with the teacher allow the meditator to express how their practice has been going and receive new instructions. The interview usually lasts a few minutes and is not meant as any kind of therapy or emotional release.

Many Thai and international meditators have participated in Ajahn Tong's meditation courses in the many temples that use his method, mostly in northern Thailand. While Ajahn Tong began teaching his meditation practice at Wat Muang Man in Chiang Mai city, he moved his center to Wat Rampoeng, just outside of Chiang Mai city, after renovating the temple. It continues today as the Northern Insight Vipassana Meditation Center at Wat Rampoeng. Wat Chom Tong, in Chom Tong, Chiang Mai Province, also has a large meditation center for Thai and international meditators.

Buddhadasa Bhikkhu Retreats in Southern Thailand

Buddhadasa Bhikkhu was a famous Buddhist scholar whose English writings cover many shelves on subjects such as comparative religion and Buddhist teachings for daily life. The temple Buddhadasa Bhikkhu (1906-93) founded, Wat Suan Mokkhabalarama, or Suan Mokkh (Garden of Liberation), in Chaiya, southern Thailand, still bears his legacy. This meditation temple, along with his nearby meditation center, the International Dhamma Hermitage, demonstrate Buddhadasa Bhikkhu's commitment to practice. His method used at these sites, like other retreat formats and vipassana methods, is a simple and replicable technique meant to be suitable for all meditators. However, Buddhadasa Bhikkhu bases his meditation technique on the *Anapanasati Sutta* instead of the more popular *Satipatthana Sutta*.

Buddhadasa Bhikkhu asserts that out of the many meditation methods and systems of samatha and vipassana created by various teachers, *anapanasati* (mindfulness of breathing) is the closest one to the Buddha's teachings. Buddhadasa finds the *Satipatthana Sutta* confusing and vague. Instead, Buddhadasa recommends using the *Anapanasati Sutta* as a framework that offers complete and clear guidance. Buddhadasa asserts that the correct practice of anapanasati is to take one truth or reality of nature and then observe, investigate, and scrutinize it in the mind with every inhalation and every exhalation. To begin on this journey, one needs awareness, and one can cultivate this by being mindful of each breath.

The ten-day retreat program for meditators at the International Dhamma Hermitage is conducted in English beginning on the first of every month and in Thai on the last week of every month. All meditation here is done as a group, and everyone follows the same schedule with periods for meditation, chores, meals, and visiting the hot springs on site. Instead of mandatory daily interviews with a teacher, there are optional ones toward the middle of the retreat. The last evening is dedicated to a dhamma sharing, where participants express their experiences.

The Thai Forest Tradition

The forest tradition of northeast Thailand does not follow the regimented, portable model of the meditation center. And yet these monasteries hold a major importance for understanding Theravada meditation. The Thai forest tradition has become well known internationally through the writings and disciples of two monks of this tradition: Ajahn Chah (1918–92) and Ajahn Maha Bua (1913–2011). Both monks are part of the second generation of forest monks, whose teacher was Ajahn Mun (1870–1949), considered the founder of the forest tradition. Before the settled forest monasteries of this second generation, Ajahn Mun and his contemporaries in the 1920s wandered the forests, villages, and capitals of north and northeastern Thailand. From encountering wild elephants and tigers to staying up all night in a graveyard site, these first-generation forest monks overcame their fear of death and cultivated trust in the dhamma. The forest monk is likened to a warrior in battle where the battlefield is his own mind, which he conquers through taming it in the challenging forest setting.

To tame the mind and steel it against fear, the forest monks cultivated samadhi. Ajahn Mun recommended reciting the mantra BUDDHO, and with one-pointed focus on this object, enter into a deep concentrative state. He sent his disciples into the forest, strategizing that fear would be a catalyst to generate samadhi and deepen wisdom at the same time. The aim is to cultivate a mind that, upon hearing a tiger's growl, would experience this as just another noise and not arouse a reaction of fright. When the mind can just note the sound and let it go, then one understands the truth of dhamma. Although these practices were risky, they taught indispensable lessons to those who were brave enough to try.

As the second generation, Ajahn Chah and Ajahn Maha Bua founded large forest monasteries in northeast Thailand. At Wat Pa Ban That, Ajahn Maha Bua recommends that one do the small tasks needed to keep the monastery functioning quickly and quietly. After this, the rest of the day is spent in walking meditation on one's individual walking path and sitting meditation in one's solitary accommodation. This way of practice is not set up for many laypeople, as there are no teacher interviews or formal instruction. In fact, it is recommended that laypeople who come to Wat Pa Ban already have developed a meditation practice or attended an intensive retreat.

Ajahn Chah stresses meditation and mindfulness in daily life rather than formal practice. In recordings of his speeches, Ajahn Chah is often described as chiding those who think that meditation can only happen on a cushion or on the walking path. For Ajahn Chah, every aspect of monastic life was to be a part of one's practice. Because of this, Ajahn Chah focused on teaching with directness, advising naturalness and self-reliance. He found that retreats in meditation centers could have some benefit but are difficult to carry over into one's daily life. Ajahn Chah advised students to interview themselves, listen to dhamma talks, and compare the teachings with their own practice. The forest tradition is unique in its lack of a retreat model and emphasis on self-motivation.

Diverse Methods and Meditators

In Theravada Buddhism, it is widely acknowledged that meditation is one of the most effective and challenging aspects of Buddhist practice. The diversity of methods available confirms that meditation is taken very seriously by its teachers in Southeast Asia. Monks of Thailand and Myanmar in particular have specialized in the study of suttas and development of meditation techniques. These various methods, all of which are based on the Theravada scriptures, are meant to help practitioners receive the benefits of meditation—from wholesome and purifying self-cultivation to reaching the final goal of nibbana.

A minority of practitioners would consider themselves "meditators," and even fewer would be aiming toward the ultimate goal of release from suffering. Some lay Buddhists may be hoping this practice will lead to a fortunate rebirth as a human or god. At the same time, international meditators, following an identical practice, might be most interested in developing tools for anger management or anxiety. Although there are different goals, Buddhist monks who created these techniques believe that vipassana will eventually lead to nibbana, no matter the motivation.

Conclusion

Places, people, and practices of Theravada Buddhism are diverse and fascinatingly complex throughout mainland Southeast Asia. The countries of Cambodia, Myanmar, Laos, and Thailand are part of a unique Theravada cultural civilization, yet they have their own regional and local variations derived from myths, local legends, histories of colonialism, and modern experiences of urbanization and globalization. I have tried to capture this multiplicity of Theravada expressions in each chapter with examples of particular temples, sacred objects, well-known monks, extraordinary female Buddhists, Thai horror films, and meditation methods.

In addition to appreciating the scope of lived Theravada Buddhism, I hope that readers continue to think through some of the themes that flow through the chapters on places, people, and practices. One of the main issues that comes through in almost every chapter is the relationship between popular and elite forms of Buddhism. *Popular* and *elite* do not describe the ways Buddhists talk about themselves, but these descriptions do reveal the ways scholars have interpreted different expressions of Buddhism. Although popular and elite exist on a spectrum with very few people occupying either extreme, the dynamic still portrays real tensions within Theravada Buddhism.

Popular Buddhism is expressed through the eclecticism of lay practices that are mixed with spirit worship, Brahminism, and Chinese religions. Buddhists on the merit-making path, rather than the path to nibbana, look to a variety of resources within the umbrella of

Theravada Buddhism for aid in their everyday life pursuits. Giving offerings to the spirits or a deity in exchange for health, wealth, and happiness, or to a Buddha statue with an aim toward a good rebirth in the next life as a beautiful human or god in a heaven realm, are some of the major practices of lived Theravada Buddhism. These practices are not only on the sidelines and are not just for laity, however. Popular forms of Buddhism are also in major urban areas, such as Bangkok with its Brahma statue known as the Erawan Shrine. Well-regarded monks create and bless amulets, wish-granting Buddha statues, and protective tattoos.

This popular aspect of lived Theravada Buddhism is at times, however, in contrast to the official version of elite Buddhism, which is more closely based on Buddhist texts and connected with scholarly pursuits within capital cities and royally sponsored temples. Elite Buddhism consists of scholar monks and meditators focused on following the Buddha's teachings and working toward nibbana. Getting out of samsara, rather than making samsara better for oneself, is the goal of elite Buddhism. Of course, not all Buddhists can follow such a path. Both paths, merit-making and nibbana, are necessary for Buddhism to thrive. Merit-making is needed to support those practicing for nibbana, and the ultimate goal of nibbana is necessary for the system of merit to be possible. Without the transcendent aspiration toward nibbana, popular Buddhism would have no power or protection to draw upon.

Popular Buddhism respects elite pursuits of nibbana, but elite Buddhists can sometimes look down upon popular Buddhism. As we have seen, conservative scholar monks criticize the use of protective devices and the buying and selling of Buddhist commodities such as amulets and services such as long-life rituals. Buddhist commercialism is a negative evaluation directed at temples or monks who appear to treat Buddhist devotional and protective items and rituals as a business concerned most with profit. Popular Buddhism, of course, does not always get charged with being commercialized. However, because there are more material objects and rituals involved in this aspect of lived Theravada, it can appear as though all popular Buddhism is based on commercialism. Yet many forms of popular practices—for example, merit-making, which includes offerings and donations—are based on the central Buddhist value of generosity.

This dynamic is an opportunity to observe Buddhists debating their own values and analyze their arguments. As a religious studies scholar, I do not take sides. It's not up to me or any person studying lived Buddhism to resolve this tension or to evaluate whether Buddhists today are living up to the teachings written in Buddhist texts. I want to make sure that those interested in Theravada Buddhism do not perpetuate a negative stereotype about popular Buddhism—that it is somehow illegitimate because the practitioners and practices are not aimed toward nibbana. Although nibbana is the ultimate goal, it is not the only goal. It is an extremely difficult end goal that takes countless lifetimes to achieve, so it would be unreasonable to expect all Buddhists to wholeheartedly embrace this goal in every lifetime. Popular Buddhism, with its more tangible and proximate goals, is what makes this lived religion extend out to everyone.

Meditation Practice Centers and Temples

This list of temples and meditation practice centers is not comprehensive but identifies the most accessible and consistently available spaces to foreigners in Thailand, Myanmar, Cambodia, and Laos.

Thailand

Suan Mokkh International Dharma Hermitage
www.suanmokkh-idh.org
Buddhadasa Bhikkhu established the International Dhamma Hermitage specifically for ten-day group retreats.

International Meditation Center, Wat Mahathat, Section 5
www.watmahathat.com/vipassana-meditation
Section 5 of Wat Mahathat has for many decades offered a practice space and instruction to both Thai and foreign meditators.

The International Forest Temple: Wat Pah Nanachat
www.watpahnanachat.org
Any English speaker can reserve a time to stay at Wat Pah Nanachat, the International Forest Temple, to experience the daily life there.

Northern Thailand Ajahn Tong Method Retreats

www.fivethousandyears.org; www.watrampoeng.com;
https://northernvipassana.org/en/about-us

There are three main temples in northern Thailand that follow the Ajahn Tong method of vipassana meditation: Wat Rampoeng, Wat Chom Tong, and Wat Doi Suthep.

Myanmar

Chanmyay Yeiktha

https://chanmyaysayadaw.org/about-chanmyay-yeiktha

Meditation master Chanmyay Sayadaw Ashin Janakabhivamsa teaches about two hundred foreign meditators and two thousand Burmese practitioners each year at this center.

Mahasi Thathana Yeiktha

In the heart of Yangon, thousands of meditators have made attainments toward nibbana here, with up to five hundred meditators hosted daily.

Pa-Auk Tawya Meditation Centre

www.paaukforestmonastery.org

The Pa-Auk Tawya Meditation Centre in Mawlamyine is a mini-city with over a thousand monastics and lay practitioners, both domestic and international.

Panditarama Forest Meditation Center

www.saddhamma.org/html/panditarama.shtml

This forest center is located forty miles outside of Yangon and is set in over one hundred acres of forest.

Shwe Oo Min Dhammasukha Tawya Meditation Centre

https://ashintejaniya.org/retreat

At this center, Sayadaw U Tejaniya accepts students during the rains retreat only, for a maximum of three months, with shorter stays available.

Cambodia

Cambodia Vipassana Dhura Buddhist Meditation Center
www.cambodiavipassanacenter.com
Although this is a space primarily for Cambodian Buddhists, it is possible to stay at this center and participate in the daily meditation routine, with practice sessions 7 a.m.–9 a.m. and 2 p.m.–5 p.m.

Wat Langka
https://english.cambodiadaily.com/news/wat-langka-meditation -130463/
Wat Langka offers weekly meditation sessions in the meditation hall on Mondays, Thursdays, Saturdays, and Sundays.

Laos

Wat Pa Nakoon Noi
https://sites.google.com/site/meditationinlaos2/ptithin-phx -sangkr
This temple, outside of Vientiane, is a forest monastery, which has some English-speaking monks experienced in teaching meditation.

Wat Sok Pa Luang
www.trip.com/travel-guide/attraction/vientiane/wat-sok-pa-luang -95861/
This temple in the capital city of Vientiane hosts short meditation sessions for foreigners hosted by English-speaking monks on Saturday afternoons.

Goenka Meditation Retreats in Mainland Southeast Asia
www.dhamma.org/en-US/locations/directory#035
These popular retreats will usually be taught in the local language and English and are managed similarly at each center.

Temple Etiquette Guide

It's important to take the time to familiarize yourself with Theravada Buddhist culture and religious settings before visiting. With some knowledge, you will be able to show respect, which will be appreciated by the monks and laypeople you encounter. When entering a Buddhist temple, observe lay Buddhists and follow their behavior. There are many customs and traditions surrounding behavior around monastics in a temple. These customs may follow local or regional norms that even native Theravada Buddhist visitors from out of town would be unfamiliar with. This does not mean that you should feel awkward or wary when entering a temple, but remember to be mindful of your actions. Monastics and laypeople will understand that you are not familiar with Theravada Buddhist ways and will appreciate that you are trying to respect the culture and rules as much as you can.

Proper Behaviors

Upon entering a temple, be sure to step over the door threshold. It is considered negative kamma to step directly on the piece of wood upon entry to temple buildings because it is believed that a protective high spirit resides there. It is also prohibited to climb or step on any temple structure or statue. In Theravada Buddhist cultures, the head is considered the highest part of the body and the most important, while the feet, being the lowest, are the most profane. Therefore, pay attention to the placement of your body and feet in relation to others.

Body Language

It is important not to stand or sit too close to a monastic, and never sit or stand in a higher location. Laypeople often bend or crouch slightly when walking past a seated monk. When walking with a monk, they try to walk behind. If approaching or taking leave of a seated monk, laypeople usually walk on their knees so that they can remain lower. Some people also try to avoid stepping on the shadow of a monk, and it is proper to give way to a monk rather than walk next to or cut in front. When monks are teaching the dhamma, lay Buddhists place both hands together at their chest, signaling their listening and respect. When inside a temple hall, laypeople sit with their legs tucked underneath their bottom or with their legs to the side. The cross-legged position is used mostly for meditation and is not considered appropriate for listening to the dhamma in the presence of monks. Other impolite positions are feet pointing toward a monk or arms clasped around the knees.

You should also be mindful of your body in relation to your travel partners. The temple is not a place for romantic affection, nor is it appropriate to joke around with a friend in an overly loud or aggressive way. You do not have to act completely serious or stoic, but you should consider your actions carefully and ensure they match the purpose and concerns of the temple environment.

Prostrating

Prostrating is another gesture of respect that is used when greeting and taking leave of monks or when entering and leaving temple halls. The prostration is usually done three times in reference to the Triple Gem of the Buddha, Dhamma, and Sangha. It is performed in the seated position by bringing the forehead to the floor while resting your bottom on your heels, and with your elbows near your knees and your thumbs near your eyebrows. This five-pointed prostration (two knees, two feet, and head) is the highest sign of respect. Often laypeople will prostrate three times to the Buddha statue and then prostrate three more times in the direction of the monk.

Respecting the Buddha Statue

The Buddha statue should be respected in any visit to a temple. Pious lay Buddhists offer incense, candles, and flowers, held in a gesture of respect, to an altar within the temple. These three objects symbolize the Triple Gem. These objects are also held on special Buddhist holidays while circumambulating a stupa three times. You can also follow along if you would like to participate in this ritual. Just like with a monk, it is appropriate to prostrate three times and never point one's feet toward a Buddha statue. If you do not feel comfortable bowing or paying respect to a Buddha statue, then hang in the back of the temple hall and just observe.

Photography

Some temples have restrictions about taking pictures or request a donation for doing so. Look for signs to this effect before taking photos. Visitors should sit or kneel when taking a picture inside a temple hall. If you would like to be in a picture, you can sit in front of the Buddha statue, with hands together at one's heart, to show respect.

Behavior for Women

There are special codes of behavior for women entering temples with male monks. Out of respect for Theravada beliefs, women should avoid touching monks or being alone with a monk. These rules are aimed at reducing feelings of lust while living a celibate life. If a woman is seen alone with a monk, rumors may spread that the monk has been impure. To avoid this possibility, usually a third person should be present if a woman has a private conversation with a monk. In a public area, however, a one-on-one conversation is usually fine. Many monks at popular tourist spots will be happy to practice their English. So, if a woman would like to talk to a monk, she should make sure she's in a public area of the temple where others are likely to pass by. If she can bring along a friend, this would also help to alleviate any tension.

Certain parts of some temples are off-limits to women because a woman menstruating is considered impure. These include sacred areas that are thought to contain guardian spirits, male monks' residence areas, some chedis with relics, and some ordination halls. You will usually see a sign in English, at temples visited by foreign tourists, if women are not allowed to enter a part of a temple. If there is no sign and other women are entering, then it is fine to enter.

Proper Dress

Travelers should consider their attire before visiting temples. At important royal temples such as Wat Phra Kaew in Bangkok, foreigners dressed inappropriately are asked to rent proper clothes provided at the gate before entering. However, less frequented temples will not have extra clothes available, so you should always plan to dress properly if your day trip includes a temple.

Usually, respectful attire consists of any shirt with sleeves and any bottom that covers one's knees. For women, more consideration is involved. Whereas men can usually wear long shorts or pants, women are expected to wear either loose pants or a long, loose skirt. Some temples are stricter and will require skirts or trousers that reach closer to one's ankles and will not accept ripped jeans. Others are less strict, and you might see laywomen wearing sleeveless shirts. However, it is best to wear sleeves in a temple to be as respectful as possible. It is not strictly necessary, but many laypeople wear white in a temple to represent purity and avoid any attention from distracting colors. Never wear a T-shirt advertising alcohol of any kind.

At temples popular with tourists, there are typically signs in English alerting visitors to take off their shoes before entering a hall or circumambulating a stupa. An exception is Myanmar, where one does not wear shoes in *any* part of the temple. You can carry your shoes with you in a plastic bag or leave them in the front of the temple to collect on your way out. At large temples frequented by many visitors, there will be a small fee for this service.

Offering to a Monk

Bringing an offering to a temple is considered proper behavior, though it is not required. Visitors can offer non-food items at any time of day to a monk at a temple. Many temples also have offerings for sale. These offerings can be made any day, but laypeople often make offerings on the weekly holy day, an annual Buddhist holiday, their birthdays, or when some good luck is needed. Along with material items, lay Buddhists also offer money in envelopes. If you do this, make sure to write your name or someone else's on the envelope so the monk knows where to direct the merit. You can indicate to any monk that you would like to make an offering by showing the offering or motioning with your hand. If offering to a monk in a temple, a man should use both hands to place the offering into the hands of the monk, and a woman should place the item on a cloth, which the monk will present in front of him. After making the offering, receive the blessing the monk will give you with your head lowered and hands held together at your chest. You can also offer cash, preferably in local currency, directly into donation boxes in the temple.

During monastic alms round, women and men can place the food directly into the monk's alms bowl. This experience is popular with tourists. In towns, villages, and cities throughout mainland Southeast Asia, between 6:30 and 7:30 each morning, monks will begin walking barefoot to collect alms for the day. They will not stop for food unless you indicate that you would like to make an offering by taking off your shoes and showing you have an offering for donation. When the monk opens the alms bowl, place the food inside. Usually, monks walk in groups. Divide your offerings into smaller parts so you can place something into each alms bowl. After you have given to all monks present, wait for them to chant a blessing. As the monk begins to chant, lower yourself with your bottom touching your calves, and your hands together at the chest. It is best to watch a layperson perform this first to understand exactly how it is done. You will see that many lay Buddhists, instead of keeping their hands at their chest, will pour water from a bottle into a glass or bowl while the monk chants his blessing. This is done to remind the layperson to share and spread the merit being made. As discussed in chapter 3, in Myanmar, monks and novices do not offer blessings.

The most convenient places to offer alms are near markets where you can buy fresh food that is packaged with the specific intention of offering to a monk. The packages usually consist of rice, curry, meat, and vegetables, within individual plastic bags. Often packages of food and flowers are sold together. After offering food, the monk will put the lid on his bowl and you can place the flower on the lid. Offerings such as juice boxes, soy milk, and bakery items are also popular. It is not necessary to offer vegetarian food, but it is common to offer what you would like to eat. Monks cannot choose what food they can eat, so think about their health and preferences when choosing the food you offer.

Proper etiquette within temples and when interacting with monastics is an important aspect of Theravada Buddhist culture. Knowing the basic rules and appropriate actions will help the traveler ease into the new environment. The rules of behavior may seem complicated, but the rewards of being a respectful and knowledgeable visitor outweigh the effort necessary. To experience lived Buddhism, it is crucial to get out of your comfort zone.

Recommended Further Reading

Buddhist Texts and Teachings

Appleton, Naomi. *Jataka Stories in Theravada Buddhism: Narrating the Bodhi-satta Path*. New York: Routledge, 2010.

Assavavirulhakarn, Prapod. *The Ascendancy of Theravada Buddhism in Southeast Asia*. Chiang Mai, Thailand: Silkworm Books, 2010.

Collins, Steven. *Wisdom as a Way of Life: Theravada Buddhism Reimagined*. New York: Columbia University Press, 2020.

Crosby, Kate. *Theravada Buddhism: Continuity, Diversity, and Identity*. West Sussex, UK: Wiley Blackwell, 2013.

Gethin, Rupert. *Foundations of Buddhism*. Oxford: Oxford University Press, 1998.

Swearer, Donald K. *The Buddhist World of Southeast Asia*. Albany: State University of New York Press, 2010.

Tilakaratne, Asanga. *Theravada Buddhism: The View of the Elders*. Honolulu: University of Hawaii Press, 2012.

Ethnographies of Theravada Buddhism

Cassaniti, Julia. *Living Buddhism: Mind, Self and Emotion in a Thai Community*. Ithaca, NY: Cornell University Press, 2015.

Cook, Joanna. *Meditation in Modern Buddhism: Renunciation and Change in Thai Monastic Life*. Cambridge: Cambridge University Press, 2010.

Davis, Erik W. *Deathpower: Buddhism's Ritual Imagination in Cambodia*. New York: Columbia University Press, 2016.

Eberhardt, Nancy. *Imagining the Course of Life: Self-Transformation in a Shan Buddhist Community*. Honolulu: University of Hawaii Press, 2006.

Holt, John. *Theravada Traditions: Buddhist Ritual Cultures in Contemporary Southeast Asia and Sri Lanka*. Honolulu: University of Hawaii Press, 2017.

Jordt, Ingrid. *Burma's Mass Lay Meditation Movement: Buddhism and the Cultural Construction of Power*. Athens, OH: Ohio University Press, 2014.

Kawanami, Hiroko. *The Culture of Giving in Myanmar: Buddhist Offerings, Reciprocity, and Interdependence.* London: Bloomsbury Academic, 2020.

Keeler, Ward. *The Traffic in Hierarchy: Masculinity and Its Others in Buddhist Burma.* Honolulu: University of Hawaii Press, 2017.

Patton, Thomas Nathan. *The Buddha's Wizards: Magic, Protection, and Healing in Burmese Buddhism.* New York: Columbia University Press, 2018.

Terwiel, Barend Jan. *Monks and Magic: Revisiting a Classic Study of Religious Ceremonies in Thailand.* Denmark: NIAS Press, 2012.

History of Buddhism, Buddhism and the State

Borchert, Thomas. *Theravada Buddhism in Colonial Contexts.* New York: Routledge, 2018.

Braun, Erik. *The Birth of Insight: Meditation, Modern Buddhism & The Burmese Monk Ledi Sayadaw.* Chicago: University of Chicago Press, 2013.

Carbine, Jason A. *Sons of the Buddha: Continuities and Ruptures in a Burmese Monastic Tradition.* Berlin, Germany: DeGruyter, 2011.

Hansen, Anne Ruth. *How to Behave: Buddhism and Modernity in Colonial Cambodia 1860-1930.* Honolulu: University of Hawaii Press, 2011.

Harris, Ian. *Buddhism and Politics in Twentieth Century Asia.* London: Continuum, 1999.

——, ed. *Buddhism, Power and Political Order.* New York: Routledge, 2017.

——. *Cambodian Buddhism: History and Practice.* Honolulu: University of Hawaii Press, 2008.

Heine-Geldern, Robert. "State and Kingship in Southeast Asia." In *Southeast Asian History: Essential Readings*, edited by D. R. SarDesai, 46-63. New York: Avalon Publishing, 2013.

Holt, John. *Spirits of the Place: Buddhism and Lao Religious Culture.* Honolulu: University of Hawaii Press, 2009.

Kawanami, Hiroko, ed. *Buddhism and the Political Process.* New York: Palgrave MacMillan, 2016.

McDaniel, Justin Thomas. *The Lovelorn Ghost & The Magical Monk: Practicing Buddhism in Modern Thailand.* New York: Columbia University Press, 2011.

Schober, Juliane, and Steven Collins, eds. *Theravada Buddhist Encounters with Modernity.* New York: Routledge, 2017.

Tambiah, Stanley J. *The Buddhist Saints of the Forest and the Cult of Amulets.* Cambridge: Cambridge University Press, 1984.

Turner, Alicia. *Saving Buddhism: The Impermanence of Religion in Colonial Burma.* Honolulu: University of Hawaii Press, 2014.

Walton, Matthew J. *Buddhism, Politics and Political Thought in Myanmar.* Cambridge: Cambridge University Press, 2017.

Southeast Asia

Owen, Norman G., ed. *The Emergence of Modern Southeast Asia: A New History.* Honolulu: University of Hawaii Press, 2004.

Rush, James. *Southeast Asia: A Very Short Introduction.* New York: Oxford University Press, 2018.

Tarling, Nicholas, ed. *The Cambridge History of Southeast Asia.* Vols. 1 and 2. Cambridge: Cambridge University Press, 1999.

Notes

1. The population and percentage of Buddhist statistics are taken from the United Nations World Tourism Organization's *Buddhist Tourism in Asia: Towards Sustainable Development* (Madrid: UNWTO Publications, 2019).

2. Translation from *Pali-English Chanting Book (Thai Tradition)* (Penang, Malaysia: Vihara Buddha Gotama, 2013).

3. Coconuts TV, "Hell's Garden," accessed May 5, 2022, www.youtube.com /watch?v=-o_DFUPwABs&t=1s.

4. Translation from *Pali-English Chanting Book (Thai Tradition)* (Penang, Malaysia: Vihara Buddha Gotama, 2013).

5. Ibid.

6. Justin McDaniel, *The Lovelorn Ghost and the Magical Monk: Practicing Buddhism in Modern Thailand* (New York: Columbia University Press, 2013), 78.

7. Translation from Itipiso, accessed May 10, 2022, itipiso.org.

8. Bhikkhu Ariyesako, "The Bhikkhus' Rules: A Guide for Laypeople," Access to Insight (BCBS Edition), December 17, 2013, www.accesstoinsight.org/lib /authors/ariyesako/layguide.html.

9. Christopher Kelly, dir., *A Cambodian Spring*. London, Dartmouth Films, 2016. Available for viewing through the documentary's website: https:// acambodianspring.com/.

10. Charles Hallisey, trans., *Therigatha: Poems of the First Buddhist Women* (Cambridge, MA: Harvard University Press, 2015), 45.

11. Pali Text Society, trans., *Gradual Sayings*, 3, p. 56 (*Anguttara Nikaya* 3:67).

12. "Where can I find the embarrassing questions that were/are asked of prospective bhikkunis?" Sutta Central, June 2019, https://discourse.suttacen tral.net/t/where-can-i-find-the-embarrassing-questions-that-were-are -asked-of-prospective-bhikkhunis/13017/6.

13. Wiriya Sati, dir., *The Buddha's Forgotten Nuns*. 2013; produced by Katrina Lucas. The film can be viewed on YouTube, www.youtube.com/watch?v =ngPkZ5zY_tQ&t=1593s.

14. I. B. Horner, trans., *The Book of Discipline (Vinaya-Pitaka)*, vol. 4 (London: Luzac, 1971), 28.

15. "The Illustrated Dhammapada: Treasury of Truth, Chapter 3, The Mind, BuddhaNet.net," accessed May 18, 2022, www.buddhanet.net/dhamma pada/d_mind.htm.

16. Ibid.

17. Amaravati Sangha, trans., "Karaniya Metta Sutta: The Buddha's Words on Loving-Kindness," Access to Insight (BCBS Edition), November 2, 2013, www.accesstoinsight.org/tipitaka/kn/khp/khp.9.amar.html.

Bibliography

Note: Sources consulted for multiple chapters of this book are listed under the first chapter for which they were consulted.

Chapter 1: The Temple

Barker, Haley. "A Comparative Analysis of the Accountability of Monks at the Tiger Temple and the Mepkin Abbey." Paper presentation at Rhodes College, Memphis, TN, April 30, 2021.

Buddhadasa Bhikkhu. *"Teaching Dhamma by Pictures": Explanation of a Siamese Traditional Buddhist Manuscript*. Bangkok, Thailand: Sathirakoses-Nagaparadi Foundation & Ministry of Education, 2006.

Chouléan, Ang. "The Place of Animism within Popular Buddhism in Cambodia: The Example of the Monastery." *Asian Folklore Studies* 47, no.1 (1988): 35-41.

Cohen, Erik. "'Buddhist Compassion' and 'Animal Abuse' in Thailand's Tiger Temple." *Society & Animals* 21 (2013): 266-83.

Cummings, Joe. *Buddhist Temples of Thailand: A Visual Journey through Thailand's 40 Most Historic Wats*. Times Centre, Singapore: Marshall Cavendish Editions, 2010.

Ferguson, John P., and Christina B. Johannsen. "Modern Buddhist Murals in Northern Thailand: A Study of Religious Symbols and Meaning." *American Ethnologist* 3, no. 4 (1976): 645-69.

Hall, Rebecca S. "Representing Heaven in Thai Painting." In *Across the South of Asia*, edited by Robert DeCaroli and Paul A. Lavy, 321-42. New Delhi, India: DK Books, 2019.

Heywood, Denise. *Luang Prabang and Laos*. Bangkok: River Books, 2014.

Kent, Alexandra. "Peace, Power and Pagodas in Present-Day Cambodia." *Contemporary Buddhism* 9, no. 1 (2008): 77-97.

Philp, Janette, and David Mercer. "Politicised Pagodas and Veiled Resistance: Contested Urban Space in Burma." *Urban Studies* 39, no. 9 (2002): 1587-1610.

Pichard, Pierre, and François Lagirarde. *The Buddhist Monastery: A Cross-Cultural Survey.* Paris: École Français D'Extrême-Orient, 2003.

Ringis, Rita. *Thai Temples and Temple Murals.* New York: Oxford University Press, 1990.

Schedneck, Brooke. "Loss and Promise: The Buddhist Temple as Tourist Space in Thailand." In *Buddhist Tourism in Asia,* edited by Courtney Bruntz and Brooke Schedneck, 66-83. Honolulu: University of Hawaii Press, 2020.

———. "Presenting 'Lanna' Buddhism to Domestic and International Tourists in Chiang Mai." *Asian Journal of Tourism Research* 2, no. 3 (2017): 1-22.

———. *Religious Tourism in Northern Thailand: Encounters with Buddhist Monks.* Seattle: University of Washington Press, 2021.

Stadtner, Donald M. *Sacred Sites of Burma: Myth and Folklore in an Evolving Spiritual Realm.* Bangkok, Thailand: River Books, 2011.

Stratton, Carol. *What's Wat in a Wat: Thai Buddhist Temples.* Chiang Mai, Thailand: Silkworm Books, 2010.

Chapter 2: Sacred Buddhist Objects

Askew, Marc. "Materializing Merit: The Symbolic Economy of Religious Monuments and Tourist-Pilgrimage in Contemporary Thailand." In *Religious Commodifications in Asia: Marketing Gods,* edited by Pattana Kitiarsa, 89-119. London: Routledge, 2008.

Baker, Chris, and Pasuk Phongpaichit. "Protection and Power in Siam: From *Khun Chang Khun Phaen* to the Buddha Amulet." *Southeast Asian Studies* 2, no. 2 (2013): 215-42.

"The Book of Protection: Paritta," translated from the original Pali, with introductory essay and explanatory notes by Piyadassi Thera, with a foreword by V. F. Gunaratna. Access to Insight (BCBS Edition). November 30, 2013. www.accesstoinsight.org/lib/authors/piyadassi/protection.html.

Chiu, Angela. *The Buddha in Lanna: Art, Lineage, Power, and Place in Northern Thailand.* Honolulu: University of Hawaii Press, 2017.

Cohen, Paul T. "Lue across Borders: Pilgrimage and the Muang Sing Reliquary in Northern Laos." In *Where China Meets Southeast Asia: Social & Cultural Change in the Border Regions,* edited by Grant Evans, Christopher Hutton, and Kuah Khun Eng, 145-61. Singapore: Institute of Southeast Asian Studies, 2000.

Conway, Susan. *Tai Magic: Arts of the Supernatural in the Shan States and Lan Na.* Bangkok, Thailand: River Books, 2014.

Cook, Joanna. "Power, Protection and Perfectibility: Aspiration and Materiality in Thailand." In *Southeast Asian Perspectives on Power,* edited by Luana Chua, Joanna Cook, Nicholas Long, and Lee Wilson, 37-50. New York: Routledge, 2012.

Germano, David, and Kevin Trainor, eds. *Embodying the Dharma: Buddhist Relic Veneration in Asia.* Albany: State University of New York Press, 2004.

Jerryson, Michael. *If You Meet the Buddha on the Road: Buddhism, Politics, and Violence.* New York: Oxford University Press, 2018.

Kinnard, Jacob. *Imaging Wisdom: Seeing and Knowing in the Art of Indian Buddhism.* London: Routledge, 1999.

Kitiarsa, Pattana. "Buddha Phanit: Thailand's Prosperity Religion and Its Commodifying Tactics." In *Religious Commodifications in Asia: Marketing Gods,* edited by Pattana Kitiarsa, 89-119. London: Routledge, 2008.

———. *Mediums, Monks, & Amulets: Thai Popular Buddhism Today.* Chiang Mai, Thailand: Silkworm Books, 2012.

Konstanz, Dale. *Thai Taxi Talismans: Bangkok from the Passenger Seat.* Bangkok, Thailand: River Books, 2011.

Marston, John. "Death, Memory and Building: The Non-Cremation of a Cambodian Monk." *Journal of Southeast Asian Studies* 37, no. 3 (2006): 491-505.

———. "Post-Pol Pot Cambodia and the Building of a New Stupa." In *Buddhism, Modernity, and the State in Asia: Forms of Engagement,* edited by John Whalen Bridge, Pattana Kitiarsa, and John Marston, 95-113. New York: Palgrave-MacMillan, 2013.

Schober, Juliane. "Buddhist Just Rule and Burmese National Culture: State Patronage of the Chinese Tooth Relic in Myanma." *History of Religions* 36, no. 3 (1997): 218-43.

———. "In the Presence of the Buddha: Ritual Veneration of the Burmese Mahamuni Image." In *Sacred Biography in the Buddhist Traditions of South and Southeast Asia,* edited by Juliane Schober, 259-88. Honolulu: University of Hawaii Press, 1997.

Soontravanich, Chalong. "The Regionalization of Local Buddhist Saints: Amulets, Crime and Violence in Post-World War II Thai Society Amulets." *Sojourn: Journal of Social Issues in Southeast Asia* 28, no. 2 (2013): 179-215.

Spiro, Melford E. *Buddhism and Society: A Great Tradition and Its Burmese Vicissitudes.* Berkeley: University of California Press, 1970.

Strong, John S. *Relics of the Buddha.* Princeton, NJ: Princeton University Press, 2004.

Swearer, Donald K. *Becoming the Buddha: The Ritual of Image Consecration in Thailand.* Princeton, NJ: Princeton University Press, 2004.

Tambiah, Stanley. "Famous Buddha Images and the Legitimation of Kings: The Case of the Sinhala Buddha (Phra Sihing) in Thailand." *RES: Anthropology and Aesthetics* 4 (1982): 5-19.

Chapter 3: Varieties of Male Monks

"Anti-Muslim Monk Forced to Disrobe." *Pratchatai English*, September 21, 2017, https://prachatai.com/english/node/7387.

Beech, Hannah, and Sun Narin. "Threatened by Facebook Disinformation, a Monk Flees Cambodia." *New York Times*, updated May 21, 2021, www.nytimes.com/2020/08/23/world/asia/cambodia-facebook-disinformation.html.

Cohen, Paul T., ed. "A Buddha Kingdom in the Golden Triangle: Buddhist Revivalism and the Charismatic Monk Khruba Bunchum." *Australian Journal of Anthropology* 11, no. 2 (2000): 141–54.

——. *Charismatic Monks of Lanna Buddhism*. Denmark: NIAS Press, 2017.

Darlington, Susan. "The Good Buddha and the Fierce Spirits: Protecting the Northern Thai Forest." *Contemporary Buddhism* 8, no. 2 (2007): 169–85.

——. *The Ordination of a Tree: The Thai Buddhist Environmental Movement*. Albany: State University of New York Press, 2012.

Dhammasami, Khammai. *Buddhism, Education, and Politics in Burma and Thailand: From the Seventeenth Century to the Present*. London: Bloomsbury, 2018.

Frydenlund, Iselin. "Buddhist Militarism Beyond Texts." *Journal of Religion and Violence* 5, no. 1 (2017): 27–48.

Harris, Ian. "Buddhism in Cambodia Since 1993." In *Cambodia: Progress and Challenges Since 1991*, edited by Pou Sothirak, Geoff Wade, and Mark Hond, 320–36. Singapore: Institute of Southeast Asian Studies, 2012.

Jirattikorn, Amporn. "Buddhist Holy Man Khruba Bunchum: The Shift in a Millenarian Movement at the Thailand-Myanmar Border." *Sojourn: Journal of Social Issues in Southeast Asia* 31, no. 2 (2016): 377–412.

Kawanami, Hiroko. "Charisma, Power(s), and the Arahant Ideal in Burmese-Myanmar Buddhism." *Asian Ethnology* 68, no. 2 (2009): 211–37.

Klinken, Gerry van, and Su Mon Thazin Aung. "The Contentious Politics of Anti-Muslim Scapegoating in Myanmar." *Journal of Contemporary Asia* 47, no. 3 (2017): 353–75.

Lall, Marie. *Myanmar's Education Reforms: A Pathway to Social Justice?* London: University College London Press, 2020.

Marston, John. "Cambodian Religion since 1989." In *Beyond Democracy in Cambodia: Political Reconstruction in a Post-Conflict Society*, edited by Joakim Öjendal and Mona Lilja, 224–49. Copenhagen: NIAS Press, 2009.

Nasee, Pisith. "Constructing the Charisma of *Khruba* (Venerable Monks) in Contemporary Thai Society." *Southeast Asian Studies* 7, no. 2 (2018): 199–236.

Rozenberg, Guilliame. *Renunciation and Power: The Quest for Sainthood in Contemporary Burma*. Translated by Jessica Hackett. New Haven, CT: Yale University Southeast Asia Studies, 2010.

Schedneck, Brooke. "Religious Others, Tourism, and Missionization: Buddhist

'Monks Chats' in Northern Thailand." *Modern Asian Studies* 52, no. 6 (2018): 1888-1916.

Schober, Juliane. *Modern Buddhist Conjunctures in Myanmar: Cultural Narratives, Colonial Legacies, and Civil Society.* Honolulu: University of Hawaii Press, 2010.

Sovanratana, Khy. "Buddhist Education Today: Progress and Challenges." In *People of Virtue: Reconfiguring Religion, Power, and Morality in Cambodia Today*, edited by Alexandra Kent and David P. Chandler, 257-71. Copenhagen: Nordic Institute of Asian Studies, 2008.

Thai Buddhism. Chiang Mai, Thailand: Mahachulalongkornrajavidyalaya Buddhist University, 2007.

Tiyavanich, Kamala. *Forest Recollections: Wandering Monks in Twentieth-Century Thailand.* Honolulu: University of Hawaii Press, 1997.

Walton, Matthew J. "Buddhist Monks and Democratic Politics in Contemporary Myanmar." In *Buddhism and the Political Process*, edited by Hiroko Kawanami, 56-77. New York: Palgrave MacMillan, 2016.

———. "Monks in Politics, Monks in the World: Buddhist Activism in Contemporary Myanmar. *Social Research* 82, no. 2 (2015): 507-30.

Weiner, Matthew. "Maha Ghosananda as a Contemplative Social Activist." In *Action Dharma: New Studies in Engaged Buddhism*, edited by Christopher Queen, Charles Prebish, and Damien Keown, 110-25. London: Routledge-Curzon, 2003.

Wijayaratna, Mohan. *Buddhist Monastic Life: According to the Texts of the Theravāda Tradition.* Translated by Claude Grangier and Steven Collins. Cambridge: Cambridge University Press, 1990.

Chapter 4: Roles for Buddhist Women

Adams, Nathaniel. "Cambodia's 'Quiet Movement': Buddhist Women in Development." World Faiths Development Dialogue, Georgetown University. May 2, 2011. https://berkleycenter.georgetown.edu/posts/cambodia-s-quiet-movement-buddhist-women-in-development.

Andaya, Barbara Watson. "Localising the Universal: Women, Motherhood and the Appeal of Early Theravada Buddhism." *Journal of Southeast Asian Studies* 33, no. 1 (2002): 1-30.

Banks, Ellison Findly. *Women's Buddhism, Buddhism's Women: Tradition, Revision, Renewal.* Somerville, MA: Wisdom Publications, 2000.

Battaglia, Lisa J. "Becoming *Bhikkhunī? Mae Chis* and the Global Women's Ordination Movement." *Journal of Buddhist Ethics* 22 (2015): 25-62.

Bhikkhu Analayo. "The Revival of the *Bhikkhunī* Order and the Decline of the *Sāsana." Journal of Buddhist Ethics* 20 (2013): 110-193.

Blackstone, Kathryn. *Women in the Footsteps of the Buddha: Struggle for Liberation in the Therigatha*. New York: Routledge, 2013.

Dhammananda Bhikkhuni. "A Journey to be a Theravada Bhikkhuni." Alliance for Bhikkunis. November 12, 2016. http://present.bhikkhuni.net/dhammananda -bhikkhuni/.

Eberhardt, Nancy. "Changing Practices, Changing Selves." Presentation given at the 13th International Conference for Thai Studies, Chiang Mai, Thailand, July 17, 2017.

Ekachai, Sanitsuda. "Female Monks Barred from Paying Respects." *Bangkok Post*, January 11, 2017. www.bangkokpost.com/opinion/opinion/1177945/ female-monks-barred-from-paying-respects.

———. "Nuns Show Us What Merit Really Means." *Bangkok Post*, October 29, 2014. www.bangkokpost.com/print/440173/.

Guthrie, Elizabeth. "Khmer Buddhism, Female Asceticism, and Salvation." In *History, Buddhism, and New Religious Movements in Cambodia*, edited by Elizabeth Guthrie and John Marston, 133–49. Honululu: University of Hawaii Press, 2004.

Ito, Tomomi. "The Path of Ubasika Ki Nanayon (1901–1974): A Thai Woman's Dhamma Practice in the Form of 'Ubasika.'" *Journal of Intercultural Studies* (Kobe University) (2017): 48.

Jordt, Ingrid. "*Bhikkhuni, Thilashin, Mae-Chii:* Women Who Renounce the World in Burma, Thailand and the Classical Pali Buddhist Texts." *Crossroads: An Interdisciplinary Journal of Southeast Asian Studies* 4, no. 1 (1988): 31–39.

Kawanami, Hiroko. *Renunciation and Empowerment of Buddhist Nuns in Myanmar-Burma*. Leiden: Brill, 2013.

Kent, Alexandra. "Shades of Gender and Security in Cambodia." In *Gendered Inequalities in Asia: Configuring, Contesting and Recognizing Women and Men*, edited by Helle Rydstrøm, 127–48. Copenhagen, Denmark: NIAS Press, 2010.

Khuankaew, Ouyporn. "Buddhism and Domestic Violence: Using the Four Noble Truths to Deconstruct and Liberate Women's Karma." In *Rethinking Karma: The Dharma of Social Justice*, edited by Jonathan S. Watts, 199–224. Chiang Mai, Thailand: Silkworm Books, 2009.

Lindberg Falk, Monica. *Making Fields of Merit: Buddhist Female Ascetics and Gendered Orders in Thailand*. Seattle: University of Washington Press, 2017.

McDonald-Gibson, Charlotte. "Buddhist Nuns Face Uphill Battle for Recognition." *Phom Penh Post*, February 28, 2003. www.phnompenhpost.com/ national/buddhist-nuns-face-uphill-battle-recognition.

Munissara Bhikkhuni. "What Buddhism Gave Me." *Present: The Voices and Activities of Theravada Buddhist Women* (2012). www.bhikkhuni.net/wp-content/uploads/2015/06/What-Buddhism-Gave-Me.pdf.

Na Thalang, Jeerawat. "If the Robes Fit…" *Bangkok Post*, February 15, 2015. www.bangkokpost.com/print/475378/.

Ohnuma, Reiko. *Ties That Bind: Maternal Imagery and Discourse in Indian Buddhism*. Oxford: Oxford University Press, 2012.

Rigby, Jennifer. "Meet Burma's Feminist Buddhist Nun." *Tricycle*. January 8, 2017. https://tricycle.org/trikedaily/meet-burmas-feminist-nun.

Schedneck, Brooke. "The Rise of Female Meditation Teachers in Southeast Asia." In *Women and Asian Religions*, edited by Zayn Kassam, 313-28. Santa Barbara, CA: ABC-CLIO, 2017.

Schubert, Kara K. "Contrasting Values: How Cambodian Women Religious Problematize NGO Prioritization of Personal Freedom." PhD diss., Claremont Graduate University, 2016.

Seeger, Martin. "The *Bhikkhunī*-Ordination Controversy in Thailand." *Journal of the International Association of Buddhist Studies* 29, no. 1 (2006 [2008]): 155-83.

———. *Gender and the Path to Awakening: Hidden Histories of Nuns in Modern Thai Buddhism*. Chiang Mai, Thailand: Silkworm Books, 2018.

Sponberg, Alan. "Attitudes toward Women and the Feminine in Early Buddhism." In *Buddhism, Sexuality, and Gender*, edited by Jose Ignacio Cabezon, 3-36. Albany: State University of New York Press, 1992.

Starkey, Caroline, and Emma Tomalin. "Gender, Buddhism and Education: *Dhamma* and Social Transformation within the Theravada Tradition." In *Gender, Religion and Education in a Chaotic Postmodern World*, edited by Zehavit Gross, Lynn Davies, and Al-Khansaa Diab, 55-71. New York: Springer, 2012.

Toomey, Christine. *In Search of Buddha's Daughters: A Modern Journey Down Ancient Roads*. New York: The Experiment, 2015.

Tsomo, Karma Lekshe. "Lao Buddhist Women: Quietly Negotiating Religious Authority." *Buddhist Studies Review* 27, no. 1 (2010): 85-106.

———. *Women in Buddhist Traditions*. Albany: State University of New York Press, 2020.

Upasika Kee Nanayon. "Pure and Simple." Translated by Thanissaro Bhikkhu. 2003. www.accesstoinsight.org/lib/thai/kee/pureandsimple.html.

Wight, Emily, and Vandy Meong. "Gender Politics in the Pagoda: The Female Voices Who Call for Change." *Phnom Penh Post*, November 8, 2013. www.phnompenh post.com/7days/gender-politics-pagoda-female-voices-who-call-change.

Wijayaratna, Mohan. *Buddhist Nuns: The Birth and Development of a Women's Monastic Order*. Kandy, Sri Lanka: Buddhist Publication Society, 2001.

Yavaprabhas, Kankanang. "New Temporary Buddhist Ordination for Women and Social Change in Thai Society." *Kyoto Review of Southeast Asia*, issue 23, July 2018. https://kyotoreview.org/yav/thai-buddhist-ordination-women/.

———. "The Values of Ordination: The Bhikkhuni, Gender, and Thai Society." PhD diss., University College London, London, UK, 2018.

Chapter 5: Theravada's Relationship with Other Religions

Ayuttacorn, Arrattee, and Jane Ferguson. "The Sacred Elephant in the Room: Ganesha Cults in Chiang Mai, Thailand." *Anthropology Today* 34, no. 5 (2018): 5-9.

Bertrand, Didier. "The Therapeutic Role of Khmer Mediums (Kru Boramei) in Contemporary Cambodia." *Mental Health, Religion & Culture* 8, no. 4 (2007): 309-27.

Brac de la Perriere, Benedicte. "Spirit Possession: An Autonomous Field of Practice in the Burmese Buddhist Culture." *Journal of Burma Studies* 20, no. 1 (2016): 1-29.

Buddhadasa Bhikkhu. *Buddhism and Christianity*. Silver Spring, MD: Council of Thai Bhikkhus, 2006.

Bun, Chan Kwok, and Tong Chee Kiong. "Rethinking Assimilation and Ethnicity: The Chinese in Thailand." *International Migration Review* 27, no. 1 (1993): 140-68.

Chandra-ngarm, Saeng. *A Buddhist Looks at Christianity*. Chiang Mai: Mahamakut Buddhist University, n.d.

Cohen, Erik. "The Vegetarian Festival and the City Pillar: The Appropriation of a Chinese Religious Custom for a Cult of the Thai Civic Religion." *Journal of Tourism and Cultural Change* 10, no. 1 (2012): 1-21.

Eddy, Glennys. "Buddhism." In *World Religions and Their Missions*, edited by Aaron J. Ghiloni, 89-121. New York: Peter Lang, 2015.

Fleming, Kenneth. *Buddhist-Christian Encounter in Contemporary Thailand*. Frankfurt: Peter Lang, 2014.

Formoso, Bernard. "Thai Buddhism as the Promoter of Spirit Cults." *South East Asia Research* 24, no. 1 (2016): 119-33.

Goh, Robbie B. H. *Christianity in Southeast Asia*. Singapore: ISEAS Publications, 2005.

Hayami, Yoko. "Buddhist Missionary Project in the Hills of Northern Thailand: A Case Study from a Cluster of Karen Villages." *Tai Culture* 4, no. 1 (1999): 53-76.

Holt, John Clifford. *Myanmar's Buddhist-Muslim Crisis: Rohingya, Arakanese, and Burmese Narratives of Siege and Fear*. Honolulu: University of Hawaii Press, 2019.

Jackson, Peter A. "Markets, Media, and Magic: Thailand's Monarch as a 'Virtual Deity.'" *Inter-Asia Cultural Studies* 10, no. 3 (2009): 361-80.

——. "Royal Spirits, Chinese Gods, and Magic Monks: Thailand's Boom-Time Religions of Prosperity." *South East Asia Research* 7, no. 3 (1999): 245-320.

Jerryson, Michael. "Appropriating a Space for Violence: State Buddhism in Southern Thailand." *Journal of Southeast Asian Studies* 40, no. 1 (2009): 33-57.

——. *Buddhist Fury: Religion and Violence in Southern Thailand*. New York: Oxford University Press, 2012.

———. "The Rise of Militant Monks." *Lion's Roar.* August 23, 2015. www.lionsroar. com/the-rise-of-militant-monks/.

Keyes, Charles. "Monks, Guns, and Peace: Theravada Buddhism and Political Violence." In *Belief and Bloodshed: Religion and Violence across Time and Tradition*, edited by James K. Wellman, 145-63. Lanham, MD: Rowman & Littlefield, 2007.

———. "Muslim 'Others' in Buddhist Thailand." *Thammasat Review* 13 (2008/2009): 19-42.

———. "Why the Thai Are Not Christians: Buddhist and Christian Conversion in Thailand." In *Conversion to Christianity: Historical and Anthropological Perspectives on a Great Transformation*, edited by Robert W. Hefner, 259-84. Berkeley: University of California Press, 1993.

Kitiarsa, Pattana. "Beyond Syncretism: Hybridization of Popular Religion in Contemporary Thailand." *Journal of Southeast Asian Studies* 36, no. 3 (2005): 461-87.

———. "Missionary Intent and Monastic Networks: Thai Buddhism as a Transnational Religion." *Sojourn: Journal of Social Issues in Southeast Asia* 25, no. 1 (2010): 109-32.

Kyaw, Nyi Nyi. "The Role of Myth in Anti-Muslim Buddhist Nationalism in Myanmar." In *Buddhist-Muslim Relations in a Theravada World*, edited by Iselin Frydenlund and Michael Jerryson, 197-226. Singapore: Palgrave MacMillan, 2021.

Marddent, Amporn. "Buddhist Perceptions of Muslims in the Thai South." ศิลปศาสตร์สำนึก [*Liberal Arts*] 7, no. 18 (2007): 47-63.

Maud, Jovan. "Fire and Water: Ritual Innovation, Tourism, and Spontaneous Religiosity in Hat Yai, Southern Thailand." In *Faith in the Future: Understanding the Revitalizations of Religious and Cultural Traditions of Asia*, edited by Thomas Reuter and Alexander Horstmann, 269-96. Leiden: Brill, 2013.

McCargo, Duncan. "Thai Buddhism, Thai Buddhists and the Southern Conflict." *Journal of Southeast Asian Studies* 40, no. 1 (2009): 1-10.

McDaniel, Justin. "This Hindu Holy Man Is a Thai Buddhist." *South East Asia Research* 21, no. 2 (2013): 191-209.

Mostafanezhad, Mary, and Tanya Promburom. "'Lost in Thailand': The Popular Geopolitics of Film-Induced Tourism in Northern Thailand." *Social and Cultural Geography* 19, no. 1 (2016): 81-101.

Pathan, Don, Ekkarin Tuansiri, and Anwar Koma. "Understanding Anti-Islam Sentiment in Thailand." Patani, Thailand: Patani Forum, 2018. www.pataniforum.com/admin/jquery/ckfinder/userfiles/files/islamophobia_ENG_PAGES. pdf.

Phra Paisal Visalo. "On the Path toward Peace and Justice" Posted August 24, 2017. Accessed May 15, 2022. http://www.visalo.org/englishArticles/peace AndJustice.htm.

Platz, Roland. "Buddhism and Christianity in Competition? Religious and Ethnic Identity in Karen Communities of Northern Thailand." *Journal of Southeast Asian Studies* 34, no. 3 (2003): 473-90.

Schober, Juliane. "Buddhism, Violence, and the State in Burma (Myanmar) and Sri Lanka." In *Religion and Conflict in South and Southeast Asia: Disrupting Violence*, edited by Linell Cady and Sheldon Simon, 51-69. New York: Routledge, 2006.

Sivaraksa, Sulak. *Conflict, Culture, Change: Engaged Buddhism in a Globalizing World*. Somerville, MA: Wisdom Publications, 2015.

Stengs, Irene. *Worshipping the Great Moderniser: King Chulalongkorn, Patron Saint of the Thai Middle Class*. Singapore: NUS Press, 2009.

Walton, Matthew J., and Michael Jerryson. "The Authorization of Religio-Political Discourse: Monks and Buddhist Activism in Contemporary Myanmar and Beyond." *Politics and Religion* 9 (2016): 798-814.

Winzeler, Robert. *Popular Religion in Southeast Asia*. Lanham, MD: Rowman & Littlefield, 2016.

Chapter 6: Lay Buddhist Practices and Beliefs

Allen, Mariette Pathy. *Transcendents: Spirit Mediums in Burma and Thailand*. n.p.: Daylight Books, 2017.

Ancuta, Katarzyna. "Ghost Skins: Globalising the Supernatural in Contemporary Thai Horror Film." In *Globalgothic*, edited by Glennis Byron, 144-56. Manchester, UK: Manchester University Press, 2015.

———. "Spirits in Suburbia: Ghosts, Global Desires and the Rise of Thai Middle-Class Horror." *Horror Studies* 5, no. 2 (2014): 233-47.

———. "That's the Spirit! Horror Films as an Extension of Thai Supernaturalism." In *Ghost Movies in Southeast Asia and Beyond: Narratives, Cultural Contexts, Audiences*, edited by Peter J. Bräunlein and Andrea Lauser, 123-40. Leiden: Brill, 2016.

Bamford, Sally. "The Nats of Myanmar." *Taasa Review* 21, no. 3 (2012): 4-6.

Brac de la Pierrere, Benedicte, and Cristophe Munier-Gaillard. *Bobogyi: A Burmese Spiritual Figure*. Bangkok: River Books, 2019.

Chandler, David P. "Folk Memories of the Decline of Angkor in Nineteenth-Century Cambodia: The Legend of the Leper King." *Journal of the Siam Society* 67, no. 1 (1979): 54-62.

Davis, Erik W. "Khmer Spirits, Chinese Bodies: Chinese Spirit Mediums and Spirit Possession Rituals in Contemporary Cambodia." In *Faith in the Future: Understanding the Revitalization of Religions and Cultural Traditions in Asia*, edited by Thomas Reuter and Alexander Horstmann, 177-96. Leiden: Brill, 2012.

Easum, Taylor M. "A Thorn in Bangkok's Side: Kruba Sriwichai, Sacred Space and the Last Stand of the Pre-Modern Chiang Mai State." *South East Asia Research* 21, no. 2 (2013): 211-36.

Evans, Grant. "The Socialist Interregnum and Buddhist Resurgence in Laos." In *Atheist Secularism and Its Discontents: A Comparative Study of Religion and Communism in Eurasia*, edited by Tam T. T. Ngo and Justine B. Quijada, 54-69. London: Palgrave MacMillan, 2015.

Foxeus, Niklas. "Spirits, Mortal Dread, and Ontological Security: Prosperity and Saving Buddhism in Burma/Myanmar." *Journal of the American Academy of Religion* 86, no. 4 (2018): 1107-47.

Greene, Paul D. "The Dhamma as Sonic Praxis: *Paritta* Chant in Burmese Theravada Buddhism." *Asian Music* 35, no. 2 (2004): 43-78.

Guillou, Anne Yvonne. "The 'Master of the Land': Cult Activities around Pol Pot's Tomb." *Journal of Genocide Research* 20 (2018): 275-89.

Hashimoto, Sayaka. "Spirit Cults and Buddhism in Luang Prabang, Laos: Analyses of Rituals in the Boat Race Festivals." *International Journal of Sport and Health Science* 6 (2009): 219-29.

Jirattikorn, Amporn. "Suriyothai: Hybridizing Thai National Identity through Film." *Inter-Asia Cultural Studies* 42, no. 2 (2010): 296-308. Johnson, Andrew Alan. "Progress and Its Ruins: Ghosts, Migrants, and the Uncanny in Thailand." *Cultural Anthropology* 28, no. 2 (2013): 299-319.

Kent, Alexandra. "Recovery of the Collective Spirit: The Role of the Revival of Buddhism in Cambodia." Legacy of War and Violence Working Paper Series, 2003, no. 9, Department of Social Anthropology, Goteborg University.

———. "Sheltered by *Dhamma*: Reflecting on Gender, Security and Religion in Cambodia." *Journal of Southeast Asian Studies* 42, no. 2 (2011): 193-209.

Kitiarsa, Pattana. "The Horror of the Modern: Violation, Violence, and Rampaging Urban Youths in Contemporary Thai Ghost Films." In *Engaging the Spirit World: Popular Beliefs and Practices in Modern Southeast Asia*, edited by Kirsten W. Endres and Andrea Lauser, 200-20. New York: Berghahn Books, 2011.

Krajaejun, Pipad. "Sceptres of Instability: Why Spirit Mediums Haunt Thailand's Junta." New Mandala. June 15, 2018. www.newmandala.org/sceptres -instability-spirit-mediums-haunt-thailands-junta/.

Malangpoo, Neeranooch. "Nationalism and Tourism: The Case of Thai Buddhist Pilgrimage in Myanmar." PhD diss., University of Wisconsin-Madison, 2020.

Marston, John, and Elizabeth Guthrie, eds. *History, Buddhism, and New Religious Movements in Cambodia*. Honolulu: University of Hawaii Press, 2004.

Nilsen, Marte. "The Spirit of a Heroine: Ya Mo—Spirit Reverence, Patriotism and Thai Buddhism." *Modern Asian Studies* 45, no. 6 (2011): 1599-625.

Patton, Thomas. "Buddhist Wizards (*Weizzā/Weikza*) of Myanmar." In *Oxford Research Encyclopedia, Religion*. Oxford University Press, 2019.

———. "The Wizard King's Granddaughters: Burmese Buddhist Female Mediums, Healers, and Dreamers." *Journal of the American Academy of Religion* 84, no. 2 (2016): 430-65.

Sadan, Mandy. "Respected Grandfather, Bless this Nissan: Benevolent and Politically Neutral Bo Bo Gyi." In *Burma at the Turn of the 21st Century*, edited by Monique Skidmore, 90-111. Honolulu: University of Hawaii Press, 2005.

Wong, Ka F. "Nang Naak: The Cult and Myth of a Popular Ghost in Thailand." In *Thai Folklore: Insights into Thai Folk Culture*, edited by Siraporn Nathaland, 123-42. Bangkok: Chulalongkorn University Press, 2004.

Chapter 7: Meditation

Ajan Tong Sirimangalo. *The Only Way: An Introduction to Vipassana Meditation*. Translated by Kathryn J. Chindaporn. Chom Tong, Thailand: Wat Pradhatu Sri Chomtong Voravihara, 1999.

Bhikkhu Analayo. "The Development of Insight—a Study of the U Ba Khun Vipassana Meditation Tradition as Taught by S. N. Goenka in Comparison with Insight Teachings in the Early Discourses." *Fuyan Buddhist Studies* 6 (2011): 151-74.

———. *Satipatthana: The Direct Path to Realization*. Birmingham, UK: Windhorse Publications, 2003.

———. "Why Be Mindful of Feelings?" *Contemporary Buddhism* 19, no. 1 (2018): 47-53.

Buddhadasa Bhikkhu. *Mindfulness with Breathing: A Manual for Serious Beginners*. Translated by Santikaro Bhikkhu. Chiang Mai: Silkworm Books, 2001.

Crosby, Kate. *Esoteric Theravada: The Story of the Forgotten Meditation Tradition of Southeast Asia*. Boulder, CO: Shambhala Publications, 2021.

Fuengfusakul, Apinya. "Urban Logic and Mass Meditation in Contemporary Thailand." In *Global and Local Televangelism*, edited by Pradip N. Thomas and Philip Lee, 219-33. New York: Palgrave Macmillan, 2012.

Hart, William. *The Art of Living: Vipassana Meditation as Taught by S. N. Goenka*. New York: HarperOne, 1987.

Mahasi Sayadaw. *Practical Insight Meditation: Basic and Progressive Stages*. Translated by U Pe Thin and Myanaung U Tin. Kandy, Sri Lanka: Buddhist Publication Society, 1971.

Sayadaw U Silananda. *The Four Foundations of Mindfulness*. Somerville, MA: Wisdom, 2002.

Schedneck, Brooke. "Meditation for Tourists in Thailand: Commodifying a Universal and National Symbol." *Journal of Contemporary Religion* 29, no. 3 (2014): 439-56.

——. "Meditation Methods in Thailand: A Map of the Field of Practice from Meditation Centers to the Forest Tradition." *International Journal for the Study of Chan Buddhism and Human Civilization* 7 (2020): 80–92.

——. *Thailand's International Meditation Centers: Tourism and the Global Commodification of Religious Practices.* London: Routledge, 2015.

Shaw, Sarah. *Buddhist Meditation: An Anthology of Texts from the Pali Canon.* London: Routledge, 2006.

Shankman, Richard. *The Experience of Samadhi: An In-depth Exploration of Buddhist Meditation.* Boston: Shambhala Publications, 2008.

Snyder, Stephen, and Tina Rasmussen. *Practicing Jhanas: Traditional Concentration Meditation as Presented by the Venerable Pa Auk Sayadaw.* Boston, MA: Shambhala Publications, 2009.

Sri Manarama Mahathera. *The Seven Stages of Purification and the Insight Knowledges.* Kandy, Sri Lanka: Buddhist Publication Society, 2010.

Stuart, Daniel. *S. N. Goenka: Emissary of Insight.* Boulder, CO: Shambhala Publications, 2020.

Websites

Ajahn Chah's books can be found free to download here: https://forestsangha.org/teachings/books/authors/ajahn-chah?language=English

Books by and about Luangda Maha Bua and his disciples can be found free to download here: https://forestdhamma.org/books/english-books/

A selection of Buddhadasa Bhikkhu's important works in English can be found here: www.bia.or.th/en/index.php/teachings-by-buddhadasa-bhikkhu/books

A great resource for reading texts from the Pali Canon translated into English is Access to Insight: https://accesstoinsight.org/.

Another resource for the Pali Vinaya is Thanissaro Bhikkhu's translations and explanations of the Buddhist monastic code in two volumes.

Volume 1: www.accesstoinsight.org/lib/authors/thanissaro/bmc1.pdf
Volume 2: www.accesstoinsight.org/lib/authors/thanissaro/bmc2.pdf

Index